Ex Libris

Thomas Spencer Jerome

BT
985
.A57
1899

CHRISTIANITY

AND ANTI-CHRISTIANITY

IN THEIR FINAL CONFLICT

BY

SAMUEL J. ANDREWS

Author of "The Life of Our Lord Upon the Earth," "God's
Revelations of Himself to Men," "Some
Thoughts on Christian Unity"

Reprinted June, 2019 by:
The Old Paths Publications, Inc.
Cleveland, GA.
www.theoldpathspublications.com
TOP@theoldpathspublications.com

SECOND REVISED EDITION

FOURTH IMPRESSION

G. P. PUTNAM'S SONS
NEW YORK AND LONDON
1899

COPYRIGHT, 1898
BY
SAMUEL J. ANDREWS

CONTENTS.

Preface to Second Edition,	v
Preface,	ix
Introduction,	xix

PART I.

The Teachings of the Scriptures respecting the Antichrist,	1
Teachings of the Old Testament,	3
Teachings of the Lord,	10
Teachings of the Apostles Collectively,	21
St. Paul and his Teachings,	28
Teachings of St. John, St. Peter, and St. Jude,	44
Teaching of the Revelation,	52

PART II.

The Falling Away of the Church,	69
Its Origin and Nature,	71
Initial Stage of the Falling Away,	87
1. In Relation of the Church to the Head,	87
2. In Relation of the Church to the Holy Ghost,	98
3. In Relation of the Church to the World,	108

PART III.

Tendencies in Our Day Preparing the Way of the Antichrist,	117
Modern Pantheistic Philosophy,	119
Modern Philosophy and the New Christianity,	139
Deification of Humanity,	159
Tendencies of Modern Biblical Criticism,	169
Tendencies of Modern Science,	185
Tendencies of Modern Literature,	201
Christian Socialism and the Kingdom of God,	221

PART IV.

THE REIGN OF THE ANTICHRIST,	237
The Personal Christ in the First and the Nineteenth Century,	239
The Pantheistic Revolution,	251
Antichrist as Head of the Nations,	264
The Morality of the Future,	284
The Church of the Future,	303
The Church of the Beast and the False Prophet,	319
SUMMARY AND CONCLUSION,	337
NOTES,	352
INDEX,	355

PREFACE TO THE SECOND EDITION.

The issue of a second edition of this book gives an opportunity to notice some objections, and, also, to remove some misapprehensions of its aim which have found expression in various criticisms.

The chief burden of these criticisms is that the book is pessimistic in its tone. It is said by one: "It does not acknowledge that there are any Christian tendencies; everything in our age is antichristian." By another: "It adopts a pessimistic theory of history." By another: "It represents the world as growing worse, rather than better."

A brief examination will show how baseless is all criticism of this kind.

We may assume that these writers accept as true the Lord's words: "All power is given unto me in heaven and in earth"; and believe that in due time He will manifest this power in a kingdom of righteousness and peace which will embrace all nations. Because Himself immortal, the final victory of Christianity is assured; and we need not dwell upon the signs of its triumph which so many are engaged in pointing out. The objection based upon pessimism is not, therefore, that the glorious goal set before the Church will not be reached; but that the present stage of its progress, and its immediate future, are presented in a pessimistic way. We are told that an Antichrist in the future is an anachronism; he has no place there. The clouds and tempests are behind us; only a cloudless sky and a smooth sea are before us, and the haven is at hand.

In all questions as to the future of humanity, we must either picture this future for ourselves, or accept Divine revelation. Those who reject revelation, and map out the course of human history as pleases them, are of two classes. The first, which embraces not a few names distinguished in science and literature, affirms that so long as men live on the earth there will be a mingling of good and evil, a perpetual struggle between them. They see no kingdom of God in the coming years. With the second class, which embraces many nominal Christians, it is the evolutionary theory which determines for them the future of humanity. Believing in its continual upward progress, they can find no place for any development of evil and an Antichrist. The kingdom must come because it lies in the ever-ascending order of nature.

If we turn to those who believe that all true knowledge of the future of man is based upon Divine revelation, we find two classes: (*a*) those who hold that Christ will establish His kingdom by the peaceable and gradual diffusion of His principles; (*b*) those who look for its establishment through His personal acts in the separation of the good and the evil, and in final judgment. These two interpretations of the Divine purpose in Christ, as it is revealed, are radically at variance. One rests upon the conception that the depths of wickedness in man's sinful nature have been already fathomed. There are no lower deeps, no new forms in which the hostility to God and Christ can manifest itself. The other conceives of depths not yet fathomed, of forms of wickedness not yet manifested. It sees actively working a spirit of pride and lawlessness which will find its culmination and highest expression in the man of sin who seats himself in the temple of God, " showing himself that he is God."

Which of these conceptions of the future shall we take? We turn to the parable of the tares and the wheat. Have the tares already ripened and brought forth their perfected fruits, and are they now withering away? "Let both tares and wheat grow together until the harvest," said the Lord. The harvest is when both are ripe, when righteousness and wickedness have both come to the full.* Is to see this growth of evil pessimistic? Who has so openly and strongly spoken of the evil days to come as our Lord Himself? Not a few in our day call any teaching of the fall of man, of the sinfulness of human nature, of the punishment of sin, pessimistic. They have ears for those only who cry, "Peace, Progress"; and eyes only to see signs of good. But if revelation clearly teaches the contemporaneous development of good and evil, why should we ignore or minimise the evil? The highest form of wickedness is at the end in him "who opposeth and exalteth himself above all that is called God, or is worshipped."

To call good evil, as the pessimist does, is not so dangerous as to call evil good. In the former case, we are at least kept on our guard; in the latter, we are taken unawares. If the blind optimist lead the blind, both shall fall into the ditch. Better that the supposed evil should prove to be good, than that the supposed good should prove to be evil. To ignore the Antichrist of whom she has been forewarned, is for the Church to expose herself defenceless to his wiles, deceptions, and attacks.

It may be said in general that all who complain of the development of evil in the future as " a pessimistic theory,"

---

*In his comment on this parable it is said by Archbishop Trench: "We learn that evil is not, as so many dream, gradually to wane and disappear before good; but is ever to develop itself more fully, even as on the other side good is to unfold itself more and more mightily also. Thus it will go on until at last they stand face to face, each in its highest manifestation in the persons of Christ and of Antichrist. . . . Both are to grow, evil and good, till they come to a head, till they are ripe, one for destruction, and the other for full salvation."

should direct their attention to these two points: first, whether or not the Scriptures foretell an Antichrist in whom the enmity to God and to His Son will culminate, "the man of sin"; and, secondly, if they do, whether or not the movements and tendencies, religious, political, social, of the present time give any signs of his appearing. If there is to be no Antichrist, all enquiry respecting him is lost labour; and if he is to come, but only in some remote future, the subject has for us no present interest.

A word may be said of the objection that the doctrine of the Divine transcendence, as here presented, denies the Divine immanence. This is an error. God is immanent in man. "In God we live, and move, and have our being." But what is said is, that the doctrine of the Divine immanence is so presented in many quarters as to be indistinguishable from pantheism. Philosophy and science in many eminent representatives agree in affirming that there is no personal God, only a universal, impersonal Spirit or Energy, of which everything that exists is a part. This, viewed on the material side, is atheism; on the spiritual, is pantheism. If the transcendence of God in His acts of creation, as declared in the Scriptures, is given up, the ordinary mind—whatever some acute metaphysicians may say of themselves—can find no final resting-place but in the humbling negations of atheism, or the deifying affirmations of pantheism.

S. J. A.

November, 1898.

PREFACE.

The aim of this book is not historical or polemical. It does not repeat in detail the opinions of the early Fathers, or of later writers, or enter into the controversy whether Nero or Mohammed, the Pope or Luther, the Papacy or Protestantism, be called the Antichrist. There is a true sense in which it may be said, "Let the dead past bury its dead." It is in the light of the present that we must re-examine the prophetical problems of the past. As the purpose of God draws nearer to its fulfillment, passing events will tend to show in their distinctive features the nature of that fulfillment. (It is, therefore, for us of to-day to note the religious tendencies of the present, and to consider carefully their bearing upon the Divine purpose in man as it has been made known to us in the Scriptures. To those who believe that God, who knows the end from the beginning, has through His prophets and His Son declared this purpose in its outlines for the guidance of His children, our inquiry is of deepest interest. We ask, To what stage of His actings have we come? What are the religious characteristics of the present time?)

If the right discernment of the religious character of an age is always to those living in it of the highest importance, the right discernment of the present time is especially important to us, if, as we are told by not a few, it is in many points to be distinguished from all that have preceded it. To-day, indeed, is always the child of yesterday. The continuity of history is never broken. Yet history tells us of successive stages of religious development, each having its own marked features. Whether we have come to a new stage, must be determined by its special characteristics. Let us, therefore, note what is said of the present time by representative men, regarding it from very different points of view. What new religious elements do we find in it? In what direction are they developing? And what is the goal?

It was said early in the century by the German philosopher Schelling, noting the tendencies of philosophic thought around him: "As regards the past, there is striving a complete new age, and the old cannot comprehend it, nor has it a distant presentiment how distinct and complete is the antagonism to it of the new."

Lecky ("History of Rationalism"): "It has long been a mere truism that we are passing through a state of chaos, of anarchy, and of transition. During the past century the elements of dissolution have been multiplying all around us.... The days of Athanasius and of Augustine have passed away never to return.... The controversies of bygone centuries ring with a strange hollowness upon the ear."

Cardinal Newman ("Patristical Idea of Antichrist") speaks of "a special effort made almost all over the world, ... but most visibly and formidably in its most civilized and powerful parts, an effort to do without Religion.... Truly there is at this time a confederacy of evil marshaling its hosts from all parts of the world, organizing itself and taking its measures, enclosing the Church of Christ as in a net, and preparing the way for a general Apostasy from it."

Leslie Stephen ("Agnostic's Apology"): "I conceive that a vast social and intellectual transformation is taking place, and taking place more rapidly now than at almost any historical period.... I cannot say what will be the outcome of this vast and chaotic fermentation of thought. ....The creed of the future, whatever it may be, exists only in germ. Philosophers, not apostles or prophets, are founding a philosophical system, not a religion."

Goldwin Smith: "There is a general feeling that the stream of history is drawing near a cataract.... There is everywhere in the social frame an outward unrest, which, as usual, is the sign of fundamental change within. Old creeds have given way."

Gronlund, the Socialist: "All signs and portents show that the face of mankind has already been set in a socialistic direction.... There has been the access of a new, rational, divine order in human life that is disintegrating the old, outward, and temporary organization, and gradually creating the new."

Kuenen, the Biblical critic: "The problem of the future is especially serious now when so much is being superseded and is passing away, when a new conception of the world is spreading in ever wider circles; when new social conditions are in the very process of birth.... In us the ends of the ages meet, the ends of the old and the new."

Prof. Sohm ("Outlines of Church History"), speaking of culture, says: "This tendency has become more and more powerful since the middle of the century, and is hostile, not only to the ecclesiastical and Christian, but to every religious theory of the universe." "The society of our day is like the earth on which we live — a thin crust over a great volcanic, seething, revolutionary heart of liquid fire." "More and more clearly are shown the signs of the movement, the aim of which is to destroy the entire social order of the State, the Church, the Family. Unbelief has grown up among us, an unbelief which is kindling the revolution of the nineteenth century."

Kidd ("Social Evolution"): "The present is a period of reconstruction. A change is almost imperceptibly taking place in the midst of the rising generation respecting the great social and religious problems of our time.... We are rapidly approaching a time when we shall be face to face with social and political problems graver in character and more far-reaching in extent than any which have been hitherto encountered." "To the thoughtful mind the outlook at the close of the nineteenth century is profoundly interesting. History can furnish no parallel to it.... We seem to have reached a time in which there is abroad in men's minds an instinctive feeling that a definite stage in the evolution of Western civilization is growing to a close, and that we are entering upon a new era."

Utterances like these, repeated in sermons and lectures, in books, magazines, and the daily press, meet us on every side; all alike proclaiming a new age at hand. Whilst differing widely as to the final result, there is general agreement that we have come to the border line that separates two eras, that we have left the old behind us and are entering upon the new. This is in itself a most remarkable fact. What is its significance? Why a new age? Are our old beliefs, our old institutions, outgrown? Are we about to break with the past, and take a sudden leap onward? What has aroused this general feeling of restlessness, this widespread discontent with the present, these eager anticipations of something better soon to come?

In considering the significance of this fact, our attention is here given chiefly to its religious bearing, although a change in religion necessarily brings with it a change in every department of human thought and action. When the new age has fully developed itself, what religion will it give us? Will it be some new phase of Christianity, or an eclectic religion, or something distinctively new? Here the anticipations of men differ widely. Let us attempt to classify them.

First, those Christians who believe that the Kingdom of God was established in the earth and the reign of Christ begun when He ascended into Heaven, or perhaps when the Roman Empire acknowledged Christianity. This is said by many, or most, in the Roman, Greek, and Anglican communions. They, therefore, look for no change in belief affecting essentially the creeds or rituals of the Church. As a

Divine Institution it is permanent, and this ensures the permanence of the present Christianity. No new religious era is to be looked for; its supposed signs are fallacious. The future will be as the past in all its main features till the Lord returns to final judgment.

Secondly, those — chiefly to be found in Protestant bodies — who think but little of the Church as a historic institution, to be preserved unchanged, but believe that there will be a wider and ever-growing spread of Christianity as a spiritual influence till the world is leavened. This class would retain for the most part the Protestant confessions of faith without any vital doctrinal or other changes. The new era they expect will come through a Christianized civilization, and the enlargement of Christendom to embrace all nations.

Thirdly, those who, having the same expectations as to the spread and triumph of Christianity, affirm that it must have large modifications in order that it may be adapted to the present conditions of religious enquiry. It is amongst these that we find many leaders of modern thought. They affirm, to use the evolutionary phrase, that the organism must be adjusted to its present environment. The Church, both as to its doctrine and polity and labours, must respond to the demands of the new age, and adapt itself to its needs. As to the extent of these modifications, there are wide diversities of opinion. Some would give up only those doctrines and rites which are most offensive to the spirit of the time; others would go further, and put away a large part of what has been regarded as distinctive in Christianity, that it may serve as a basis for an universal religion. But most have apparently no clear conception of what they must give up or retain.

Fourthly, those in all sections of the Church who see clearly enough the rapid religious changes all around them, and feel the power of the growing revolutionary tendencies, and are greatly perplexed what to think of the future, or what to do. They ask anxiously: Where are the proposed modifications of Christianity to end? Is it true that we are at the beginning of a new and better age? Is it the light of a glorious dawn that is beginning to illumine the heavens, or the lurid gleam of far-off volcanic fires? They know not what to believe in the present, or what to expect in the future. Faith in God, in the Scriptures, in the Church, does not wholly fail, but they are disquieted in spirit and sad at heart.

On the other hand, there are many in Christendom, and apparently a continually increasing number, who affirm that mere modifications of Christianity, greater or less, cannot permanently save it. Christendom has proved it for many centuries, and found it a practical failure. Its fundamental principles conflict with the growing intelligence of the world. We have come to a new age, and a new age must bring with it a new religion, not a revivification of the past; one based upon a new conception of God, simple, comprehensive, and fitted to be a world-religion. Some, indeed, think to make it eclectic, and to incorporate in it more or less of Christianity; but those of clearer vision see the impossibility of this, and affirm that Christianity must be taken as a whole, or rejected as a whole. Of these Renan is a sample, who says: "The future will no longer believe in the supernatural, for the supernatural is not true, and all that is not true is condemned to die. The pure truth will triumph. Judaism and Christianity will disappear." In the same way speaks the learned Jew, Darmesteter: "All Europe is in quest of a new God, and seeking everywhere for the echo of a coming gospel." And all those who, like Herbert Spencer, substitute an impersonal Force for a personal God, will have nothing of Christianity but its ethics. Of the attempts to formulate the new religion, we shall, later, have full occasion to speak. But in them all we shall see ample proof that Christianity, with its vital doctrines, the

Trinity, the Incarnation, Sin and Atonement, Resurrection and Judgment, must give place to some form of belief better suited to the modern conceptions of a Supreme Being, of the reign of Law, and of the goodness and dignity of human nature.

It is almost inevitable that but few in a time of transition like the present can have any definite conception whither they are going, for such a time is always one of obscurity and confusion. Christendom is a battlefield where the old elements and the new are struggling together, assailants and defenders inextricably mingled. It is in such a transition period that the light of the prophetic word is indispensable to clear vision. Knowing what God has said of His purpose in His Son, and in humanity, and illumined by it, we may discern the signs of the times, and the real nature and significance of passing events, and thus know the meaning of the present, and the goal to which it leads.

Assuming here (what the examination of the Scriptures will soon show us) that the antichristian spirit, which has often had its partial representatives in the past, is to be finally summed up in a single person, who is distinctively the Antichrist — the last product of the antichristian tendencies — we are brought to the vital question, What will be the relations of the coming new age to him? Do we see in its spirit and principles a preparation for him? We are taught by the Apostle Paul that "he shall sit in the temple of God, shewing himself that he is God." Are we to have a new religion in which the Saviour from sin can have no place, but will be supplanted by one who will present himself as the representative of a Divine humanity, and so an object of worship? It is the purpose of this book to answer these questions. To those who look upon the present tendencies as the harbingers of a new and higher evolution of Christianity, it will be both false and offensive. Why, they will ask, these pessimistic utterances? Why dishearten the spirits of zealous men by forebodings of evil? Why speak of an apostasy when the Church is just arising into the full consciousness of its mission, and girding itself anew for its accomplishment? Why speak of an Antichrist when the world is honoring the Christ more than ever before?

To those, also, on the other hand, who think that the world is outgrowing Christianity, and that there is no longer a place for the Church or its Head, and that humanity, freeing itself from its old and burdensome religious traditions, is entering upon a new and higher development, this book will be an offense; if it be not rather wholly disregarded and despised as a vain attempt to revive an antiquated belief which the Church of to-day itself rejects.

Thus, both by Christians who believe that the trials and perils of the Church are in a great measure over, and the day of triumph at hand, and by Antichristians who believe that Christianity will soon pass away, or be merged into a larger religion, the belief in a coming Antichrist as here presented will be rejected. But for all who accept the Scriptures as an intelligible revelation of a Divine purpose, the first duty is to ask what they teach us. Putting away all prejudices and unreasoned beliefs, we must ask what the Holy Ghost, speaking by the prophets of old and by the Lord and His apostles, has told us of the final stages of the great conflict between good and evil so long waged in the earth, and of its chief actors in the time of the end.

It is only through Scriptural light that we can fully know the character and work of the Antichrist; and to this light it is of vital importance that we give heed, for we are forewarned that he will present himself to men under an aspect best fitted to deceive. Those despising the prophetic word, and not believing in his appearing, will be attracted and fettered by the power of his person:

and those whose conception of him is that of an open blasphemer of God, a bitter enemy of all religion, detestable because of his vices, will not discern him should he appear as a saviour of society and a religious leader. It is only through the attentive study of the Scriptures, and its prophetic outlines of the future, and especially of St. Paul (2 Thess. ii. 2), that we can be kept from fatal misconceptions. He who seats himself in the temple of God, "shewing himself that he is God," is not, as is often said, one who compels the world to pay him Divine homage by brute violence; it is done voluntarily. That he can present himself to men as the object of Divine honour, and receive it, shows a community of belief already existing between him and his worshippers. They see in him the representative of their own religious ideas. He will not come as a spectre of the night, but as an angel of light, the morning star of a new day; and the age that will welcome and worship him will not think itself irreligious, but the most religious of all the ages. In him the modern spirit will find its truest representative and exponent. We may believe that he will be regarded by his generation as the highest type of our developed humanity, the noblest embodiment of its dignity, its "consummate flower." He will be recognized as a natural king of men, and his kingdom, rising grandly before the world, will be welcomed as the full evolution of the democratic idea, the realization of popular aspirations, the end of social strife, the unity of nations, the natural outcome and highest product of our civilization, and the goal of human history. It will be welcomed by the multitude as the long promised "Kingdom of God."

It need not be said that this man and his kingdom are not the accidents of an hour; there is a long preparatory process. As with our Lord, so with him. There is a "fulness of time" for his appearing, and this is not till the antichristian leaven has spread through Christendom.

Then will be the final test of Christian faith and discernment. Before the world will be two kings and two kingdoms. He who will set up the kingdom of God, is the Incarnate Son returning from Heaven; he who will set up the kingdom of man, is a son of the earth; and the question which must then be answered is, Which king and which kingdom will Christendom and the nations have?

The order of our enquiry is, therefore, this: First, what do we learn from the Scriptures — from the prophets and from the teachings of the Lord and of His apostles — respecting the religious condition of the world and of the Church at the period immediately preceding His return? And what is predicted of the Antichrist? And in this enquiry we are especially concerned with the doctrine of St. Paul and of St. John respecting the nature of the apostasy as preparatory to the coming of the man of sin, its final product. Having a clear conception of that apostasy, its origin, its nature, and final development in the man of sin; we may proceed, secondly, to examine the religious and the philosophical tendencies of the present time, that we may know its real character, and how far it is a preparation for the fulfilment of the Scripture predictions. This enquiry necessarily embraces many distinct points, which must be separately discussed. But it will be noted that the present purpose is to state and illustrate the religious tendencies and movements of the time, and not to confute them. Their confutation lies in seeing the goal to which they lead.

Perhaps more space has been given to the philosophic tendencies of our times than many may think to be necessary. But no one can truly know them who does not discern the pantheistic spirit which underlies them, and determines their practical working, manifested in all departments of human life. To understand the prophetic descriptions of the Antichrist, as claiming Divine homage, we must see how the prevalent philosophy tends to the deification of man, and so helps to prepare his way.

INTRODUCTION.

The term Antichrist is to many, perhaps to most Christians of our day, a term of great vagueness. But to the early Christians, and to the Church for several centuries, it was of very definite and fearful meaning. It designated the last and greatest of the enemies of God and of His Christ — an apostate who would sum up in himself all wickedness. Endowed by Satan with all his power, he would receive from him the kingdoms of this world, and rule over the nations. He would make war with the saints, and would overcome them, and reign supreme for a little time; but be himself destroyed at the coming of the Lord.

It is the purpose of this essay to enquire what the Scriptures teach concerning the Antichrist and his times; and how far we may see in the history of the Church, and in the movements and tendencies of our day, the foreshadowing of him, and the preparation for him. This involves a consideration of the place of Christ in the Divine purpose, and of His person and prerogatives.

But, before entering upon this enquiry, it will be well to define the term antichrist, and to give a brief outline of the several phases of belief in the Church in regard to his person and work.*

---

* Among the more important writers on the Antichrist are the Roman Catholics, F. T. Malvenda, *De Antichristo Libri undecim*,

The term "antichrist" plainly denotes an enemy of Christ, but leaves indefinite whether a person or a series of persons; whether one arising from within the Church or without it; whether one who has appeared or is yet to appear. Nor does the word itself determine whether he is simply an enemy of Christ, or both an enemy to Him and a substitute for Him. Many find only the element of hostility. This certainly is the predominant idea, but does not exclude that of substitution. This appears if we note that the work of Christ in our redemption has two chief parts, that of atonement — the propitiation for our sins and the heavenly intercession based upon it; and that of judging and ruling, or the administration of the Messianic kingdom. The first of these Antichrist wholly denies. He will know no atonement, no cross, no priesthood. Here his hostility to Christianity is openly avowed. For the second of these, the Messianic kingdom, he will substitute an earthly kingdom, the elements of which will be fraternity, liberty, equality, and in which will be the highest development of man. It is here that he offers himself as a substitute for Christ. He will be the Messiah of the nations, and under him all will be blessed. As said by Archbishop Trench ("Synonyms," *sub voce*),

---

Romæ, 1604 A.D.; Cardinal Bellarmine, *De Controversiis Christianæ Fidei*, 4 Tomi, 1622. In Tomus I he treats at length the charge of Calvin that the papacy is Antichrist. A good summary is found in Stern's Commentar, Die Offenbarung, ch. xiii, 1854. Among recent Protestant writers, aside from the commentators, are C. Maitland's "Apostolic School of Prophetic Interpretation"; Dr. J. H. Todd's "Discourses on the Prophecies Relating to Antichrist," Dublin, 1840. For a very recent statement of early and mediæval belief see Wadstein in Hilgenfelds Zeitschrift, 1895–6.

"He will not call himself Christ, for he will be filled with deadliest hate, both against the name and office, against the whole spirit and temper of Jesus of Nazareth, now the exalted King of Glory. . . He will not assume the name of Christ, and so will not in the letter be a false Christ, yet assuming to himself Christ's offices, presenting himself to the world as the true centre of its hopes, as the satisfaction of its needs, and healer of its hurts, he will, in fact, take upon himself all names and forms of blasphemy; will be the false Christ and the Antichrist both at once."

In giving a brief outline of the various beliefs in the Church respecting the Antichrist, we find three periods clearly marked.

First, the belief in the early Church, and in general down to the Reformation. Second, from the Reformation to the French Revolution. Third, from the French Revolution to the present time.

I. In the first period, extending over some fifteen centuries, there was not absolute uniformity of belief, but substantial agreement. To quote in detail the words of the early fathers would demand more space than we can give, nor is it at all necessary for our purpose. That there is such agreement is affirmed by all who have investigated the matter, both Roman Catholics and Protestants. Some quotations from the more recent writers will be sufficient here. Thus it is said by Greswell ("Parables," Vol. II), "Another article of belief on which the fathers are unanimous is this: That before the end of the world Antichrist must be expected to appear. It made no difference whether they were advocates or opposers of the doctrine of the millennium in particular; in the reception of this opinion there was perfect agreement among all parties. . . . The fathers are likewise agreed in considering Antichrist to be a real person, and not merely a figurative or symbolic character. . . . They are unanimous that the appearance and rise of the Antichrist would be accompanied by the persecution of the followers of the true Christ, and that his kingdom would be established on the ruins of the Church." It is said by Bishop Wordsworth (Com. on 2 Thess.), "The general opinion of the fathers was that a personal Antichrist would appear a short time before the second coming of Christ."

In like manner it is said by Todd ("Discourses," note p. 18), "All more ancient writers unanimously agreed that an individual Antichrist was described in the prophecy, and that he was to appear at the end of the world immediately before the second coming of the Lord." After stating the early opinions in brief, S. R. Maitland says: "I believe that the opinions which I here attribute to the early Church, were held by all Christian writers until the twelfth century." Prof. Eadie remarks ("Essay on Man of Sin") "That the man of sin was to be one human being, one man, . . was the first and prevailing interpretation." So also J. H. Newman ("The Patristical Idea of Antichrist"), "That Antichrist is one individual man was the universal tradition of the early Church." Perhaps these statements should be somewhat modified as regards the Alexandrian School.

This agreement of the fathers embraced the following points:

1. That before the end of the world or age, there would be an apostasy, which in its culmination would be not merely a corruption of the Christian faith, but

a total denial of it — an apostasy not universal, but very general.

2. That the last representative and leader of this apostasy would be a man, "the man of sin," "the wicked one," "the son of perdition," or "the Antichrist."

3. That this man would attain to universal dominion, all nations becoming subject to him.

4. That this dominion would continue but a short time, forty-two months, or three and a half years.

5. That he would claim divine honours for himself, and persecute all upholding the faith of Christ, and suppress, as far as possible, all Christian worship.

6. That the time immediately preceding and during his reign would be one of great tribulation.

7. That many of the Jews would receive him as their Messiah.

8. That he would be destroyed with his adherents by the Lord at His appearing.

Besides these points of general agreement, there were diverse particular opinions about the person of the Antichrist, of which we may mention: *a*. That he was Satan incarnated. *b*. That he was a son of Satan by a human mother. *c*. That he was a man possessed by Satan. *d*. That he was a man who voluntarily gave himself up to do Satan's will, and was endowed by him with miraculous powers — *Organum diaboli* — and to him Satan would give the rule of the kingdoms of this world. *e*. That he was a man raised from the dead by Satan, and so a counterpart of the risen Christ.

The surmises of some of the fathers as to his birth in Bethsaida, and his education in Babylon, are of no importance. It was held by many that he was to be a Jew, and of the tribe of Dan, chiefly on the ground that Dan is not mentioned among the sealed tribes of The Revelation (ch. vii). It was said by Lactantius and some of the fathers, that he would come from the East and subdue the West.

The points enumerated as those of general belief in the first age of the Church, are still held in substance in the Roman Catholic and Greek communions, and probably in the small Eastern sects. But some important modifications gradually came in, the grounds of which will be better understood after speaking of the nature of the apostasy. It need only be said here that, as the expectation of a speedy return of the Lord gradually passed away, and it was believed that the prophecies respecting the success and glory of the Church were to be fulfilled during His absence, and that this might be indefinitely prolonged, the fear of Antichrist's speedy appearance ceased, and comparatively little interest was taken in it; and the matter became practically of little importance.

It does not really affect the unanimity of the pre-Reformation Church that in the twelfth and following centuries some small sects began to apply the prophecies respecting Babylon to the Church of Rome, and identified the Papacy with the Antichrist; since this seems to have been done rather out of anger because of real or supposed oppression, than upon any clear view of the character of Antichrist, or upon any consistent principle of prophetic interpretation. At this time, too, or a little later, when the Roman Church was much distracted with the contentions of rival popes, it was not unusual for zealous partisans to brand the claimants they opposed with the title of Antichrist. Thus St. Bernard of the twelfth century called Pope Leo, whom he regarded as an usurper of St. Peter's chair, the beast of the Apocalypse. (See Todd, " Discourses," p. 28, Note A.) But it will be noted that it was the usurper, not the real pope, whom he so called. It was not the bishop of Rome, the true vicar of Christ, as such, to whom the title of Antichrist in these disputes was applied, but to one who falsely claimed to be His vicar. And it was not until the Reformation that it was applied to the popes officially without distinction — a series of Antichrists. Some changes during this period of the primitive belief will be spoken of later.

II. Second Period, from the Reformation to the French Revolution.

The application of the term Antichrist to the pope in his official position, or its application to the Papacy as a system, marks the Reformation period. It is said by the Roman Catholic commentator, Estius, in his remarks on Second Thessalonians II, that " Luther, instigated by the Devil, was the first who applied the term to the pope as pope." ("*Adversus execrabilem bullam Antichristi,*" 1520.) But it is not clear that at first Luther meant it to apply to the whole series of popes. This was done later by many of the leading Reformers, and marks the growing estrangement from the Papacy. It shows also a wide departure from the early belief in affirming: *a.* That the Antichrist was not an individual; *b.* That he had already appeared; *c.* That the apostasy would not be a total denial of the truth.

The designation of the papal system as antichristian, and its head as Antichrist, is found in several of the Confessions of the Reformed Churches. (See " Hutterus Redivivus " of Hase, p. 342; and Schaff's

"Creeds of Christendom"; also the Address of the translators of the Bible to King James.) In the Westminster Confession we read: "The Pope is that Antichrist, that man of sin, and son of perdition, that setteth himself in the church against God, and all that is called God." (The references in proof are, Matt. xxiii, 8–10; 2 Thess. ii; Rev. xiii, 6—.) The same is said in the Savoy Declaration of 1658 with this addition: "We expect that in the latter day, Antichrist being destroyed, the Jews called, and the adversaries of the Kingdom of God's Son broken, the Church of Christ, enlarged and edified through a free communication of life and peace, will enjoy in this world a more quiet, peaceable, and glorious condition than it has enjoyed."

The belief of the Protestant churches as to the papal Antichrist continued to be generally held, though with some modifications, down to the time of the French Revolution. It was, however, held less and less firmly, and by some was openly rejected. The glaring inconsistency of calling those antichristians who offered all their worship in the name of Christ, was more and more felt.

III. Third Period, from the French Revolution to the present time.

After this Revolution the belief of the Reformers as to the papal Antichrist was much modified, and by many Protestants is now entirely given up. Several causes for this may be given — the natural decay of the old animosity and bitterness of feeling toward the Roman Church; and the growing consciousness that a church which holds and repeats in its services the three great Creeds, and claims its head to be the vicar of Christ, cannot in any real sense of the term be called antichristian. Still more important in effecting this change was the French Revolution, which brought into view a new and most deadly element of hostility to the Christian faith, not its corruption merely, but its total denial; and, therefore, affecting alike all Christian Communions. Not a few Protestants now accept the primitive belief that the Antichrist is a single man, and that he is yet to come. Others distinguish between the Roman Church and the Papacy, the last being the Antichrist. Others still find two Antichrists, the papal and the infidel, the first fulfilling one part of the Scriptures, and preparing the way for the last, who will completely fulfil them. Dr. Hodge says ("Systematic Theology", Vol. III): "There may hereafter be a great antichristian power concentrated in an antichristian ruler, who will be utterly destroyed at the coming of the Lord; and at the same time the belief may be maintained that the Antichrist, designated by Daniel and St. Paul, is not a man but an institution or organized power, such as a kingdom or the papacy."

There are probably many Protestants in our day who have no definite belief, and, while they may regard Roman doctrine in important points as corrupt, do not look upon the Papacy itself as antichristian; and there is, doubtless, a very considerable and increasing number in all Christian communions who wholly disbelieve in any Antichrist to come, and who think the matter to be of no practical importance, and not worthy of consideration; some because they believe in a victorious future of the Church, and others because they expect on evolutionary grounds a gradual but continuous development of humanity, and reject all supernatural interpositions.

In the Roman Church there seems to be no authoritative teaching, and various beliefs are expressed. The belief of Malvenda (*De Antichristo*) that the Antichrist will be an individual, and is still future — *Antichristum futuram unum certum et singularem hominem* — is probably the more general belief.* It is said by Bellarmine (*De Controversiis*): *Catholici omnes ita sentiunt fore Antichristum unum quandam hominem.*

We may add here some remarks of J. H. Newman (1835) as to the value of this enquiry: "In the present state of things, when the great object of education is supposed to be the getting rid of things supernatural . . I must think that this vision of Antichrist, as a supernatural power to come, is a great providential gain as being a counterpoise to the evil tendencies of the age. It must surely be profitable for our thoughts to be sent backward and forward to the beginning and the end of the Gospel times, to the first and second coming of Christ."

---

* A late distinguished member of the Paulist Fathers, Rev. F. A. Hewitt, in a recent article (*Catholic Quarterly*, April, 1894), attempts to show that the predictions respecting Antichrist were fulfilled in Mohammed; and that "the Kingdom of Christ is advancing on a steady line of progress towards a development which shall surpass anything in its past history."

CHRISTIANITY
AND ANTI-CHRISTIANITY

PART I.

THE TEACHINGS OF THE SCRIPTURES RESPECTING THE ANTICHRIST.

THE TEACHINGS OF THE OLD TESTAMENT.

THE TEACHINGS OF THE LORD.

THE TEACHINGS OF THE APOSTLES COLLECTIVELY.

ST. PAUL AND HIS TEACHINGS.

THE TEACHINGS OF ST. JOHN, OF ST. PETER, AND OF ST. JUDE.

THE TEACHINGS OF THE REVELATION.

THE TEACHINGS OF THE SCRIPTURE.
OLD TESTAMENT.

We now come to the inquiry, What do the Scriptures teach us respecting the Antichrist? We begin by asking whether the Old Testament speaks of him as the Antimessiah? and this leads us to enquire as to the Messianic expectations of the Jews in our Lord's day. These, as based upon the covenants and the prophets, had their culmination in the Kingdom to be set up by the Messiah. Into the conception of the Kingdom there entered three chief elements: (*a*) the authority of Jehovah, their covenant God, would be established over all the earth; (*b*) to the Jews as the covenant people would be given the highest place among the nations; (*c*) the government under Jehovah would be administered by a Son of David, under whose rule all peoples would dwell in unity and peace. Jehovah would everywhere be honoured as the supreme God, but in Jerusalem would be His temple, and the centre of all worship.

In regard to the time and manner of the setting up of the Messianic Kingdom, it was believed that it

NOTE — Passages speaking of the Kingdom of the Messiah:

(*a*) Its King, a Son of David, Jer. xxiii, 5, xxxiii, 15; Isa. ix, 7; Isa. xi, 1.

(*b*) Under it the Jews will be saved, Jer. xxiii, 6, xxxiii, 7; Isa. xxvii, 6, lx, 21.

(*c*) Under it all nations will dwell in peace, Ps. lxxii; Is. lx, 8; Isa. ii, 4.

(*d*) Under it all peoples will worship Jehovah, Isa. ii, 3, xi, 9, lxvi, 23; Zech. xiv, 16.

would be when the Jews were in great trouble and distress (Dan. xii, 1). They would be scattered abroad in all lands, and subject to cruel oppression, and encounter the hostility of all nations. But the Messiah would appear, and through Him Jehovah would deliver them from their oppressors, gather them together into their own land, and fulfill to them all the promises made through the prophets of the prosperity and glory of the Messianic Kingdom. The period of trial and judgment immediately introductory to the Kingdom would be one of brief duration. At its beginning, the enemies of the Messiah would be active and triumphant, but at the end would be overthrown, and the authority of the Messiah everywhere be recognized. This period of trial, preceding the coming of the Messiah, and followed by the Kingdom, was known by various names, "the day of wrath," "the day of judgment," "the great and terrible day," "the time of the birth-throes"; as the end of the age or dispensation, it was "the last day," or "last days;" and as forming the transition to the Messianic age, it was the conclusion or "end of this world" and "the beginning of the world to come."

It was in "the last days" that both good and evil would come to the full, and the distinction between them be most manifest, and, therefore, the hostility the greatest. Among all peoples there would be division and strife and hatred; and in the physical world, great disturbances and cosmical changes (Joel ii, 30; Zech. xiv); the end of all being "new heavens and a new earth" in which the righteous would dwell (Isa. lxv, 17).

But whilst the Jews believed that the nations would

assemble together, and fight against the Messiah at
His appearing (Ps. ii, Joel ii, Zech. xiv, 2), did
they believe that their enemies would then be united
under one head — the Antimessiah? It is not wholly
clear what the Jews believed on this point.* The
prophecies of Daniel were much read, and largely
moulded the popular expectations as to the future.
This prophet uses the symbol of a beast to represent
the kingdoms which wasted and oppressed his people.
He saw four different beasts coming up from the sea
— four successive kingdoms — each with its special
characteristics, but all hostile to the Jews (Dan. vii).
In the image seen by Nebuchadnezzar (Dan. ii, 31),
four kingdoms were symbolized by its differing parts
of gold, silver, brass, and iron. That the fourth and
last is the Roman has been generally held.† This
beast (vii, 24) has ten horns (the horn being everywhere a symbol of some form of power), which
here represent the fullness of its kingly power:
"The ten horns out of this kingdom are ten kings
that shall arise." Among these came up "a little
horn," having eyes like the eyes of a man, and a
mouth speaking great things, whose look was more
stout than his fellows, and who thinks to change
times and laws. That this eleventh horn symbol-

---

* What is said by Bertholdt (*Christologia*, 16) of the Antichristus is taken from later, and for the most part Christian,
sources. Eisenmenger, "Entdecktes Judenthum," quotes only
from the later Rabbis. It is said by Jowett, "Essay on Man of
Sin": "It was a current belief of the time in which St. Paul
lived that the coming of Messiah would be preceded by the coming of Antichrist," referring to Gfrörer as his authority.

† Dr. Todd "Discourses" affirms that the fourth kingdom
is that of the Antichrist. Against this interpretation there are
very strong objections.

ized some great persecutor is plain from the words spoken of him; and it is not likely that the Jews of the Lord's day believed that they had had their fulfillment in Antiochus Epiphanes, or in any persecutor of the past. It is more probable that they saw in Antiochus a type of a greater enemy to come, and the last, for after his destruction the kingdom would be given to the saints of the Most High. Understanding the one "like unto a Son of Man" (vii, 18) to be the Messiah, who now takes the Kingdom, this would certainly lead to the conception of this last enemy as an antimessiah; but that the Jews so understood it, is more than we can positively affirm.

The same may be said of "the little horn" (Dan. viii, 9), and interpreted as a symbol of "a king of fierce countenance," who "shall destroy the mighty and the holy people." And also of "the willful king" (xi, 36), though not a few now understand the fulfillment of this prophecy to be wholly in the future. Of the prediction of the "one that maketh desolate" (ix, 24 —) we shall speak in considering the Lord's teachings.

If we turn to the other prophets, the words of Isaiah xi, 4: "With the breath of His lips shall He slay the wicked," are translated in the Targum, "With the breath of his lips shall he slay Armilus." This shows that at the time of this translation there was a belief that the Messiah would be confronted by a chief personal enemy whom He would destroy. St. Paul applies this to the man of sin (2 Thess. ii, 8). Of this passage Delitzsch ("Messianic Prophecies") says, "We have an indication that the apostasy of the earth will finally culminate in the Antichrist." Other typical references to the Antimessiah in this prophet are found by many interpreters in x, 5, where the "Assyrian" is mentioned; and in xiv, 12, where "Lucifer," "the shining one," or "son of the dawn," is spoken of, who says, "I will ascend into heaven, I will exalt my throne above the stars of God. . . I will be like the Most High." In the mention of Leviathan (xxvii, 1), "the swift serpent," "the crooked serpent," "the dragon that is in the midst of the sea," some find a symbolic pointing out of the Antimessiah.

A reference to an Antimessiah is found by some in Psalm cx, 6. "He shall wound the heads over many countries" (in R. V. "He shall strike through the head in many countries"). The singular "head" being used in the Hebrew, they understand it as equivalent to "prince," and to foretell that many countries are to be united in that day — "the day of God's wrath" when He shall judge among the nations — under one man as their chief.

A union of many peoples under one head is spoken of by Ezekiel, xxxviii, 2. But it is not easy to identify Gog, "the chief prince of Meshech," with the blasphemous oppressors of Daniel. He seems rather to be a distinct enemy, and not improbably a Christian power, hostile to the Jews, who will invade their land and oppress for a short time the Jewish people; but at what time or under what conditions we cannot now understand.

Whilst then we do not find in the Old Testament any distinct mention by name of an Antimessiah, we do find predictions that at the time when the Messiah was expected to appear and take the Kingdom, there would be arrayed against Him the nations acting together in unity. This implies a head, some one who is the leader, and possessed of great, if not supreme power. (See Joel iii, 2. "I will gather all nations against Jerusalem," and Zech. xiv, 2, "I will gather all nations against Jerusalem to battle," also Ps. ii.) The characters of the oppressors mentioned by Daniel, their hatred of the holy people, their selfish exaltation, their contempt of God and of His times and laws — all mark a period when "wickedness is come to the full," and the most bitter enemies of God and His Christ appear. It is not without ground that we may believe that the imprecatory Psalms, especially cix, may prophetically refer to this man in whom would be concentrated all hostility to Jehovah and the Saints.

We may, then, accept the language of Prof. Briggs ("Messianic Prophecy"), "It is not unnatural, but rather in accordance with the analogy of prophecy, that the hostile kingdoms should not only increase in extension, but also increase in intension; we might reasonably expect that a great hostile monarch, an Antimessiah, would precede the advent of the Messiah Himself. . . The sufferings of the people of God would reach their climax under the Antimessiah."

That the Jews of the Lord's day, or at least many of them, believed that the general hostility of the nations to them as the Covenant people, would find its last expression in some mighty one, their leader, who would be overthrown by the Messiah, although nowhere distinctly asserted by the prophets, cannot well be doubted. But was this Antimessiah to be a heathen man, or an apostate Jew? Some have seen a prophetic intimation that he would be a Jew, in the mention by the prophet Zechariah (xi,

17) of "the idol (foolish) shepherd." Thus Delitzsch says: "If the good shepherd is the image of the future Christ, the foolish shepherd is the counterpart of Christ, that is, the lawless one in whom the apostasy from Christ culminates. A heathen ruler is not meant, but one proceeding from the people having the name of the people of God."* But on the other hand, those whom the later Jews regarded as types of the Antimessiah were heathen, as Balaam and the Assyrian. It is not likely that the Jews believed that anyone of their number would so fall from the faith as to deny the special calling of his people; or that an apostate Jew would be received by the heathen as their head. They saw rather in the Antimessiah, if, indeed, they had any definite conception of him as an individual, one who did not recognize their claim to be God's chosen people, or the claim of their Messiah; a Gentile who hated the Jews for their religious exclusiveness and pride, and who presented himself as the leader of their heathen enemies.

* It was long before said by Jerome: *Pastor stultus aut imperitus haud dubium quin Antichristus sit, qui in consummatione mundi dicitur esse venturus, et qualis sit venturus, indicatur.*

THE TEACHINGS OF THE LORD.

In considering these teachings, we must distinguish between those spoken to His own disciples and those spoken to the Jews. So far as His words concern us here, they refer to three points. First, His own Messianic relations to the Jews, and their national future; Secondly, The future of the Church, immediate and remote, down to His return; Thirdly, The person and work of the Antichrist.

I. (*a*) We have seen what were the Messianic expectations of the Jews in the Lord's day. Presenting Himself to them as their Messiah, the Son of David, He asserted His prerogative, as Judge and King. "The Father judgeth no man, but hath committed all judgment unto the Son, that all men should honour the Son even as they honour the Father." (John v, 22—.) The time of this judgment is at His return. "When the Son of man shall come in His glory .. then shall He sit upon the throne of His glory." (Matt. xxv, 31. See also in same discourse the parables of the "Talents," and of the "Virgins"; and of the "Nobleman," Luke xix, 12—.)

(*b*) He confirmed the predictions of the prophets that at this time the Jews would be scattered abroad, and Jerusalem trodden down by the Gentiles, and the temple left desolate. (Luke xxi, 24; Matt. xxiii, 38.) He confirmed, also, the predictions that this would be a time of great trouble, and distress of all nations. "Then shall be great tribulation, such as was not since the beginning of the world to this time, no, nor ever shall be." (Matt. xxiv, 21—.) "These be the days of vengeance, that all things which are written may be fulfilled." "There shall be great distress in the land and wrath upon this people." "Except those days should be shortened, there should no flesh be saved."

(*c*) He confirmed God's promise that after these judgments had brought them to repentance, the Jews would be gathered to their own land, and acknowledge Him as their King. This is plain from His promise to the Apostles of the circumcision:— "In the regeneration, when the Son of man shall sit on the throne of His glory, ye also shall sit upon twelve thrones, judging the twelve tribes of Israel." (Matt. xix, 28; Luke xxii, 29–30.)

II. The Future of the Church, immediate and remote.

We must, as already said, distinguish those teachings of the Lord addressed to the Jews respecting their national future, from those addressed to His disciples respecting their immediate future, and the future of the Church; though much which He said concerned both the Jews and the Church as standing to Him in like Covenant relations. His return to establish His kingdom would equally concern both, but would present to each its special aspect. Now, His words respecting His Church, its relations to the world, its history and its spiritual condition at the time of His return, demand our most careful consideration.

We may best consider these teachings under several particulars.

1. The permanent antagonistic relation of the Church to the world. As not of the world, but called out of it, and witnessing against it as evil, the relation is one of inherent hostility. The Lord in His last discourse to His disciples emphasises this. "If ye were of the world, the world would love his own; but because ye are not of the world, but I have chosen you out of the world, therefore the world hateth you. Remember the word that I said unto you, The servant is not greater than his Lord. If they have persecuted Me, they will also persecute you; if they have kept My saying, they will keep yours also." (John xv, 19–20.) In His intercessory prayer, He says: "I have given them Thy word; and the world hath hated them, because they are not of the world, even as I am not of the world." (John xvii, 14—.) He also foretells how deadly this hostility will be: "They shall put you out of the synagogues; yea, the time cometh that whosoever killeth you will think that he doeth God service." (John xvi, 2.) That this was not a transient outburst of enmity, and confined to the Jews, and only for a brief period at the beginning, but the result of a permanent antagonism between sin and holiness, righteousness and unrighteousness, truth and falsehood, and, therefore, an antagonism between the Church and the world to the end, appears everywhere from His teachings; of which the parable of the tares and the wheat may be taken as an illustration. That this antagonism is not one of abstract principles simply, but is embodied in persons, the Lord shows by His recognition of the fact that there is "a Power of darkness," the head of which is Satan —"the prince of this world," the personal adversary of God and of His Son. To the special attacks of

this great enemy He had Himself been exposed, and knew that so long as Satan continued to be the prince of this world, His disciples would have no exemption from his subtle temptations and deadly assaults. They were in an enemy's country, and he would not cease in his attacks until he was cast out of the earth. All expectations of peace between his followers and the followers of the Lord were vain; but he might disguise his hostility and assume the attitude of a friend, and so lull the Church into security, and into a forgetfulness, or even a denial of his existence. But this peace was only seeming. The more the Church manifested the holiness of her Head, and affirmed the sinfulness of human nature, and the necessity of His atonement; the more clearly she proclaimed Him as the incarnate Son of God through whom alone is salvation; the more pronounced and bitter would this hostility become. The only way in which this antagonism could be set aside, was either by the conversion of the world to faith in Christ, which would deprive Satan of all his following and power; or by the entire apostasy of the Church from that faith, which would make Satan's power supreme. Either the Church or the world must lose its distinctive character before there could be peace between them.

As to the conversion of the world through the preaching of the Gospel, it must be noted that although the Lord gave the command that the Gospel should be preached to all nations, He nowhere speaks of it as being universally received. In sending forth His Apostles upon a temporary mission during His earthly ministry, He said to them, in words which plainly looked forward beyond that mission, and embrace all missionary labour, that every form of opposition and suffering would meet them. (Matt. x, 5—.) "I send you forth as sheep in the midst of wolves... Ye shall be hated of all men for My name's sake... Think not that I am come to send peace on earth; I came not to send peace, but a sword." Even the closest family bonds would be severed: "A man's foes shall be they of his own household." All who would be His followers must bear His cross, and be willing even to die for His sake.

Nowhere in all His teachings did the Lord say, that this hostility of the world to the Church would cease through the conversion of the world. On the contrary, it would continue, though it might be in a latent condition, and would become most intense at the time of the end; for then His actings in preparation for His return, the assertion of His authority, and the quickened faith of many, would call forth the latent hatred, and rouse into activity "the prince of this world" who would put forth every power of evil to destroy. His disciples could not be "hated of all nations for His name's sake," until "the gospel had been preached in all the world for a witness unto all nations." The tares would grow and ripen till the harvest came.

If peace would not be made by the conversion of the world to the Gospel, could it be through the whole Church becoming worldly in her spirit and aims? Of a total apostasy we cannot think. The Lord has said that "the gates of hell shall not prevail against His Church." She cannot cease to be the body of Christ, and the temple of the Holy Ghost. But though the Church cannot ever become wholly apostate, and therefore she cannot be at absolute peace with the world, she may become worldly-minded; and thus the enmity of the world to her may be blunted, and the appearance of peace exist. The Church may forget her high calling, and become earthly in her spirit. She may corrupt the Gospel, mingling the leaven of error with the truth, may refuse to set forth the claims of Christ in their fulness, may seek the honour which cometh from men, and in many ways propitiate the world; and the line of distinction be thus almost effaced. She may become "the unjust steward," lowering her Lord's claims upon the faith and obedience of men in order to gain their favour. Those who have the spirit of this world, the world will not hate. To His own brethren, who did not then believe on Him, the Lord said (John vii, 7): "The world cannot hate you, but Me it hateth, because I testify of it that the works thereof are evil." A seeming concord may be established between the Church and the world on the basis of a common worldliness, but it is superficial and unreal. The true antagonism will reappear so soon and so far as the Church bears a faithful witness in word and life to her living Head. And as the consciousness of her high calling is reawakened and strengthened in the last day, and she rises into her true heavenly position, so will the antagonism then be sharpest and most intense.

We have dwelt the longer upon this point of essential and permanent hostility, because the belief that the Church and the world can dwell peaceably together, and jointly serve God, though in different ways; and that to this end the claims of Christ, as held at first in the Church, may now be greatly modified, and His headship made of little account, is one very powerful means, as we shall see later, in preparing the way of the Antichrist.

2. Let us now note what the Lord said of the spiritual condition of the Church just before His return. It would be one of great worldliness. "The love of the many shall wax cold." (Matt. xxiv, 12.) It would be at the coming of the Son of man as in the days of Noah and of Lot, when the ordinary pursuits of life, building, planting, marrying, and the like —things in themselves right and necessary — so engrossed men that they were wholly unmindful of God's warnings, and therefore His judgments would come upon them unawares. (Luke xvii, 26—.) He speaks of the time as one of greatest temptation, when false Christs and false prophets would arise, showing great signs and wonders, and through them many would be deceived.* (Matt. xxiv, 23–4.) Iniquity — lawlessness — would abound, and many be offended, and hate and betray one another. The faith that prays for His return, though greatly

---

* There seems to be good reason for believing that the clause in the prayer of the Lord which He gave His disciples: "Lead us not into temptation, but deliver us from evil," "Bring us not into temptation, but deliver us from the evil one," (R. V.), refers to the great temptation, and to the power of Satan, at the time of the end. As the second petition is a prayer for the coming of the kingdom, so the last petition a prayer that the disciples may escape the great and final temptation immediately preceding it, and be delivered from the Tempter, who would then put forth all his power through "the son of perdition." (See Rev. xii, 12: xiii, 6—.) This is wholly in accordance with the Lord's general teaching with reference to the future, and especially to the tribulation of the last days. This time of trial and temptation He does not put far distant, but would have it ever remembered, and it was clearly in the mind of the disciples as near at hand.

strengthened in a few, would be well nigh extinguished in most; and that day come upon all that dwell upon the face of the whole earth, as a snare. It would be a time so fearful, that He commands His disciples "to watch and pray always that they may escape the things which shall come to pass"; for there are some who, like Noah and Lot, shall escape the sore judgments. (Luke xxi, 36—.)

Let us consider the Lord's actings as Judge at His return. The time having come when the tares and the wheat must be separated, the Lord begins with His Church, and separates in several successive judicial acts the faithful from the unfaithful, and gathers the faithful to Himself. (Matt. xxiv, 40; xxv, 10, 11, 31—) This done, He proceeds to set the Jews in their place, separating in like manner the believing from the unbelieving among them; and finally judges the nations, making a like separation among them. Thus His kingdom is fully established — all things that offend and them which do iniquity being gathered out, and all classes of His subjects put in their right places — and the predictions of the prophets are fulfilled. These events, doubtless, occupy a considerable period of time, and this whole period is "the day of judgment," "the great day of the Lord."

This summary of the Lord's teaching shows us that anything like a conversion of the world before His return by the preaching of the gospel, was not in His thoughts. Had it been, He could not have failed to comfort His mourning disciples, and encourage them to vigorous action by assurances of the success of their mission. But he persistently holds up before them hatred, persecution, death. His life on earth was prophetic of the history of the Church; and the greatest manifestation of hostility to her, as to Him, would be at the end. Then would she go down into her Gethsemane; then would be "the hour and the power of darkness"; and it would be the time of "the perplexity and distress of the nations." Only His return could bring deliverance; for that she must ever watch and pray.

III. The person and work of the Antichrist.

1. Let us examine the Lord's words to the Jews. We have already seen reason to believe that the Jews looked for some great one to appear in the last days, in whom the enmity of the nations against them would be headed up, and by whom they would be grievously persecuted and oppressed; and who would set himself in opposition to the Messiah, and finally be destroyed by Him. Does the Lord in His teachings to the Jews allude to such a person? The only passage bearing on this point is that in John (John v, 43), "I am come in My Father's name, and ye receive Me not; if another shall come in his own name, him ye will receive." It is here clearly intimated that someone would come presenting himself to the Jews as their Messiah, and would be received by them. Jesus, the true Messiah, had come in His Father's name, and they had rejected Him; another would come claiming in his own right the Messianic rule, and him they would receive. The Lord does not say that he would be a Jew, and yet we can scarce suppose that, with the then prevalent conceptions of their high place as God's covenant people, they could have thought of a heathen Messiah. It is possible that he may be both a Jew and a Christian, an apostate from both covenants.

2. The Lord's words to His disciples. In these does the Lord speak of an individual in whom the enmity of the world to the Church would be headed up? We find no distinct reference to one, except in the words already quoted which were spoken to the Jews, and have no direct reference to His Church. He speaks of false Christs, but not of an Antichrist. Yet there may be one implied in His reference to Daniel. (Matt. xxiv, 15.) "When ye, therefore, shall see the abomination of desolation, spoken of by Daniel the prophet, stand in the holy place (whoso readeth, let him understand),—then let them," etc. The question arises, what did the Lord mean by "the abomination of desolation"? The phrase occurs three times in the prophet. (ix, 27; xi, 31; xii, 11.) In the last two it is rendered "the abomination that maketh desolate"; but in the first (R. V.), "and upon the wing of abominations shall come one that maketh desolate; and even until the consummation, and that determined, shall wrath be poured out upon the desolator." Most interpreters suppose that the Lord referred to this passage of the prophet, and if so, He intended to have the disciples understand that some one person would come — an abominable desolator — who would stand in the holy place. Thus understood, this teaching of the Lord would serve as the foundation of the later teaching of St. Paul (2 Thess. ii, 4).

If, however, we suppose the Lord to have referred to all the passages in which "the abomination that maketh desolate" is spoken of, and His general warning — "Let whoso readeth, understand," implies this, we can scarce avoid the conclusion that He would teach us that at the end the enmity against

God would be summed up in a person. What He said to the Church after His ascension respecting the beast and false prophet, will be considered when The Revelation is before us.

This brief survey of the Lord's words will serve to shew the importance of His Person and work as distinguished from His teachings. These were necessarily adapted to the spiritual and mental understanding of those to whom He spake. But He Himself was the Way, the Truth, and the Life. The salvation of the world was not to be effected by the mere enlargement of its religious knowledge, but by its acceptance of Him as the Saviour. Not by His words, but by His works must it be saved. What He said was to explain who He was, and what He was then doing, and what He was still to do; and one stage of His work prepared the way for another; the Cross for His priesthood, the priesthood for His Kingdom; all must be done by Him personally. To substitute His teachings, spiritual or ethical, as the means of saving society or the world, is to hide Him and His future work from sight, and thus tends powerfully, as we shall see, to prepare the way for the Antichrist.

THE TEACHINGS OF THE APOSTLES COLLECTIVELY.

Before entering upon the enquiry as to the teaching of the several Apostles, whose Epistles we have, in regard to the Antichrist, and the spiritual condition of the Church before the coming of the Lord, let us first note what they all have in common. And in our examination we must bear in mind that they all looked for the return of the Lord in their own lifetime, or in the lifetime of some then living. This must affect our interpretation of their words so far that we may not impute to them a conception of a long period as intervening.*

Accepting their Lord's words as the very truth of God, the Apostles make them the rule of all their teachings to the Church. What He said of the future of the Jewish people, and of His Church, they repeat; and as time went on, and His words became more and more clear through their partial fulfilment; and the Holy Ghost also gave new light through the Christian prophets (John xvi, 13; 1 Tim. iv, 1), they bring forth some particulars which He had not made known. This gradual enlargement of prophetic knowledge need not surprise us, for it lies in the very nature of prophecy that, as the purpose of God goes on from stage to stage, He makes known to His children what He is about to do, that they may be His helpers.

* It is well said by Bengel: "*Gradatim profetica procedit, apocalypsis explicatius loquitur quam Paulus; Paulus explicatius quam Dominus ante glorificationem.*

1. The Apostles agree in affirming that the return of the Lord was to be continually watched for by the Church as an event that might occur at any moment. This was only to repeat His express teachings. (Matt. xxiv, 44; Luke xii, 35—.) They, therefore, so taught the Church. St. Peter said: "The end of all things is at hand; be ye therefore sober, and watch unto prayer." "The day of the Lord will come as a thief in the night... What manner of persons ought ye to be in all holy conversation and godliness, looking for and hastening the coming of the day of God."

St. Paul said: "The day of the Lord so cometh as a thief in the night.. therefore, let us not sleep as do others, but let us watch and be sober." "The night is far spent, the day is at hand; let us therefore cast off the works of darkness, and let us put on the armour of light." St. James said: "Be ye patient, for the coming of the Lord draweth nigh: the Judge standeth before the door."

It is often said that in their expectation of the nearness of the Lord's return, the Apostles were mistaken, as the long centuries since have shown. Mistaken in this, they may also have been mistaken in other matters. The objection is invalid. The Lord commanded them to watch for Him alway on the ground that of the day of His return neither Himself, nor any man, nor any angel knew, but the Father only. (Matt. xxiv, 36; Acts 1, 7.) Not to have watched for Him, and not to have taught the disciples to do so, would have been in the face of His command; and would have brought upon them the judgment pronounced upon the evil servant, who said: "My Lord delayeth His coming." (Matt.

xxiv, 48.) But the Apostles also knew from the Lord's own words, and from the light given them by the Holy Spirit, that, as the harvest is not reaped until it is ripe, so there must be a certain spiritual ripening, a going on unto perfection, in those ready for His appearing. Not upon the unready and unprepared could the great and sudden change from the mortal to the immortal pass. (1 Cor. xv, 51—.)

So great is the dislike now felt to the Lord's return by many, and so little the faith in it, that His command to watch must be explained away. By some it is said that the Apostles misunderstood Him. He used words in the spiritual, not literal, sense; and did not mean that He would ever return to earth, but that at their death they would come to Him. Thus Prof. Jowett (" Essay on Belief in the Coming of Christ,") says: " St. Paul at first was waiting for and hastening to the day of the Lord, but in the course of years He grew up into a higher truth, that to die and to be with the Lord is far better."* But

---

*How wholly foreign the patient waiting for the Lord is to the modern spirit, may be seen in Jowett's words: "The language which is attributed in the epistle of St. Peter (2 Pet. iii, 8—) to the unbelievers of that age, has become the language of believers in our own. . . No one can now be daily looking for the visible coming of Christ, any more than in a land where nature is at rest, he would live in expectation of an earthquake. The experience of eighteen hundred years has made it impossible, consistently with the laws of the human mind, that the belief of the first Christians should continue among ourselves." Prof. Jowett overlooks the essential distinction that to wait for the Lord is to wait for a living Person who has promised to return, and therefore may be daily looked for; but an earthquake is an event which may or may not be, and of the time of its occurrence we know, and can know, nothing.

others more bold say, that the Lord was Himself mistaken. He shared the common but erroneous Messianic expectations of His day. He thus led the Apostles into error, and they led the Church.

It was when the Apostles discerned that the churches under them did not, as a whole, leave the things that were behind, and press onward toward the mark, the goal, the perfected likeness to Christ, that they knew that the Lord, though "not slack concerning His promise," would delay His return, "not willing that any should perish, but that all should come to repentance." But how long He would delay, they did not know. They, therefore, did not cease to hold up before the Church His speedy return, for this was ever the highest incentive to spiritual sobriety and watchfulness. Whilst there was the growing consciousness that they themselves would not be able to present the Church as one body to Christ, yet they knew not but some might be made ready through His special spiritual dealings with them. The Lord had taught them in the parable of the wise and foolish virgins, that some at His return would be ready, and some not ready to meet Him; and, as in the wheat field, some stalks ripened before others, so would it be in the Church; and they knew not when His all-discerning eye would see His wise virgins, His first ripe fruits, and come to take them to Himself. This done, an interval might elapse during which He would purify those not ready yet not apostate, by the fires of the great tribulation. These last, many or few, would, like the builders of wood, hay, and stubble, "suffer loss, but be saved, yet so as by fire." (1 Cor. iii, 12—.)

Of the two chief Apostles, St. Peter and St. Paul,

the first knew from His Lord's words (John xxi, 18) that he himself would not live to His return. But his knowledge of his own death did not prevent him from keeping the Lord's speedy coming before the Church, rather it made him more earnestly do so. (2 Peter i, 13—.) So St. Paul knew that he would not live to present the Church to Christ, but the knowledge only redoubled his desire to warn it of its perils, and exhort it ever to watch for the Lord. (2 Tim. iv, 6—.)

2. The Apostles agree in teaching that the preaching of the Gospel — the sinfulness of men, the call to repentance, the atoning sacrifice of Christ, and salvation through His death and resurrection,— is offensive to our fallen nature; and that His disciples, therefore, must always be exposed to hostility and hate. In this, also, they only repeat what He had taught them. Says St. Paul: "We preach Christ crucified, unto the Jews a stumbling block, and unto the Greeks foolishness." "All that will live godly in Christ Jesus shall suffer persecution." "For we which live are alway delivered unto death for Jesus' sake." "We must through much tribulation enter into the kingdom of God." Says St. Peter: "For even hereunto (suffering) were ye called; because Christ also suffered for us." St. James says: "Take, my brethren, the prophets . . for an example of suffering affliction, and of patience. Behold, we count them happy which endure." In the apostolic teaching, the offense of the cross is never to cease. "The friendship of the world is enmity with God," and this enmity will reach its highest point just before the Lord's return. "In the last days perilous times shall come." "Evil men

and seducers will wax worse and worse deceiving and being deceived." "There shall come in the last days scoffers, walking after their own lust, and saying, where is the promise of His coming?" "Remember the words which are spoken before of the Apostles of our Lord Jesus Christ, that there shall be mockers in the last time."

If the Apostles expected that the preaching of the Gospel would bring all men, or a very large part of them, to repentance and faith, they would not have spoken in this way. How long would be the period of the Lord's absence, they did not know, or how many would be gathered into the Church. Had they looked for any conversion of the world, or the reception of the gospel by all nations, they could not have looked for the Lord's return in their own lifetime. They knew the Church to be an election, and it might be speedily gathered. But the whole period, whether longer or shorter, they knew to be one of trial and suffering for those faithful to their absent Lord. Of honour, wealth, power, rule, they say not a word, but shame, reproach, persecution — these are ever on their lips.

3. The Apostles agree in teaching that Satan is "the prince of this world," and that he will continue to show to the Church the same hostility that He showed to the Lord. He will remain to the end the enemy and tempter. St. Paul says: "The God of this world hath blinded the minds of them that believe not." "I fear lest, as the serpent beguiled Eve through his subtility, so your minds should be corrupted from the simplicity that is in Christ." "The prince of the power of the air, the spirit that now worketh in the children of disobedience." "Put

on the whole armour of God, that ye may be able to stand against the wiles of the devil." St. Peter says: "Be sober, be vigilant; because your adversary the devil, as a roaring lion, walketh about, seeking whom he may devour." St. John says: "He that is begotten of God, keepeth himself, . . and the evil one tempteth him not." "The whole world lieth in the evil one." (R. V.) "For this purpose the Son of God was manifested, that He might destroy the works of the devil."

The supremacy of Satan as the prince and god of this world continuing to the end, the Church must expect to be tempted as the Lord was tempted, and to meet with every form of subtle deception as well as of open opposition. He would come in "the guise of an angel of light." He would even suffer himself to be scoffed at as a nonentity. He would make use of all devices to deceive and to destroy. The Church, therefore, must never think herself secure, but be always on the watch, "putting on the whole armour of God." (Eph. vi, 11—.)

ST. PAUL AND HIS TEACHINGS.

Having briefly examined the teachings of the Apostles collectively as to the religious character of the last days, we proceed to examine those passages in each where mention is made of an individual man as the great enemy of God and of His Son at the time of the end. And, as St. Paul speaks most fully and distinctly on this point, we begin with him.

This Apostle, in his second Epistle to the Thessalonians (written about 54 or 55 A. D.), speaks of the apostasy or falling away, out of which would come "the man of sin," "the son of perdition," "that wicked." This man, it is said by Prof. Eadie, "the fathers as a body identified with Antichrist." (Com. on Thessalonians.) As a chief source of our knowledge respecting him, the right understanding of St. Paul's words is of the highest importance in our enquiry.

It is not necessary here to go into exegetical details, we need note only the chief points of the Apostle's statement: These are, First, The working of the mystery of iniquity in his day. Secondly, The apostasy, or falling away. Thirdly, The coming of the man of sin, or of the lawless one. Fourthly, The hindrance to his revelation. Fifthly, His destruction at the Lord's coming.

First, " The mystery of iniquity," or, as in the R. V., " the mystery of lawlessness." (2d Thess. ii, 7.)

Here two things are affirmed by the Apostle, the fact of a lawless spirit already working in the Church, and that this working was "a mystery." A mystery is not a thing in itself unknowable, but something hidden from the general knowledge and revealed only to the initiated. (*Arcanum iniquitatis*, Tertul.) Thus the Lord spoke of "the mysteries of the kingdom" which His disciples alone could know; from others they were hidden. (Matt. xiii, 11, Eph. iii, 3.) It is said by Campbell ("Four Gospels"), "The spirit of antichrist hath begun to operate, but the operation is latent and unperceived." And it is said by Bishop Wordsworth *in loco*, "What St. Paul was thus describing was then a mystery, and not as yet revealed, but working inwardly." It was made known to the Apostle by the Holy Ghost because of his position as a ruler under Christ over the Church. In like manner the Apostle John saw the spirit of antichrist already active. (1 John iv, 3.) Both discerned, what was hidden from others, that there was already working a spirit of lawlessness, a rejection of apostolic authority, which, if fully developed, would set aside the rule of the Head, and make the Church her own lawgiver and ruler; and in its last manifestation would reject not only Christ's authority, but all authority of God over men. Out of it would come "the lawless one," who would make his own will the supreme law of his action. As said by Bishop Ellicott: "In the apostasy of the present, the inspired apostle sees the commencement of the fuller apostasy of the future."

But, in what form did this incipient lawlessness so early manifest itself? We have only to read St.

Paul's Epistles to find the answer.* In almost all of them we find complaints that his apostolic authority was not recognized, and that he could not effectually fulfill his ministry. As the fundamental condition of all true obedience in the Church there must be love. The Lord said: "If ye love Me, keep my commandments." Obedience based on any other motive was seeming, not real. And St. Paul himself speaks of the ministers of the Church as able to build it up only in or through love. (Eph. iv, 16.) As this point will again meet us, we need not dwell upon it here. It is sufficient to say that in the loss of "the first love," we find the hidden root of the lawlessness, the first workings of which the apostles saw.

Secondly. The apostasy, or falling away.†

This means, generally, a falling away from some given standard; a defection. Here it means a falling away from the true standing of the Church as appointed by God. This meaning is confirmed by the use of the word elsewhere (Acts xxi, 21), "Thou teachest the Jews to forsake Moses"; literally, "apostasy from Moses." The word is used by St. Paul (1st Tim. iv. 1), "Some shall depart from the faith," "shall apostatize from the faith." This general meaning leaves undetermined the degree of the apostasy or

---

* See Bernard, "Progress of Doctrine in the New Testament," Lecture viii : " In the Epistles we seem, as it were, not to witness some passing storms which clear the air, but to feel the whole atmosphere charged with the elements of future tempest and death. Every moment the forces of evil shew themselves more plainly. . . New assaults are being prepared, new tactics will be tried, new enemies pour on, the distant hills are black with gathering multitudes."

† As to the meaning of this term in the Fathers, see Todd's note, p. 206; in Vul. *discessio;* Tertullian, *abscessio.*

falling away, whether a total or partial denial of the truth. In its culmination, as represented in the man of sin and in his adherents, it is undoubtedly a total denial of the Christian faith. He denies both the Father and the Son. The Apostle distinguishes two forms of the apostasy, one being the corruption of Christianity, the other its absolute rejection. At the first, the working of evil was rather in the heart than in the intellect; and was seen not so much in the loss of truth as in the loss of love. The great Creeds of the Church, and their continued repetition in the past, are the witness that " the Spirit of truth " has worked powerfully in it, preserving the form of sound words, and true rites of worship. But fulness of truth can be held only where is fulness of love; and Church history teaches us that many were early infected with doctrinal error, and rejected more or less of the truth without absolutely denying the Father or the Son. But any falsehood cherished, like the unclean spirit of the Lord's parable, soon takes to itself seven other falsehoods; and thus it is that at the end, when the development of truth and falsehood is completed, we have the absolute truth and the absolute lie standing face to face. Antichrist and his adherents will contemptuously reject whatever the Church has believed respecting the Father and the Son, and all the articles of her faith.

But the falling away, beginning with the loss of love, is not to be confined to doctrine; it embraces the whole spiritual life; and therefore the whole external order of the Church. There cannot be a loss of life without a corresponding decay in the entire ecclesiastical constitution, its ministries, its sacraments, its activities, and also, in practical godliness.

We may now ask in what relation does the mystery of lawlessness stand to the apostasy? Are they to be distinguished or identified? There seems no good reason to doubt that they are essentially the same, the same spirit ruling in both. The distinction is one of development, the lawlessness of the first days culminating in the apostasy of the last. What St. Paul saw in his day was but the beginning of the apostasy, manifesting itself in disobedience to Christ's rule, and discernible only by the Apostles in the light of the Holy Ghost. As it progressed, there would enter into it other elements, so that at the end "the lawless one" is, also, "the man of sin," "the son of perdition,"—the representative of all that is evil in man. That this initial lawlessness is for a time checked by some hindrance, so that the lawless one does not appear until the end, does not show that the mystery of lawlessness did not continue active after the Apostle's day, but only that its activity was, and continues to be, partially repressed.

We must, therefore, reject the interpretation of those who separate "the mystery of iniquity" from "the falling away" as essentially distinct in nature, and separated by a long period of time; and who affirm that the apostasy is caused by the man of sin, and cannot take place till he appears. This point will meet us again.

The question arises here, does the Apostle in the use of the article, "the apostasy," refer to some apostasy already predicted, and known to the Thessalonians? This is most probable. This knowledge may have come from the Lord's predictions known to them, where He speaks of the spiritual condition of the Church just before His return, or from the previous teachings of the Apostle, or from words of prophecy spoken in the Church, or possibly from traditional interpretations of Old Testament prophecies. (See 2 Thess. ii, 5.)

Again, The numerical extent of the apostasy. It is clear that the Apostle expected that many would be infected by the spirit of lawlessness already working, and fall away from their heavenly standing. In other and later epistles, he expresses his fear that the Church will fall as Eve fell, and that he could not present the disciples as a chaste virgin unto Christ. (2 Cor. xi, 2—.) He often speaks as if many of those he had gathered were unfaithful. Thus he says, writing to the Philippians (iii, 18), "Many walk, of whom I have told you often, that they are the enemies of the cross of Christ." Again (ii, 21) "All seek their own, not the things which are Jesus Christ's." To the elders of Ephesus he said (Acts xx, 29): "I know this, that after my departing shall grievous wolves enter, not sparing the flock. Also of your own selves shall men arise, speaking perverse things, to draw away disciples after them." In his last Epistles he speaks of "the perilous times" to come and of those who would yield to the temptations, in terms that imply large numbers.

Thirdly. The Man of Sin. ("Man of lawlessness." Westcott & Hort.) The question which first meets us is, Does the Apostle speak of an individual, or of a series of persons, or of anti-christian principles? As we have seen, it was the early belief that he spake of a person, and this is justified by his language. The use of the article in the designations, "the man of sin," "the son of perdition," "the lawless one," does not of itself show that an individual must be meant, but, taken in connection with the other parts of the Apostle's description, it makes this conclusion certain. It is said by Bishop Ellicott: "Antichrist, in accordance with the almost uniform tradition of the ancient church, is no mere set of principles, or succession of opponents, but one single personal being." This man seats himself in the Temple of God, showing himself that he is God. This could not be said of a polity, much less of principles, and not naturally of a series of persons, but of one person only. There is, also, a clear contrast drawn between Christ and this His rival; as Christ has His revelation "in His day," so the man of sin is to be revealed in "his own time." As Christ has His coming, παρουσία, so the man of sin has his coming, παρουσία. As the Lord received power from the Father to do His works, so he is endowed by Satan with all power and signs and lying wonders, and he is to be destroyed by Christ at His coming.

All this points decisively to a person, and as we shall see, this is confirmed by all that we find in the other Epistles, and in The Revelation. But this does not forbid that the antichristian spirit may have been working in individuals all along from the beginning, and so there have been already many antichrists, as said by St. John in his Epistle.

If, then, St. Paul speaks here of the last antichrist in whom the antichristian spirit culminates, we next ask, In what relation does he stand to the apostasy? It is said by some, and in general by Roman Catholic commentators, that he is its cause. He leads the Church astray by the miracles and signs he is able to do in confirmation of his lies. The apostasy, therefore, does not really begin until he appears, and so is still future. But we have already noted that the beginning of the apostasy was seen by the Apostle in the mystery of lawlessness then working. There was then, indeed, some restraining power, something that hindered its full development; and we may say that so long as this hindrance remains, the apostasy is not fully manifested. The mystery of lawlessness still continues. In this sense it is still future. The last and greatest of the antichrists has not yet come. But it is nevertheless true that he is not the cause of the apostasy; on the contrary, he is its product. The spirit of lawlessness is consummated in the lawless one, and he cannot, therefore, appear until its last stage — the last time — and thus will be its last and truest representative. And the influences that will mould his character, will also prepare the way for his reception. This interaction permits him to be both product and, in a limited sense, the cause, as Napoleon was both the child of the Revolution and its leader. These influences moulding him and preparing his way, will be considered later.

Although the term, "lawless one," expresses most clearly the characteristic and leading feature of this last enemy, yet the other terms applied to him by St. Paul must be considered as adding many important particulars to our knowledge. He is called "the man of sin," the man in whom sin is, as it were, embodied. In him the fallen nature of man, which is not subject to the law of God, nor can be, is most fully summed up and revealed. As the risen Christ is the representative of the redeemed and holy humanity, so is the man of sin of the sinful humanity which refuses redemption. As the essence of sin is "lawlessness," ἀνομία (1 John iii, 4, R. V.), this lawlessness, in its final development, is the absolute rejection of the law of God. Thus, as the man of sin, fully pervaded by it, he is, on the one hand, fitted to be the perfect instrument of Satan, and can be endowed by him with all power; and so, on the other hand, is he fitted to be the head of all lawless men, and the leader of all the enemies of God and Christ.

He is also called, "he who opposes," the opposer, the adversary. As Satan is God's inveterate enemy, so is he. He sets himself in opposition to all that God would do.

He is also "the son of perdition." This designation was applied to Judas by the Lord. (John xvii, 12.) It implies that he who is so described, is by his own acts devoted to perdition, one to whom above all, perdition is the proper retribution; he cannot escape it.

He is, also, one who "exalteth himself above" ("against," R. V.) "all that is called God, or that is worshipped, so that he as God, sitteth in the temple of God, showing himself that he is God." The spirit of pride, of self-exaltation is so developed in him that he claims Divine honour. He will not worship any God, but will be himself worshipped.

As to this claim to be God, three suppositions may be made. That he claims to be the God of the Jews, Jehovah, and therefore seats himself in the Jewish temple, and as such is to be worshipped. This, though affirmed by some early fathers, is wholly incredible. Still more is it incredible that he claims to be the Christian God, the Father. Antichrist denies both the Father and the Son.

That he claims such limited Divinity as was

affirmed of the Roman emperors — apotheosis. But the emperor was deified because he was regarded as the embodiment of the State, which had a sacred or divine character. As such embodiment he was enrolled among the Gods. This apotheosis was an honour originally given by the Roman senate, and only to the emperor, and usually after his death; though later given by the emperor himself, in occasional instances, to some member of his family. It is said by Tiele ("Hist. of Religion") that "the Cultus of the emperors was pursued with such zeal that games were instituted in their honour, temples were built, and special priests appointed." But it clearly appears from the Apostle's words that this man does not regard himself exalted by any act of man, or as merely one of many deified men. He comes not in the name of another, but "in his own name." He exalts himself above all that is called God, or is an object of worship. He claims a homage that is paid to none beside. He shews himself that he is God, and thus is exalted above all that is called God, above all polytheistic deities, all deified men, whether demons or spirits of heroes; above every being who can be an object of worship. A fuller discussion of the ground on which this assertion of Divinity is made, will come up when we speak of the pantheistic tendencies of our time.*

*As all prophecy which finds its complete fulfillment in the remote future, has something in the present which serves as its foreground, and gives it form and meaning, so is it here. It is said by Burton (Church Hist.), that the Gnostic philosophy in St. Paul's day was beginning to be widely spread, and that he probably alluded to it in the passage now before us. It is generally agreed that in Simon Magus (Acts viii, 9), we meet a representative of this philosophy. The Gnostics occupied them-

We have still to speak of the relation of the man of sin to Satan. His "coming is after the working —energy— of Satan, with all power and signs and lying wonders." As his endowments are superhuman, so also his energy. (This term is said in G. and T. Lexicon, to be used in the N. T. only of superhuman power.) Here, also, he appears as the counterpart of the Lord. As the Son received power from the Father to do His works, so does Antichrist from Satan. As the Son had no will of His own, but did the Father's will, and so was His perfect instrument; so the man of sin is the perfect instrument of Satan, doing in all things his will. As to his endowment with all satanic power and authority, this point will meet us again in our examination of the teaching of The Revelation.

But it is said by some that the Apostle here speaks of pretended miracles, wonders, and signs, which are only illusions and deceptions. This is affirmed on the ground that Satan has not the power to work miracles, God giving to His messengers only this power, in order to serve as their infallible credential. But in calling them "lying wonders," the apostle does not affirm that they are unreal, but that they are wrought to confirm lies. This appears from the con-

---

selves with the old problem how to pass from the Infinite to the finite. This they did by means of a series of emanations, or of spiritual beings, interposed between God and the human race, and appearing as occasion demanded in the human form. Such a being was Simon Magus. He was believed to be the greatest of these, "the great power of God." It is, therefore, not improbable that the Christians to whom St. Paul wrote, may have better understood his words about "a man claiming Divine honour," than later generations wholly ignorant of Gnostic ideas. (See note of Meyer, Com. *in loco*.)

text: "And with all deceivableness of unrighteousness in them that perish, because they received not the love of the truth." As they who had the love of the truth, believed the Lord's words, and needed not the miracle for confirmation, so they who have not the love of the truth, will believe Antichrist's word; but as the Lord confirms the words of His servants by signs following, so Satan will confirm his lies by miracles that he may take all captive. (See Mark xvi, 20; Rev. xiii, 13, 14.)

Fourthly. The hindrance to his revelation. The Apostle, enlightened by the Spirit of God, saw the mystery of lawlessness then working, and knew what its ultimate product would be; yet he, also, saw that its speedy development would be hindered by an obstacle; and that the lawless one could not be revealed until it was taken out of the way. What was the obstacle he does not say, but it seems to have been made known by him earlier to the Thessalonians, and therefore was no secret. "And now ye know what withholdeth." A very common interpretation, dating from the time of Tertullian (*Quis, nisi Romanus status?*), is, that the Roman Empire as the preserver of political order in the earth was intended by the Apostle, but not expressed lest the mention of its being "taken out of the way," or, in other words, its overthrow, might be offensive to the Roman rulers. In favour of this interpretation is the use of the masculine and neuter articles, "what withholdeth" and "he who withholdeth." But this interpretation, though approved of by many, was by no means universally received, and is not well sustained. The Apostle is speaking of lawlessness then working in the Church, of disobedience to spiritual rulers and to

Christ their Head ; and with this the preservation of legal order in a heathen State had nothing to do. Obedience of Christians to Christ and to His apostles was based on faith and love, and dependent on no political institutions. It remained the same whether the Roman Empire survived or perished. It may, indeed, be said that the regard for law which marked the Roman State, and the habit of obedience enforced, were opposed to the lawlessness of the man of sin, and so an obstacle to his revelation. Without doubt the habit of obedience, whether to civil rulers or to parents, tends to help obedience to God. But the Apostle is not speaking of him in relation to civil authority, or as himself a political power. It is in the Church that this lawlessness is seen, and in the Church the hindrance is to be sought. The disposition to find the hindrance in something external, arose at a later period; and, as we shall see, from the unwillingness to believe that the apostasy began so early in the Church, and would continue to develop itself until it ended in the man of sin. And it is to be borne in mind that, as the Apostle expected the Lord to return in the lifetime of some then living, and that by Him the Antichrist would then be destroyed, if the hindering power were the Roman Empire, it must be overthrown before the Antichrist could appear. Did St. Paul look for any such speedy overthrow ? It is scarcely credible that he did.*

---

* A friend has made some remarks on this point from which I quote : "I can not help thinking that the hindrance and the hinderer or restrainer must include a spiritual element, must imply some long-suffering acting of God which at last comes to an end. . . In many passages of Scripture I see the possibility of such a departure of the Holy Spirit from an apostate Chris-

If, then, the lawlessness spoken of by the apostle was within the Church, and found here the sphere of its activity, we must find that which hindered it, also, in the Church. What can this have been but the presence and power of the Holy Ghost? That He could be grieved and not able to do His full work, the Epistles shew us, and thus we understand how the spirit of disobedience could so early manifest itself. But He, nevertheless, continued in the Church, and His presence has been in all the past the power restraining the tendencies to lawlessness. That He is called both "what withholdeth" and "he who now withholdeth," may refer to Himself in person, and to His work in ministries and ordinances. But, however this may be, there is no ground for supposing the Apostle to have referred to a Roman emperor as the hindering power. Civil authority could do nothing in repressing spiritual lawlessness. It was the authority of Christ as represented in His Apostles which was rejected. Any fixed legal order may, indeed, serve as

tendom as would justify the view that the restrainer is in some sense the Holy Spirit. . . Putting all these hints together, I am led to think that, while the Roman Empire may be the outward and mechanical hindrance, the more efficient and spiritual hindrance is found in these faithful ones in whom the Holy Ghost can work His full work."

If we believe that St. Paul distinguished in thought between those who would escape the tribulation under Antichrist, and those who would pass through it, as intimated in the Lord's teachings (Luke xxi, 36; Matt. xxv, 1—), and more clearly brought out in The Revelation under the symbols of "the first fruits" and "harvest" (xiv, 1, 15), and in the two companies,—those who escape and those who pass through the great tribulation (vii, 4, 9,)—we find a ready solution of the question of the hindrance. It is seen in this first company which must be taken away before Antichrist can be revealed.

an obstacle to the lawless one in his political action, for such order rests upon the Holy Spirit who acts both in the Church and in the State; and if lawlessness prevail in the former, it will do so also in the latter. But the apostle is not speaking of the Antichrist in his political relations.

Some other questions remain. What is meant by "the temple of God" in which the man of sin seats himself? This was understood by many from the Apostles' days as the temple at Jerusalem, which will be rebuilt before his time, or which he will rebuild. (So Malvenda.) This is supposed to find confirmation in the words of Daniel (xi, 45), "He shall plant the tabernacles of his palace between the seas in the glorious holy mountain"; and, also, in the words of the Lord respecting "the abomination of desolation standing in the Holy Place." But most of the earlier interpreters affirm the Christian Church to be meant, and think this to be another form of the statement as to the generality of the apostasy. A few, however, do not understand this of the Church as a spiritual body, but of the church edifices, taken collectively, in which Divine honours will be paid Him. (Suicer, *Thesaurus, in omni divino templo sedebit.*)

Fifthly. The destruction of the man of sin by the Lord at His return: "Whom the Lord Jesus shall slay with the breath of His mouth, and bring to naught by the manifestation of His coming." (R. V.) Those who apply the Apostle's words respecting the apostasy to the Papacy, understand by "the breath of His mouth" the power of the Gospel by which the Church is delivered from papal errors. The Revised Version gives the true force of the verb by substituting "slay" for "consume" in the author-

ized version; it is not a conversion but an act of
judgment. (Isa. xi, 4.) A distinction is to be taken
between the Lord's "epiphany," or manifestation, and
His "coming"; and some make it to be that His coming, or bodily presence, precedes the manifestation of
that presence to the world. He fulfills the promise
to His disciples: " I will come again and receive you
unto Myself," before He reveals Himself to the world,
and executes judgment upon His enemies. The first
of these judgments is that upon the man of sin. In
The Revelation xix, 20, the beast and the false prophet
are cast alive into the lake of fire before the binding
of Satan. But with an inquiry as to the exact order
of events we are not here concerned.

Godet, Article " Revelation," in Johnson's Cyclopædia, 1895, thus writes: " Antichrist's theological
system may be summed in the three following theses:
1. There is no personal God without and above the Universe. 2. Man is himself his own god — the god of
this world. 3. I am the representative of humanity,
by worshipping me humanity worships itself."

THE TEACHINGS OF ST. JOHN, OF ST. PETER, AND OF ST. JUDE.

ST. JOHN.

This Apostle alone makes mention of the Antichrist under this name (1 John ii, 18, 22, iv, 3 ; 2 John 7). The same question meets us here that we have met in considering St. Paul's Epistle: "Does St. John speak of one individual as the Antichrist, or only of many in whom is manifested the antichristian spirit? We find the expressions, "Antichrist," "the Antichrist," "many Antichrists," "the spirit of the Antichrist." (R. V.) Comparing the teachings of the Apostle we reach the general result: 1. That which constitutes the essential characteristic of Antichrist, or of the antichristian spirit, is the denial that "Jesus Christ has come in the flesh," or that "Jesus is the Christ,"—a denial of the Incarnation. 2. This spirit of the Antichrist was already in the world, and had infected many : " Even now have there arisen many antichrists." 3. This antichristian spirit would find its last and highest manifestation in some one man, distinctively, the Antichrist. This clearly appears from the words, ii, 18. "As ye have heard that Antichrist cometh." Upon this Westcott remarks, " The absence of the article shows that the term has become current as a technical or proper name." 4. The appearing of the Antichrist marked "the last hour." 5. The many antichrists were apostate Christians. "They went out from us."

As this Apostle twice speaks of the knowledge which his readers had of the Antichrist, we must conclude that he had already taught them verbally, or that the knowledge came from the earlier teaching of some other of the apostles. As St. Paul had so long before written to the Thessalonians, what he had taught may have become known to all the congregations of Greece and Asia Minor. But we cannot doubt that this point was more or less explained by all the apostles, and not by St. Paul only, and was familiar to the early disciples, so that the Antichrist could be alluded to without express description.

Does St. John give us any *datum* as to the time of the Antichrist? He says: "It is the last time (hour); and as ye have heard that Antichrist shall come, even now there are many antichrists, whereby we know that it is the last time" (hour). Is it the object of the Apostle to prove from the appearance of the many antichrists that it is the last time? If so, it shows how clear in his mind was the belief that the last days would be marked by the prevalence of the antichristian spirit. But his meaning may be that, being the last time, antichrists are to be expected. By "the last time"—hour— we are to understand the whole Christian dispensation, all the period from the ascension of Christ to His return; the duration of which was wholly unknown to the Apostle, but believed by him to be brief.* He could, therefore, well speak of it as if near its end, the last hour. This

---

* "The last hour, *i. e.*, the end of this age, and very near the return of Christ from heaven." Grimm's Lexicon, by Thayer.

whole period, longer or shorter, is the time of the trial of the world in regard to Christ, His acceptance or rejection.

"Every spirit which confesseth not Jesus, is not of God; and this is the spirit of the Antichrist, whereof ye have heard that it cometh, and now it is in the world already." (R. V.) No earlier form of hostility to God could have been antichristian; Christ must appear in the world before His claims could be rejected. As the Incarnate Son, and God's representative, it is the hostility to Him,— the antichristian spirit— which distinguishes this whole dispensation, but comes into highest manifestation at the end. It is the Christian apostasy which produces the Antichrist.

As St. Paul had spoken of "the mystery of lawlessness" working in the Church in his day a few years earlier, so St. John speaks of its further development. "Even now are there many antichrists. . . They went out from us, but they were not of us." This marks them as apostate Christians. They had a name among the disciples, but had fallen away from the faith. They were the first fruits of "the scoffers and mockers" predicted by St. Peter and St. Jude. Some of the early writers speak of them as Gnostic teachers and leaders.

The mention of the Antichrist is not that the Apostle may speak of the last Antichrist in detail, but that he may warn the Church against the workings of the antichristian spirit already active. As said by Ebrard, "the Apostle's design is warningly to testify that the many antichrists then appearing were in their character like the nature of the Antichrist to come." There is no good reason to doubt that he, like St. Paul, looked to see this spirit reach its full development in an individual Antichrist, who should deny both the Father and the Son. (I. ii, 18, 22.) All who had yet appeared were but his heralds and forerunners; the growing, but not the ripened tares. The Apostle's teaching is doctrinal, to show in what the spirit of Antichristianity consisted — the denial that Jesus had come in the flesh, or the denial of the Incarnation. It is from the knowledge which his readers already had of the Antichrist to come, that he can explain the true character of the errors now seen among them, and their great significance and danger.

It deserves to be noted in considering the emphasis which this Apostle lays upon love in his Epistles, that he wrote at Ephesus, and that it was he by whom the Lord sent the Seven Epistles to the Seven Churches; in the first of which, addressed to the Church at Ephesus, he reproved it for "the loss of the first love." Whether his own Epistles were written earlier or later than the Seven, it is evident that he marked the same loss; and therefore enforced the value of this grace, both in its relation to the Head of the Church, and in that of the members to one another. "God is love, and he that dwelleth in love, dwelleth in God, and God in him." "If we love one another, God dwelleth in us." The loss of this love opened the way to many forms of evil, both doctrinal and practical.

NOTE. — It is said by Prof. Stevens ("The Johannine Theology," 1894), that the prevailing view in the Church in the past, that Antichrist in this epistle designates a person, is not well founded, because "the man of sin" of St. Paul, "the Antichrist" of St. John, and "the beast" of The Revelation, are representatives of different forms of evil ; the first being the representative of Jewish hostility, and the last of the persecuting power of Rome. But our examination of St. Paul's words has shown us that he is speaking of the spirit of lawlessness in the Church, and not of Jewish hostility ; and that the beast does not symbolize Roman persecution, will clearly appear in the examination of The Revelation. That the Gnostic heresy was in the mind of the Apostle John, may be admitted, and the Apostle Paul seems, as we have seen, to have alluded to it; but this is wholly compatible with its union with other forms of evil, and all these are to be summed up in the Antichrist. It is observed by Plummer ("The Epistles of John") that "there is a strong preponderance of opinion in favor of the view that the antichrist of St. John is the same as the great adversary of St. Paul." Bishop Wordsworth (Com. *in loco*) thinks that "the man of sin and the Antichrist do not correspond accurately to each other," but it is not "impossible that they may eventually coalesce." He identifies the man of sin with the Beast (Rev. xiii, 1—).

THE TEACHINGS OF ST. PETER.

There is no mention of an individual antichrist by this Apostle, but much is said of the evil tendencies which he saw already active. In his first Epistle he speaks fully of the trials and sufferings, present and future, of those to whom he wrote, but very little of false teachers and their heresies. He tells them that though already tried by manifold temptations, there was a time of "fiery trial" yet to come before the glory of the Lord could be revealed. This trial by fire is doubtless the same as that spoken of by St. Paul, when "the fire shall try every man's work of what sort it is." (1 Cor. iii, 13.) It is the same as the day when the Lord returns "in flaming fire" to punish His enemies, and to be glorified in His saints. (2 Thess. i, 8.) When this shall be, St. Peter does not say, but he says: "The end of all things is at hand." (1 Pet. iv, 7.)

It is to be noted that St. Peter knew through the word of the Lord spoken to him (John xxi, 18) that he himself should not live till His return, but this did not prevent him from warning the disciples to be ever expecting Him and hoping to the end. (2 Peter i, 12—.) He, no more than St. Paul, speaks of a long interval before that revelation, but he knew that, however short the interval, the Church would be subject to manifold temptations through the craft and malice of its great adversary, " walking about as a roaring lion."

It is in his second Epistle that he speaks distinctly of the false teachers who would arise and bring in damnable heresies, whose pernicious ways many would follow. (2 Peter ii, 1—.) He speaks prophetically, yet evidently the present mirrors for him the future. He saw in his own day the germs of the heresies which would ripen into all evil fruits. He describes the leading features of these false teachers and their followers, " walking after the flesh in the lust of uncleanness," despising governments, presumptuous, self-willed, speaking evil of dignities, servants of corruption, though boasters of liberty. He is not speaking of heathen enemies, but of Christians, those who, having " escaped the pollutions of the world through the knowledge of the Lord and Saviour, are again entangled therein and overcome; those who have forsaken the right way, and have turned from the holy commandment delivered unto them." That these are the same as those mentioned by St. Paul (2 Tim. iii, 1—) as " having a form of godliness, but denying the power thereof," and by St. John as the antichrists who "went out from us," there can be no doubt. That St. Peter expected this apostasy to increase, is plain from his words that there would "come in the last days scoffers, walking after their own lusts, and saying, Where is the promise of his coming?" As scoffers and scorners are the ripened tares — the last and highest product of the apostasy — so, on the other hand, there must be the ripened wheat, those "looking for and hastening the coming of the day of God," those "diligent to be found of Him in peace, without spot, and blameless."

But St. Peter does not speak of any individual as the head of these apostates, or of them as forming an organized body, unless the mention of "false teachers" implies this. As he himself was soon to end his ministry — "knowing that shortly I must put off this my tabernacle" — others whom the Lord would raise up, must be the guides of the Church in the coming days of the great antichristian trial. Both St. Paul and himself had given the churches full warning, and he could therefore say: "Beloved, seeing ye know these things before, beware, lest ye also, being led away with the error of the wicked ($\tau\hat{\omega}\nu$ $\dot{\alpha}\theta\acute{\epsilon}\sigma\mu\omega\nu$, the lawless), fall from your own steadfastness."

THE TEACHINGS OF ST. JUDE.

This Epistle, like the second of St. Peter, speaks of a class already existing, who had crept into the Church unawares, against whom he would warn the faithful. They were "ungodly men, turning the grace of our God into lasciviousness, and denying the only Lord God, and our Lord Jesus Christ," "speaking evil of the things they knew not," "defiling the flesh, despising dominion, and speaking evil of dignities," "clouds without water," "raging waves of the sea," "wandering stars." He calls to mind the words of the Apostles foretelling that there would be in the last time "mockers," "separatists," "sensual," "having not the Spirit." But he does not speak of one who should be the leader among them. The reference to the prophecy of Enoch (v. 14) shows that the separation of these from the faithful would not be till the Lord came. Till that day the disciples must build themselves up on their most holy faith, and keep themselves in the love of God.

THE TEACHING OF THE REVELATION.

This book is to be regarded as a continuation from Heaven of the teaching which the Lord began when on earth. (Acts i, 1.) A considerable number of years had passed since His ascension, and He had seen in His Church the working of "the mystery of lawlessness" of which St. Paul wrote, and its gradual develment in "the scoffers" of St. Peter, and the "many antichrists" of St. John. Now it seemed good to Him to give, through the last surviving Apostle, fresh instructions, and admonitions, and warnings, adapted to that condition of trial and peril upon which His children had entered. In Epistles addressed to seven then existing churches, He outlined the whole spiritual history of the Church, from the loss of the first love of Ephesus to the lukewarmness and self-exaltation of Laodicea. Following upon these Epistles He proceeds to give, under various figures and symbols, such teachings and openings of the future as were necessary to guard His children amidst the temptations and dangers of their way. As everywhere in Divine revelation respecting things to come, the object here is practical, to make known the future so far as needful for instruction and guidance. As His words when on earth were only understood by those "who had ears to hear" (Matt. xi, 15), so is it with His words from Heaven. Neither the unfaithful nor the curious can understand them; only those illumined by the Spirit, the obedient and faithful. Only the spiritual ear can understand "what the Spirit saith unto the churches." He alone through His prophets can interpret these symbols, and bring forth the meanings hidden under them; and this He does only so far as the needs of the time demand.

It is to be noted that the Lord in this book speaks to His Church only. He is not addressing any others, Jews or Gentiles; if they are mentioned, or events in their history, it is only as symbols of parties or events in the Church.

To interpret the apocalyptic symbols in general, or to enter upon details of fulfillment, as it is beyond our power, is beyond our present purpose. We confine our attention to the one point: What are we taught in this book as to the apostasy, and as to the Antichrist? As to the apostasy, we find two symbols of the Church that claim our attention, that of the woman, and that of Babylon; and as to the Antichrist, the symbol of the Beast. Rightly understanding these three symbols — the Woman, Babylon, and the Beast — we have all we now seek.

First. (*a*) The woman as the Bride. Under the figure of the marriage relation is often set forth in the Old Testament the relation of God to His covenant people. The same figure, which is the highest expression of love, is used by the Apostle to explain the relation of Christ to His Church. (Eph. v, 23—.) This relation is to be perfected at the marriage of the Lamb (Rev. xix, 7), when the Church enters into the immortality and glory of her Lord. Till then she is an "espoused virgin," waiting for the Bridegroom. (2 Cor. xi, 2; Matt. xxv, 1—.) But as, in the human relation, the espoused virgin may be unfaithful, so in the Divine. Thus we have the Church, as symbolized by the woman, presented under two aspects. In the one (Rev. xii, 1), we see her in that spiritual and heavenly condition in which she was placed at the beginning, and in which she should have continued, ready to be presented unto the Bridegroom at His coming, without spot or blemish. (Eph. ii, 6; v, 27.)

(*b*) The woman as a harlot. The Church did not abide in the heavenly condition. Becoming earthly-minded, a resident on the earth, seeking its honours, and in alliance with its rulers, "glorifying herself, and living deliciously," she is presented under the figure of a harlot, arrayed in purple and scarlet, and sitting upon a scarlet-coloured beast. (Rev. xvii, 3.) Under this symbol the Church is presented to us in the final stage of her apostasy, retaining some of the outward signs of her high calling, but borne by the Beast, upheld and supported by him.

The sin of the Church which at last brings upon her the fierce anger of her Lord, is fornication with the kings and rulers of the world. (Rev. xvii, 2; xviii, 3.) This points to the crime of permitting them to usurp authority over her, and to exercise for their own ends the rights and prerogatives which belong to her Lord alone. To Him it belongs to appoint her ministers, to inspire her teachings, to direct all her action. She cannot serve two masters. Allied with the rulers of the world, controlled in her action by their interests, dependent upon their bounty for her support, and seeking the honour which cometh from men, she can no longer be a faithful witness to her absent Lord, or do His present work, or wait with longing desire for His return. Spiritual fornication is, therefore, the grievous charge brought by the Lord against her, and its last and highest stage is reached when she becomes the handmaid of the Beast. (Rev. xvii, 3.) Then her harlotry is open and unconcealed. The absent Lord is wholly forgotten. She is no longer "the espoused virgin" waiting for the Bridegroom, diligent to make herself ready. There is no sense of any bereavement in His absence, or desire for His return. She is no more " the widow who cried day and night" for deliverance from the bondage which oppressed her (Luke xviii, 3—), but she proudly says: "I sit a queen, and am no widow, and shall see no sorrow." (Rev. xviii, 7.)

But it will be noted that the symbolism of the marriage relation is imperfect in setting forth the full relations of the Church to Christ, in that an espoused virgin cannot be at once both faithful and unfaithful. This symbol does not admit of partition; another symbol, therefore, is needed, through which the fact can appear that the Church may have at the same time both faithful and unfaithful members; and that there is never an entire falling away. Always, even in the darkest hour, there are those that remain true to their Lord — "the remnant," the seven thousand who do not bow the knee to Baal. The symbol which permits this distinction of the faithful and unfaithful as co-existing in the Church, is found in a city.

Secondly, Babylon, a city, symbolizes the Church not in its immediate vital relation to its Head — His body — or as His espoused wife; but as an organized institution, a polity with laws, ordinances, and offices; and thus able to be brought into relations with civil governments,— the visible as distinguished from the invisible Church, and known to the world as the sphere of Christ's rule. As in every well-ordered city, justice, equity, and peace prevail; so above all in the Church, the Heavenly city. Here all God's statutes and ordinances are kept; all His servants are in their places, and fulfil their duties, and His children dwell together in righteousness and love. Of such holy order and peace the heavenly Jerusalem is the symbol. (Gal. iv, 26; Rev. xxi, 2.)

Sacred history presents Babylon under two aspects, first, as a city of confusion — Babel — where no one understood another's speech. (Gen. xi, 7.) Secondly, as the city where the covenant people were held in captivity. (Ezra v, 12.) In the first, we see symbolized the Church as divided into many sects and parties, holding little or no communion with one another, without unity of belief, or of purpose, or of action. This confusion of religious speech is seen in the chaotic period of the second and third centuries, and most clearly since the Reformation; but has marked in large degree the whole history of the Church; and will, we may believe, reach its culmination just at its close, when the term "Babel" will have its fullest application.

The second aspect in which the historical Babylon is presented, is as that city to which God removed His people as a punishment for their disobedience. He had chosen for them a place where He would dwell — His holy city — and there ordered the building of His temple, where only His appointed worship could be offered; but they had profaned His Sanctuary, and He gave city and temple up to destruction. In Babylon must His people dwell till they had been brought to repentance, and been made to pray earnestly for deliverance. (Ps. cxxxvii, 1—.) Till this hour should come, they must pray for the peace of Babylon, and be submissive to the powers over them. (Jer. xxix, 7.) Thus this city could be the symbol of a condition in which the Church, having lost her highest ministers, and unable to offer worship in its appointed fulness, came into a relation of dependence upon secular powers. Very early she entered into an alliance with the Roman State for her protection and help, and this alliance has continued in various forms under all rulers succeeding the Emperors. Thus has arisen that great structure, both ecclesiastical and civil, sacred and secular, which we call Christendom. Although Christendom embraces the nations which as such profess the Christian faith, and is ruled by those who bear Christ's name; yet the relation between them and the Church is one contrary to the appointment of God, who has set His Son to be her Head and sole Ruler. Christ, indeed, is the King of Kings as well as Head of the Church, yet He would not have these two spheres of His rule to be confounded. His rulers in the State may not interfere with His rulers in the Church. Each has its defined border, over which it may not pass. The State may not appoint priests, or dictate their teaching or action, or the Church control the State in its legitimate functions.

It is not necessary to follow in detail the union of Church and State since the time of Constantine. In general, it may be said that for the protection and help of the State the Church has assented to a measure of secular control over her, both as to her polity and administration, and, in a degree, also, as to her doctrine; a control wholly incompatible with the prerogatives of her Head. Her whole history shews a continued struggle between the ecclesiastical and civil rulers, the

Church attempting to rule the State and the State to rule the Church, priests striving to be princes, and princes exercising the functions of priests. The right of interference in spiritual matters once obtained, secular rulers have attempted to exercise it more and more; attempts which have often been strenuously, sometimes successfully, resisted. Each party has sought to make use of the other for the accomplishment of its own special ends. With the sword of the magistrate would the Church put down all religious dissent, and with the sanction of the Church would the State justify its acts of cruelty and oppression.*

The application of this symbol is not to be limited to the Church of Rome, as is often done. It embraces the whole Christian Church in so far as it symbolizes a condition of things in which the Lord is deprived of the full exercise of His prerogatives as her Head by her unhallowed alliance with secular rulers, whether the alliance be on her part voluntary or coerced. The sin is the same whether the State be monarchical or democratic in its government, whether the Church be established by law, or, if nominally free, is controlled by the popular will expressed through majorities. Babylon is found wherever there is interference on the part of princes or people with His absolute rule; and His children are thus brought under bondage. But, if this has been a common sin,

---

* A recent historian, Parkman ("The Jesuits in North America") writing with no reference to prophecy, but as a student of the practical workings of a system, says: "Holy mother Church, linked in sordid wedlock to governments and thrones, numbered among her servants a host of the worldly and the proud, whose service of God was but the service of themselves. . . This mighty Church of Rome, in her imposing march along the high road of history, heralded as infallible and

it has been most manifest in the Roman Church, whose organization and claims to supremacy have brought it into closer relations, sometimes of peace, sometimes of hostility, to both kings and peoples.

But this intermingling of the religious and political elements, making the Church to be a component part of the State, was more than a denial by the Church to her Head of His prerogatives of rule; it was the sin of fornication, already spoken of, a sin by which He was most deeply wounded and dishonoured. The Church was His espoused virgin, whom, under His own ministries and ordinances, He would make and preserve holy and without blemish to the day of the marriage. Therefore, how great her fall to play the harlot with the kings of the earth, and be their handmaid to promote their selfish interests, and minister to their pleasures. This was to infuse the spirit of harlotry into her own children by effacing the distinction between the Church and the world, between the sacred and the secular; and to intoxicate the nations with vain expectations of the prosperity and glory to be given them under her administration, and before the coming of their Judge and King. (Matt. xxiv, 48—.)

We may now understand why upon the forehead of the woman sitting upon the Beast the name was written: "Mystery, Babylon the great." (Rev. xvii, 4, 5.) Under the combination of the two symbols — the harlot and Babylon — we have presented the last stage of the alliance between the Church and the

divine, astounds the gazing world with prodigies of contradictions; now the protector of the oppressed, now the right arm of tyrants, . . now beaming with celestial truth, now masked in hypocrisy and lies; now a virgin, now a harlot, an imperial queen, and a tinselled actress."

State. Through its corrupting influence upon her own spiritual condition, and her growing spirit of pride and ambition, she is ready to make an alliance even with the Beast, thus utterly rejecting the headship of her Lord. This fall into harlotry is a mystery, like "the mystery of lawlessness," something known to all and yet not known; now dimly discerned by the spiritual eye, but not clearly to be seen till the last trump shall sound, and "the mystery of God shall be finished." (Rev. x, 7.) It is at this time that the long-suffering of the Lord comes to an end. He will now separate the faithful from the unfaithful. The command goes forth: "Come out of her, my people, that ye be not partakers of her sins, and that ye receive not of her plagues." (Rev. xviii, 4.) This separation made, "Babylon becomes the habitation of devils, and the hold of every foul spirit, and a cage of every unclean and hateful bird." The apostate Church, the faithful having been all gathered out, becomes the church of the Antichrist.

As we have seen, Christendom being the product of Christianity, an amalgam of the religious and political, is presented in both its elements under the symbol Babylon, the great city. As a political system, it must stand or fall with the Church with which it is in such close alliance; and its destruction is sudden and complete. An angel casts a great millstone into the sea, saying: "Thus with violence shall that great city, Babylon, be thrown down, and shall be found no more at all." The Christian Church and the Christian State fall together, for the enmity of the Antichrist embraces both, and both must be overthrown before his kingdom can be set up.

This same distinction of the faithful and the apostate, and their separation at the time of the end, is elsewhere taught us in this book under the symbols of "the harvest" and "the vintage" (Rev. xiv, 14–20); the harvest embracing those who have lived in Babylon and been infected with its errors and vices, but are at last gathered out of it, and ripened — dried — by the fire of judgment; the same as "the great multitude" that comes purified out of the great tribulation. (Rev. vii, 14.) The vintage embraces those gathered to the Antichrist — "the vine of the earth," the counterfeit of the true Vine. This is "cast into the great wine press of the wrath of God." (Rev. xiv, 19—.)

Thirdly, The Beast. (Rev. xiii, 1—.) Of a beast as a symbol of a cruel and oppressing nation or State, we have already spoken in treating of the visions of Daniel. This prophet saw four beasts coming up from the sea — four successive kingdoms — each with its special characteristics, but all standing in hostile relations to the Jewish people. The Beast seen by St. John to arise out of the sea, has the same symbolic character. It represents some persecuting power; but the object of its persecution is not the Jewish people, for the teachings of The Revelation directly concern only the Christian Church. When mentioned in this book, the Jews appear in their symbolical, not historical, character. (vii, 4.) There has been much discussion whether this Beast is to be identified with the last beast of Daniel (vii, 7), the symbol of the Roman Empire; and also what its relation to the eleventh horn of this beast, but into this discussion it is not necessary to enter. But it is important to notice that, while the beasts of Daniel are representative of kingdoms with a succession of rulers, yet this is probably not the case here. As the Messianic kingdom has but one King, both King and kingdom may be spoken of as identical, as in the petition "Thy kingdom come;" and as the kingdom of the Antichrist has but one king, both king and kingdom may be represented by the Beast. This kingdom, as the last of the series of hostile kingdoms, may unite in itself all the characteristics of those that preceded it, as symbolized by the bear, the leopard, and the lion; and this kingdom may be said to be universal, since the dragon, "the prince of this world," gives the Beast from the sea "his throne, and great authority." It deserves, also, to be considered that this Beast is described under the same form as the dragon, with seven heads and ten horns, implying co-extensive authority.*

We find, then, no difficulty in believing that the Beast of St. John symbolizes the Antichrist as king;

---

* Doubtless, there is a distinction to be taken between the heads and the horns of the Beast. The horns are, by general consent, symbols of power, and here of kingly power. "The ten horns are ten kings." (xvii, 12.) The head cannot be a symbol of the same thing; nor can the seven heads symbolize a succession of kings, or successive forms of government. This cannot be the case with the seven heads of the dragon, for he is described as he is at the time when he waits for the birth of the man-child. (xii, 8.) The heads of the Beast seem rather to symbolize that ecclesiastical power or headship which civil rulers have usurped for centuries over the Church. The Lord as its Head is its only ruler, yet civil rulers have called themselves its heads, and exercised authority over it. As we see symbolized in the ten horns the fulness of political power, so in the seven heads we see the fulness of that ecclesiastical authority which the several kings, calling themselves heads of the Church, have exercised in its history, and which the Beast as supreme civil ruler now claims for himself. Therefore, upon the heads, not upon the horns, are the names of blasphemy; and with the mouth he speaks great things and blasphemies.

and, also, the nature of his kingdom as both political and ecclesiastical. That there is much obscurity still in regard to the interpretation of chapter xvii, 9-11, we know, and it probably will not be removed until the Antichrist appears, and begins to run his course.

The transfer of the crowns from the heads of the dragon to the horns of the Beast, may point to some outward establishment of the authority of Satan, which has to this time been exercised secretly, the world seeing it not; but now in the Antichrist, his representative, it is seen in full manifestation.

This beast arises out of "the sea," not out of the sea of the heathen nations as did the beasts of Daniel, but out of the sea of Christendom — the peoples of Christendom democratized — the sea being the symbol of that state of society in which man measures man, as in the sea all drops of water are equal; and also of instability, that form of rule where the unstable popular will is supreme. At that period, kingly governments — the mountains — have been swallowed up in the depths of the sea (Ps. xlvi); or if the name of kings is retained, their kingdoms are in fact democracies. Out of the stormy sea, "casting up mire and dirt," comes the Antichrist. (Luke xxi, 25.)

Let us now consider what we are taught of this ruler from the sea. (Rev. xiii.)

First, as to his relations to God and to His faithful children. "Upon his heads were names of blasphemy." "And there was given unto him a mouth speaking great things and blasphemies. . . And he opened his mouth in blasphemy against God, to blaspheme His name, and His tabernacle, and them that dwell in Heaven." By blasphemy we are to understand all kinds of speech injurious to the Divine majesty ; bold and contemptuous denial of God, and of His claims to obedience and worship. The Beast himself claims Divine homage, and it is given him. "All that dwell upon the earth shall worship him, whose names are not written in the Book of life of the Lamb slain from the foundation of the world."

Such being his hostile relations to God, it follows that the same hostility will be shown to His Son, and to all who honor and fear Him. "And it was given unto him to make war with the saints, and to overcome them."

Secondly, his relations to Satan. "The dragon gave him his power, and his throne, and great authority." Here the dragon, or Satan, is presented as having power or authority in the earth, according to his words to the Lord: "All this power (authority) will I give thee, and the glory of them, for that is delivered unto me; and to whomsoever I will, I give it." (Luke iv, 6.) St. Paul speaks only of the endowment of the man of sin by Satan "with all power ($\delta\upsilon\nu\dot{\alpha}\mu\epsilon\iota$) and signs, and lying wonders,"— that evil spiritual endowment by which he is prepared to be Satan's effectual instrument. Thus spiritually prepared, the prince of this world gives to him his throne, and sets him as his vicegerent; and as such, authority is given him over all kindreds, and tongues, and nations. His character and success amaze the nations, who ask, "Who is like unto the beast ? who is able to make war with him ?"

Thirdly, his relation to the kings of the earth. We are told (xvii, 12) that the ten horns of the Beast symbolize ten kings which are "to receive authority

THE TEACHING OF THE REVELATION. 65

as kings with the Beast for one hour;" and that these, though nominally heads of States, will in fact be subject to him. "These have one mind, and shall give their power and strength unto the Beast. . . For God hath put in their hearts to fulfil His will, and to agree, and give their kingdom unto the beast." We are thus pointed forward to a political status in which there will be a confederacy of the nations of Christendom under one head, and this head the Antichrist; yet each will preserve in some degree its own independent government. But of this confederacy we shall have occasion later to speak.

Fourthly, his attainment of power, and time of its duration. In the progress of the Beast to supreme power, there seem to be two stages presented under different forms. He is wounded as unto death (xiii, 3), but his wound is healed. He is also spoken of as "ascending out of the abyss,"—bottomless pit,— (xi, 7), into which he must first have descended, and from this time on overcomes all enemies. From these expressions it may be inferred that for a time after his appearance he meets with some special resistance, probably the testimony of the two witnesses (xi, 3—), and at this time receives a deadly wound, or in other words, descends into the abyss. His wound being healed, or rising from the abyss, he makes war upon the witnesses and kills them. From this time on no one is able to resist him, and "power is given him over all kindreds, and tongues, and nations." Interpreting "the abyss" as the place of the dead, some early fathers believed that Antichrist would be a man raised from the dead. But the language, "as it were wounded to death," does not affirm his death; and we may understand the abyss into which he

descends, to be presented here as the abode of demons.
(See ix, 1, 11; xx, 1, 3.) Thus taken, we are
taught that by the Spirit of God in the mouths of the
two witnesses Antichrist is unmasked, and successfully resisted for a time in his efforts to deceive the
faithful; but, strengthened anew with demoniac power,
he enters upon his victorious career. The period of
this career may be the same as that of the sounding
of the "three woe trumpets," which begins with the
opening of the abyss, and the coming forth of the
locusts — symbols of the false teachers, scoffers, and
mockers who will then destroy the faith of men in all
Christian truth. (viii, 13; ix, 1—.) At this time,
also, it may be that the ten kings give their kingdom to the Beast; and the harlot Church is made
desolate, and burned with fire. (xvii, 16—.)

The duration of Antichrist's rule seems to be for
forty and two months, or three and a half years. (xiii,
5.) If, as has been said by some, this period is to be
distinguished from that xii, 6, and later, the whole
time of the Antichrist will be seven years: three and
a half in attaining power, and three and a half in
its exercise. But upon our interpretation of these
chronological data we cannot rely; we may, however,
believe that events will move very swiftly. (See
xii, 12.)

Fifthly, his destruction. This is described under
the symbol of a battle, in which appear on one side the
Lord and His army, and on the other the Beast and
the kings of the earth, and their armies. (xix, 19.)
"And the beast was taken, and with him the false
prophet. . . These both were cast alive into a lake
of fire burning with brimstone, and the remnant
were slain with the sword of Him that sat upon

the horse." Upon their destruction follows the binding of Satan, and the establishment of the Messianic kingdom. The tares are now gathered up and burned with fire, and "the righteous shine forth as the sun in the kingdom of their Father."

We have yet to ask, who is symbolized by the second beast that comes up out of the earth? and what his relation to the first Beast? (xiii, 11—.) These points will be considered in speaking of the church of the Antichrist.

We may here sum up those chief teachings of the Scripture which are directly contradicted by the teachings of the latest forms of Anti-Christianity.

1. There is a personal God, Creator of heaven and earth.

Contra. There is no personal God, but an Eternal Energy or Force; and there has never been an act of creation.

2. Besides man there are created Intelligences — Angels; and there is a kingdom of darkness under the rule of a fallen Angel, Satan, the enemy of God and man, and " prince of this world."

Contra. There are no Angels, good or evil, and there is no kingdom of darkness.

3. Man fell from his original goodness, and so came under the law of sin and death; and needs a Redeemer.

Contra. Man has never fallen; his nature is not sinful, and needs no redemption, but is capable of highest development in wisdom and goodness.

4. The only-begotten Son of God became man to redeem man from sin and death through the Cross;

and is now our High Priest making intercession for us.

Contra. Jesus was but one of the Sons of God, for God is incarnate alike in all men. He is not now our High Priest; His work as Saviour was completed in giving us a moral Ideal.

5. There is to be a Kingdom of God set up at the return of the risen Lord, in which His Church, made like Him in resurrection life, shall reign with Him, and all nations dwell in peace.

Contra. There will be no return of Christ to earth, and no resurrection of the dead. Death itself is the ascent to a larger and better life. On earth will be seen a perfected Humanity, and a new Social Order; under which all evils of the past and present will be done away, and the Kingdom of Man will come.

6. The contest of good and evil will come to its final decision in the persons of the man Christ Jesus from heaven and of "the man of the earth," inspired and aided of Satan, but who will be cast into the bottomless pit.

Contra. There is no bottomless pit, and there can be no such contest, for all evil is imperfect good, and will disappear as humanity is developed.

PART II.

THE FALLING AWAY OF THE CHURCH.

THE FALLING AWAY — ITS ORIGIN AND NATURE.

INITIAL STAGE OF THE FALLING AWAY AS SEEN

  I. IN THE RELATION OF THE CHURCH TO THE HEAD.

  II. IN THE RELATION OF THE CHURCH TO THE HOLY GHOST.

  III. IN THE RELATION OF THE CHURCH TO THE WORLD.

PART II.

THE FALLING AWAY—ITS ORIGIN AND NATURE.

Having seen that the Lord and His apostles foretold the fact of the falling away of the Church, let us consider more particularly the origin and nature of that falling away. But this cannot be rightly understood unless we have a true conception of that standing or condition from which the Church fell. We must, therefore, enter into some particulars as to the ends which God purposed to accomplish by it, so far as He has made them known, and how those ends were to be attained.

Before entering upon this enquiry, it is important to keep certain points in mind: First, that the Church is an election, some taken from among others for a special purpose. Revelation of Himself and of His will to the world through election has always been God's method. He chooses some to prepare them to be His instruments of instruction and blessing to others. This He did through individuals, as with the patriarchs; or, as in the case of the Jews, through a nation. They were separated by His act from other nations, and brought into a special Covenant relation to Him. The Christian Church constitutes a new election, wholly distinct from that of the Jews; its members gathered, indeed, from all nations, yet made one community under one Head.

Secondly, That this election may fail partially to fulfil the purpose for which God chose it. It was so with the Jews (Is. i, 2; v, 2), "I have nourished and brought up children, and they have rebelled against me." But His purpose in them cannot fail forever, nor his Covenant be broken. (Jer. xxxiii, 20.) And, as with the Jews, so with the Church. It is not preserved from all falling away, but cannot become wholly apostate. "The gates of hell shall not prevail against it." From this it is preserved by the headship of Christ, and the indwelling of the Holy Ghost.

Thirdly, That as there was salvation out of the pale of the Jewish election, so is there outside of the Christian. The principle rules in all God's elections, that the greater grace given to the elect takes no present grace from the non-elect. That there are higher workings of the Spirit within the Church, does not forbid or diminish His lower workings without it.

Fourthly, That the Church is not the kingdom, but preparatory to it. It serves for the gathering and preparation of those who shall be Christ's helpers in the administration of the kingdom when it shall be set up. This election is but a part, the kingdom will embrace all the saved.

It is only by keeping clearly in mind that the Church is an election, a part, that we can understand the full meaning of the name so often given it, the Lord's body. As the human body is that through which a man acts upon things without, so is it with Christ's body. The Church is not the totality of men, or of the saved, but is a part brought into a special relation to Him that it may be the instrument of His action upon others.

With these preliminary remarks upon the Church as an election — the body of Christ — we may now consider the ends which God would accomplish through it. Regarded in its relation to men, it is a means whereby He effects their salvation; regarded in its relation to Christ, the Head, it is a means of His self-manifestation. First, as a means of salvation. The Church, indwelt of the Holy Spirit, is to gather into itself through the preaching of the Gospel all who believe; and, through its ministries and ordinances, instruct and prepare them both for the present time and for the kingdom to come. This is its appointed work toward men in the present dispensation. Upon this, as familiar to all, we need not now dwell.

Secondly, as a means of the self-manifestation of the risen Lord as its Head. To this end, the Church must be brought into closest union with Him that His will may first be done in it; and that through His actings by it the world may know that He is the living and ruling Head. And here we meet that which constitutes the essential and unique characteristic of the Church, the headship of Christ.

The Apostle Paul (Eph. i, 22) teaches us when this headship was established. The Son of God, having fulfilled His work in mortal flesh, rose from the grave in the power of an endless life. It was not till made immortal and glorified that He could receive and send down the Holy Ghost to build His Church through the impartation in regeneration of His own resurrection life. (John vii, 39; Acts ii, 33.)

Thus the Christian Church is wholly unlike any

other religious community in that it is founded on life, not on abstract religious truth or doctrine. Many teachers, claiming Divine inspiration, have taught more or less of truth, and founded religious sects or schools; but no one has ever pretended to make his disciples partakers of his own life. Their community with him is only that of opinion or belief. But all symbols used to describe the relation of His disciples to Christ imply a vital union — the temple made of living stones, Himself being the chief corner-stone; the vine and the branches; Eve made from the side of Adam, "bone of his bone and flesh of his flesh." None are brought into this vital union by natural birth; all must be regenerated, born again.

Again, this life, common to the Head and body, is a supernatural life; Jesus risen from the dead, immortal, glorified, the second Adam, the quickening Spirit, the Heavenly Man, is its source. As His body — one with Him — the whole constitution of the Church is supernatural and heavenly.*

---

* It is much to be regretted that the term "supernatural" should be used in so vague and general a way as greatly to obscure its meaning in the Biblical presentation. In this we see three distinct and successive conditions of nature: The first, or natural, the world as it was made, and which God pronounced good; the second, the fallen, or unnatural, that into which it came through the sin of man; the third, or supernatural, that into which it comes through Christ, when all things are made new.

It is the second of these conditions, the fallen, which is the sphere of special Divine interpositions, or of the miracle. These could have had no place in the primitive order; here could be only growth, progress; nor will they have a place in the future and perfect order. Redemption is the deliverance of man from the law of sin and death, and the world from the bondage of corruption. To effect this, the Son of God became man, and was in mortal flesh, and suffered death. In His resurrection He entered

We have here, in the fact of Christ's headship, the foundation of the organic unity of the Church. No organic unity is possible where there is not a common life. No community of belief, or of interest, or of action, can make an association of individuals an organism. And the constitution of an organism — its principle of life, and the organs through which this life is put forth, and the mode of their action — can never be changed except by the same power that gave it being. There may, indeed, be weakness of life, and disuse and mutilation of organs, and consequent partial failure of activities, but the organic structure abides. The Church, not the body alone, but the Head and body, is an organism through the life of the Head pervading it; and thus all the members are one with Him and with one another. Separated from Him, the Church would cease to be an organism, and be only an organization. But this common life does not take away individual freedom and responsibility. There

into the third and perfect condition of humanity; upon the natural was superinduced the heavenly. In Him as the Incarnate Son we see the foundation of the supernatural laid, but it was not realized and manifested till He rose from the dead. Then the fallen and mortal passed in Him into its final and perfect condition of immortality and glory. Made the Head of the Church, He gives in regeneration His supernatural life to His children, and to nurture this supernatural life, He feeds them at His table with supernatural food. The Church in all its constitution is thus supernatural, but "mortality is not swallowed up of life" till the Head returns; then will be "the manifestation — apocalypse — of the sons of God"; and then will the creation be delivered from the bondage of corruption into the liberty of their glory. It is this perfected and supernatural condition, not any development of the natural, much less any evolution of the fallen, which is the great object of Christian hope and prayer.

may be "withered branches" in the vine, which shall be cast forth and burned. (John xv, 6.) It is possible for the members of Christ so to separate themselves individually from Him that the whole body may become spiritually enfeebled, and so fail to fulfil its purpose; but the Church, however weak or mutilated, cannot cease to be Christ's body, or its members cease to be members one of another. Divisions, separations, even bitter hate and bloody persecution, cannot break this organic unity.

As a consequence of this community of life, there is such a community of feeling, purpose, and action between the Head and the body as cannot otherwise exist. Not as a king who makes laws for his subjects, or as a general who gives commands to his soldiers, or even as Jehovah giving ordinances to His elect people, does the Lord direct His Church. It is one with Him; the law of His life is the law of its life, and, therefore, so far as it abides in Him, it is in full sympathy with Him, His truth is its truth, His purposes are its purposes, His strength is its strength. It loves and hates what He loves and hates. As the human body, when in full health and vigour, responds to every volition of the man, so the body of Christ to His volitions. As one with Him, it can join in His present intercessions, and hereafter sit with Him in His throne.

Thus we see that the Head in Heaven has a twofold work: first, in the Church — to fill it with His life; and, secondly, through the Church — to manifest Himself to the world; and the unity of life is the basis of both. Himself perfected and endowed with all power at His ascension, He became the Father's perfect instrument for all His future work, both that in heaven before God as High Priest, and that to be done on earth in the formation of His body. The first He carries on alone. But He must have His helpers in His earthly work of preaching the Gospel and gathering and perfecting His disciples. To this end He sends down the Holy Ghost, and by the impartation of His life His body is formed.

In this Divine order we see, first, the Head risen and glorified and clothed with all authority, but Himself invisible in the heavens; secondly, the Church, a visible community on the earth, through which He can act and manifest Himself to the world. Accordingly as He can do His will in the Church, so can He manifest Himself through the Church. The measure of the manifestation of Himself to the world, and of its knowledge of Him, is, therefore, found in the spiritual condition of the Church as affected by its unity with Him; if it abide in Him according to the Divine appointment, it will be the perfect instrument by which He can carry on His work in the earth. As He has no will separate from the Father's will, so the Church should have no will separate fron His will. As He said: "I can of mine own self do nothing." "The Father that dwelleth in Me, He doeth the works;" so the Church of its own self can do nothing. It can have no independent activity. In all things taught or done in or by the body, it is the Head who teaches and acts. He is the Apostle, the High Priest, the Prophet, the Elder, the Evangelist, the Pastor. It is He who acts by His ministers, and leads the worship of the Church. In nothing, Godward or manward, can the body act separate from Him; and only as His will is fulfilled in the Church, can it answer the end of its calling.

With these remarks on the nature and place of

Christ's headship, we are able to see clearly what is meant by "the falling away" of the Church. It is such a change in its corporate relation to its Head, that He cannot carry on His perfect work, first in it and then by it. The vital union of the Head and body is not, indeed, broken, but it is weakened; the body is no longer filled with the fulness of His life, and, therefore, He is not able to put forth His full power, either in gathering and in perfecting its members, or in His action upon the world. There may be in individual members much zeal and activity, but the corporate action is enfeebled, and comparatively ineffective. The world does not see in the Church the reflection of the truth, the love, the power of the invisible Head, and He is dishonoured.

If we now ask for the cause of this change, its deepest root, we find it in the Lord's words addressed from heaven to the Church at Ephesus — the representative of the Church of the apostolic age: "I have this against thee, that thou has left thy first love." (Rev. ii, 4, R. V.) Here was the first step in the falling away. In all other respects the Lord highly commends the Church. Let us carefully note the significance of this first downward step — the loss of the first love.

The Scripture reveals God to us as a Person; in His essence, indeed, unknowable, but One who can so reveal Himself to men that they can know and love Him. "He is love, and he that loveth dwelleth in God, and God in him." In our religion we are not dealing with principles, but with Persons, with the Father, the Son, and the Holy Ghost. In the Son made man, we have the visible embodiment of Divine love, and, therefore, His Person is the special object of Christian affection. Love is the bond of all true spiritual unity and communion, and finds its fullest scope in the relation of the Church to her Head. If it fails, there comes estrangement, separation. If the Church ceases to be one with the Head through her loss of love, she no longer has full communion with Him, and cannot grow up into Him in all things, and come unto the measure of the stature of His fulness. (Eph. iv, 15—.) He is hindered in all His teachings and actions. Though the loss of the first love is not the loss of all love, yet it is in His eyes a fall, as declared to the Church in Ephesus, and calls for repentance: "Remember, therefore, from whence thou hast fallen, and repent, and do the first works." The first works can be done only where the first love is found; and this failing, the Lord — the Doer of the works — is unable to put forth the fulness of His power. Hindered in doing His perfect work in the Church, He cannot, through the Church, do His perfect work in the world. The Lord cannot fulfil His promise: "Greater works than these shall ye do, because I go to my Father." He is the all-powerful Head, but through the weakness of the body He is "as a strong man that is bound."

It is thus in the loss of the first love, not in doctrinal errors, that we find the root of the falling away in the beginning, and the key to the whole subsequent history of the Church. Then began that spiritual separation from the Head which cannot cease till the first love has been regained. The Church has not, indeed, ceased to be His body; the Holy Ghost has not ceased to dwell in it, and to act through its various ministries, and has continued to make the preaching of the Gospel effectual to individual salvation, and to fill sacraments and ordinances with supernatural power, and to embody Divine truth in Creeds and Professions of Faith; but it early ceased to be so responsive to the will of the Head that His full headship could be put forth. Its members did not "attain unto the unity of the faith, and of the knowledge of the Son of God." It has been like a human body partially paralyzed. Its history shows that the words of the Lord: "I will remove thy candlestick out of its place," began early to find a partial fulfilment. He did what he threatened to do if the Church did not repent, and do the first works; His attitude to the Church was changed. The candlestick was removed out of its place, the communion of the first love has never been restored.

Let us now note briefly some of the consequences to the Church of the loss of the first love.

First, as to its Unity. We must here distinguish between the unity of life and the unity of love. The first cannot be broken by man. Whatever divisions and enmities may arise in a family, its members remain one. Love may cease, the vital bond remains, they cannot cease to be brethren. It is so in the Church. All its members are one in the unity of a common life, and cannot cease to be one. But the unity of love may be broken. The baptized may be divided into jealous and hostile sects, and cease to regard each other as brethren. Each acting for itself and its own interests, the common good is neglected, the one Head is dishonoured. To build up his own sect becomes more important than to build up the Church.

How powerful was brotherly love in the beginning, we see in the records of the early Church: "And the multitude of them that believed were of one heart and one soul . . and had all things common." (Acts iv, 32.) With the loss of this love, the external bonds of unity gradually relaxed. Each man began to look at his own, and not at the things of others. What divisions and strifes prevailed even in the second century, all Church history attests. The early persecutions of the brethren by the heathen rulers, indeed, bound them together for a time in an external unity; but the inward bond being weakened, the divisions soon reappeared, and have continued to increase even down to our day. Those organizations that have been compacted by time, like the Greek and Roman Churches, present, indeed, a show of unity in themselves, but it is not the unity for which the Lord prayed, "that they all may be one"; and this very solidity of partial ecclesiastical organizations is a barrier against its realization. The first step to a true and full reunion of the members of the body is their full reunion with the Head, and this can be only by the regaining of the first love.

Secondly, as to Obedience. The ground of all true obedience to God and to His Son is love. It was so amongst the Jews; only as they loved Jehovah, could they obey His laws. But this is true in a far higher degree in the Christian Church. "If ye love Me, keep My commandments," said the Lord. As His work in humanity was through love, so all that His children can do for him must be through love; and only where there is full love can there be full obedience. The loss of this first or full love was followed by the disobedient and lawless spirit of which St. Paul speaks as seen in his day; and in proportion as love decays does this spirit increase, and

His children come to care less and less for God's commands and appointments. The fear of Him may remain with many, and lead to an outward observance of His laws; but the desire to please Him in all things, and do His perfect will, be found only in a few.

Thirdly, as to the Truth. Our Lord said, "I am the Truth." To know the truth we must know Him, as our knowledge of persons must be through our personal communion with them; otherwise we know of them, but do not know them. This is in the highest sense true of the Divine Persons. We know them only as they reveal themselves to us, and this revelation is as we are able to enter into communion with them. The basis of this communion is love. "Love is of God, and everyone that loveth . . knoweth God." "If any man love me, I will love him, and will manifest myself unto him." Communion with Him who is Himself the Truth, is the surest and speediest way to attain it. The self-manifestation of Christ to us is something far higher than any mere intellectual apprehension of His words, and gives a knowledge of Divine truth in all its relations which it is not possible otherwise to obtain. It was the visions of the risen Lord, not any reasonings or persuasions of the disciples, that made Thomas and afterwards St. Paul believers; and made this Apostle the great teacher of the Church. (2 Cor. xii, 1—.)

We may thus see how the loss of love brings with it the loss of truth through the loss of communion. As when on the earth it was to the loving, and to them only, that the Lord could make Himself fully known, either as to His person or office; so is it now. No error can be greater than that any man, no matter what his official position in the Church may be, pope, patriarch, or bishop, can cease to be in full personal communion with Him, and yet enter into the fulness of His truth. The Spirit of truth can show the things of Christ only to those who delight to hear them, and who are sanctified through the truth. "It is with the heart that man believeth unto righteousness." "He that hath ears to hear, let him hear." As love grows cold, the power to perceive and apprehend Divine truth fades away, our spiritual discernment is blunted; the intellect formulates logical but lifeless systems of doctrine; and theologians, ceasing to dwell in God's presence, and in communion with Him, theology soon becomes a mass of learned disquisitions about the Divine Persons, and heavenly things. Even if they hold to the old Creeds, and walk in the old paths, and count themselves orthodox, yet the Lord cannot use them to lead His people on in the further knowledge of His ways. There can be no true growth in knowledge where there is not growth in love.

We may thus understand why there have been such almost endless disputes as to the higher truths — the Trinity, the Incarnation, the work of Christ; and in general, as to the purpose of God in man. Because the right knowledge of His own Person is the key to the Divine purpose, He said when about to send the Spirit of Truth: "He shall glorify Me, for He shall take of mine, and shall declare it unto you." His disciples had been gradually growing into a larger knowledge of His Person from the time He first met them on the Jordan till the day He ascended. Ascending, He entered into a new condition of being, was glorified, and made Head over all to the Church.

Now will He through the Spirit reveal Himself as
thus exalted, and the Church come to a further and
higher knowledge of His Person as the Heavenly Man,
and so be able to bear a clear and distinct witness to
Him. But if hindered in this revelation of Himself
from heaven through the spiritual incapacity of the
disciples to receive it, they must fall back on the
records of His earthly life, and find in this its lower
stage the proof that He is the Son of God to be given
to the world.* The true witness is to Him as He is;
and this witness can be borne only by the Holy
Ghost through His Church abiding in full communion
with Him.

Fourthly, as to the desire for the return of the Lord,
and for the perfected union with Him in the new
life of immortality and glory. This was most ardent
in the beginning when love was most ardent. Nor was

---

* It need not be said that a knowledge of the earthly life of
the Lord is necessary to understand aright His present heavenly
life; but as every later stage in a Divine work illustrates and
confirms the earlier, so is it here. The life on earth gave the
basis for the life in heaven, but the continuity of the two must
be proved by the last; and from the present we look back, and
judge the past. Thus the gospels can be rightly read only in
the light of the Lord's present heavenly life. If this life be
denied or ignored, the Lord's words recorded in them become in
many points unintelligible, the true significance of His works is
not seen. Criticism, however learned and acute, seeing only the
earthly life cannot comprehend it, or enter into the largeness of
its meaning as the initial stage of a work which embraces the
whole redemptive age. As the full-grown oak shows what was
hidden in the acorn, so is it the Heavenly Man who fully reveals
the powers hidden in the Babe of Bethlehem, and only partially
manifested in the Man of Galilee. The living man is always his
own witness that he lives; and the Lord in heaven will be His
own witness, unless hindered, as at Nazareth, by the unbelief of
His people.

it merely a natural desire for His personal presence, such as pupils might feel for a beloved teacher; but a spiritual longing for His return because it would bring to them that perfect and holy likeness to Him, and that higher communion with God through Him, for which they prayed. Then also would His prayer be answered that "they might be with Him, and behold His Glory." He spoke of the Church under the figure of a widow during His absence, who prayed day and night for His return. (Luke xviii, 1—.) But this feeling of widowhood was only of brief duration, and with its decay came purposes and plans in which His return, and the higher glory of His kingdom, had little or no place. The first love failing, the spirit of self-sacrifice grew weak, His honour, His interests, ceased to be paramount. The Church was puffed up by the honour which the world gave her, and pleased that she should be flattered and caressed by the great ones of the earth. She became willing that the day of the marriage should be put off into the distant future. The Holy Ghost could not work that internal and spiritual transformation which is necessary before the change in the twinkling of an eye from the mortal to the immortal, can take place. (1 Cor. xv, 51-2.) The groaning in spirit for "the redemption of our body," for perfect deliverance from sin and death, and the longing for the heavenly inheritance, in great measure ceased; and "the little while" of His absence has lengthened into long centuries. (Rom. viii, 23; John xvi, 16—.)

We have thus spoken in some detail of the peculiar relation of the Church to Christ as His body, partaking of His life, and so one with Him; of the falling away as a spiritual separation from Him; and of the root of this separation, the loss of the first love. We have seen that while the union of life cannot be dissolved, and He cannot cease to be the Head of the Church, the union of love may be; and that the loss of the first love on her part brought about an estrangement, and in a measure a separation from Him, which has been felt in all her subsequent history. As her strength was in union with Him, so her weakness was in disunion. Ceasing to be one with Him in the unity of love, her members soon ceased to be one in the same unity. With the loss of love came disobedience, and the mystery of lawlessness. She failed to attain to the full truth, and to the unity of the faith, and lost more and more the desire for His return. This estrangement from the Head, thus early begun, reaches its full measure in the last days, when as He declared, "lawlessness shall abound, and the love of the many shall wax cold." (Matt. xxiv, 12, R. V.)

INITIAL STAGE OF THE FALLING AWAY.

Having spoken of the nature of the falling away, and of its origin in the loss of the first love, let us consider its bearings: 1. On the relation of the Church to her Head as affecting the exercise of His headship; 2. On her relation to the Holy Ghost as affecting the fulfilment of His office in her; 3. On her relation to the world as set to prepare the way for the return of its King, and the establishment of His Kingdom.

I. The headship of Christ as affected in its exercise by the loss of the first love.

When we recall the nature of the Lord's headship as already set forth, we cannot well doubt that it was in the purpose of God in constituting this vital relation that He, exalted into the heaven, and set as Head of the Church, should continue to bear witness to Himself before the world by His acting in it and through it. Thus acting, and putting into full exercise His prerogatives as the Head, it would be impossible for the world to ignore or deny Him, and His headship would be manifested more and more plainly as the Church grew in grace and strength. As the living Lord, He must be the central figure in its history; but if hindered in the exercise of His headship, and hidden from view, men first ignore, and then deny His official place and supremacy; and finally question His personal existence.

We have, then, to ask, How the ascended Lord could prove to the world through the Church, not only His continued personal existence in heaven as the risen One, but also His official power and authority? Of both these the world may rightly demand proof.

The death of Jesus being universally known and unquestioned, the fact to be proved, first of all, was His resurrection. Must this proof be limited to the testimony of those disciples who saw Him after He was raised from the dead?

It need not be said that this proof, however convincing at the first, becomes weaker with the lapse of years, and demands corroboration. This corroboration has been found by many, and rightly found, in the existence and history of the Church. Its existence proves both His existence, and, in a measure, also, His authority. The Church is a living witness to a living Head. Neither her continued existence nor her history can be explained if we deny His headship. Still, we know that the fact of His resurrection, and, therefore, of His headship, is doubted by many who profess and call themselves Christians. The history of the Church, they say, may prove continual Divine help and guidance, but so does Jewish history. And religious systems may be vigorous long after their founders are dead, as we see in Mohammedanism. Because Christianity exists, we may not say that Jesus personally lives and has any present functions; it holds its place upon its ethical merits. He lives in His principles and example.

But such an explanation of the continued existence and progress of Christianity is satisfactory to no thoughtful mind. If Jesus had not risen from the dead and ascended to heaven, and does not still live,

Christianity as a religion would long since have lost its distinctive character.

Whilst thus the Church, as a visible body, and in every right form of its activity, bears continued witness to its Head as living in heaven, we still ask, How can His headship be so manifested that the world everywhere shall know it? The answer is, in the unity of the rule and administration of the Church as one whole, thus manifesting a personal will controlling all. Beholding the Church, composed of men of all races, of the most diverse classes gathered from discordant religious faiths; its members scattered over all the earth yet all united under one authority, not a multitude of little independent communities, but one great community, with common ordinances and rites of worship; and all acting in harmony to one common end, the world must ask, How is this unity of administration and action obtained? We see every proof of the control of one personal will, yet there is no one visible personal ruler. There must be somewhere a centre of authority, or such widely dispersed and discordant elements could not act in unity. We see divers kinds of ministries, some of universal and some of local jurisdiction; who is it that sets these various ministers in their places, and defines their official relations, and makes them to work together in harmony? To these questions the Church can answer: We are under the control of one personal will. We have a Head, but He is in heaven. We do not see Him, but He has those among us who are chosen by Him, and who act for Him, both in the Church universal and in the local churches. To these as His ministers, clothed with His authority, we render obedience. We are one because we have one Head and Lord, and act in unison because His will is one.

This is the visible proof which the Church, fully united to her Head and obedient to Him, should always have given to the world of His existence and authority. Of the Spirit of truth dwelling in the Church — the internal bond of unity — the Lord said: "The world seeth Him not, nor knoweth Him." It is not His holiness and truth revealed through the Church, but the unity of administration through the Head, which the world can see and know. (John xvii, 21.) On His part such proof is simply the exercise of His headship. The prerogative of the appointment of His ministers lies in the nature of His office as the Head, and cannot be separated from it. It had been exercised by Him in the choice of the twelve Apostles, and later of St. Paul. Whether He called them personally, or by the Holy Ghost, there was the definite expression of His will as to those who should serve Him, both in the higher and the lower ministries; the voice of the Holy Ghost through prophets designating them, as in the case of Timothy. (1 Tim. i, 18; iv, 14.) As He Himself was called of God to His ministry as High Priest, so no man could hold priestly office in His Church who was not called by Him (Heb. v, 4); and only through those thus called could He put forth the fulness of His power.

Such was the order of God in the Church at the first in establishing the headship of Christ. The Head, personally or through the Holy Ghost, made known who should officially serve under Him, and teach and rule His people; and thus unity of doctrine and of administration was preserved, and to the world a visible witness was borne both of His existence and authority. Whatever the moral attitude of the world toward the Church, it could not deny the fact of His headship and rule in it.

But a few years later we see all changed. A new method of appointment of all ministers has come in, that of popular election. Each congregation or diocese chooses for itself who shall rule and teach it. The ministers of universal jurisdiction have disappeared; only local ministers remain, and thus all unity of administration is lost. Why this change? Was it in the Divine purpose that the Head should voluntarily give up His prerogative of appointment to the Church? The answer usually made, and almost universally accepted, is, that such appointment on His part was extraordinary; it was not an essential element of His headship, and was necessary only at the beginning. Being once organized, and the several orders of ministers set in their places, the Church, like other religious communities, should perpetuate its own existence by the election of its rulers and teachers. And it was affirmed that such election was, in fact, the Lord's election, since the electors in their choice were guided by the Holy Ghost.

We have thus, after the death of St. John, the last of the Apostles, the spectacle of the Church in its several divisions choosing all its ministers, even the highest. But it scarcely need be said that these highest ministers were local, not universal. They were heads of single churches, or of several united. In the nature of the case no minister of universal jurisdiction could have been chosen by popular election. The election was, indeed, made in the Lord's name, and to a certain extent with the help and counsel of those already in office; and thus a witness, though imperfect, was borne to Him as ruler over the Church through the local ministries. But the change was a most momentous one, and has powerfully affected its whole subsequent history, both as to polity and doctrine.

Assuming that the choice of the people is the choice of the Lord, popular election of all teachers and rulers is affirmed to be the normal and permanent mode. It is taken for granted that there can be no such separation between the Head and the body that the popular will can be other than the expression of His will. Therefore, it is said, if the Lord cease to use His prerogative of appointment, He can as fully act and bear witness to Himself through those whom His people choose, as through those chosen by Him; and there has been, in fact, no such contrariety of purpose and action between Him and those popularly elected, that the history of the Church has been in any respect abnormal.

But this optimistic view of the past and of the present of the Church has no historical basis if judged by its own records. Very few outside of the Roman Catholic pale will say that its history has been such as it would have been had the Lord's will been carried out in it by the ministers of His own appointment. The evils, past and present, of popular appointment are too manifest. Yet very few will trace them to their true source — the loss of the first love — and consequent loss of the spirit of obedience, without which His holy rule, in general, and especially His prerogative of appointment, cannot be exercised. We can explain the history of the Church, its divisions and ceaseless strifes, only by the fact that He could not by His own appointed ministries preserve unity, and lead

His people on to the full knowledge of His ways. This could be done only when there was the full obedience springing from love. Through its loss the Church, very early even in the Apostolic age, came into such a spiritual condition of estrangement from the Head that He could no longer exercise His prerogative of appointment.

We have already spoken, in examining the teachings of St. Paul, of the beginning of disobedience and lawlessness as seen in the resistance made to Apostolic authority, and therefore to the Lord's authority, for it was of His Apostles He said: "As Thou hast sent Me into the world, even so have I also sent them." "He that receiveth you receiveth Me." The refusal to be ruled and guided by them, of which their Epistles give such ample evidence, was the practical rejection of His authority.

But to say that the Lord no longer, through the Holy Ghost, declared His will respecting those who should serve Him in the various ministries, is not to say that the Holy Ghost did not so guide the electors that faithful and good men were in general chosen. This all Church history attests. Beyond question, many, perhaps most, of the ordained servants of God of every grade, in every generation, and in every part of the Church, have sought to do His will so far as it was known to them; and those under them were blessed through their labours. Yet Church history shows, also, that not a few in the highest places in all the centuries greatly dishonoured His name in their lives, and were fomenters of division and abettors of heresy.

How marked the difference as to the rule and guidance of the Church by those appointed by the

Head and by those appointed by the Church after the death of the Apostles, both as to statements of doctrine, practical wisdom, catholicity of spirit, and unity of action, was clearly manifested in the second century, and has often been commented upon by Church historians.

It is here in the loss of the first love and in the consequent disobedience to His Apostles, His immediate representatives, that we find the ground of the Lord's inability to appoint the ministers of His Church after those He had appointed had passed away. His prerogative of appointment remained, but He could not then exercise it. If the spiritual condition of the disciples was such that those whom He first appointed could not fulfil their ministry, to appoint others could serve only for judgment. They could not give what His children would not receive. Why send a second Paul, when the first could not do his work? The Lord, therefore, did as God had done to the Jews under like conditions (Ps. lxxx, 8—); He permitted the Church to walk in the path of discipline and trial, and thus prove by a bitter experience that only by giving to the Head the full exercise of His headship, and walking in obedience to His ministers, could the full grace of God be ministered unto it, and the purpose of its calling be realized.

Let us note some of the consequences of this election by the Church of its ministers.

First, the loss of unity of administration through the loss of ministers of universal jurisdiction. It is obviously impossible that many and widely-scattered congregations could choose by popular vote any but their own deacons, priests, and bishops. How could these bishops be brought into unity? Two ways were attempted, first, by giving the Emperor the right to call a general Council, and the power to execute its decrees. This made him the virtual head of the Church, and led to its division into the four great Patriarchates after the model of the prætorian Prefectures. But this established no unity. Between the Patriarchates, and especially those of Rome and Constantinople, there was continued strife for pre-eminence.

The second attempt, the result of the failure of the first, was the claim by the Bishop of Rome to be universal bishop, and this claim found large recognition. But the division of the Empire, and its two rival emperors, each supporting its own patriarch, made it impossible that the claims of Rome should be recognized by the Oriental Churches. After the death of St. John there was no ministry of universal jurisdiction, and popular election, in the sense of general suffrage, could not in the nature of the case furnish such a ministry; nor the appointment of bishops by civil rulers; nor the election of a single bishop by an oligarchy of cardinals. If the Head did not send those clothed with His authority, all other attempts to preserve unity must fail; and we know that, in fact, ecclesiastical Christendom has been a counterpart to the political — a number of independent and warring communities, each seeking to promote its own interests, with little regard to the common welfare, and unable to establish any permanent bonds of union and concord.

Secondly, the growing feeling of independence of the Head on the part of the Church. Appointing its own ministers and teachers, and thus able, like a close corporation, to perpetuate its own existence, it soon learned to look upon the Lord's prerogative of appointment as no more to be used by Him. Why indeed, should He use it, since the choice of the people is His choice? If, as said by Rome, her bishop, elected by cardinal electors appointed by himself, is His vicar set to execute His will, and preserved from all error, why look beyond him to the Heavenly Head? Having given it a perfect constitution under the earthly head, whom he Himself appoints through the mediation of the cardinals, why should the Lord in heaven interfere at all in the internal administration of the Church? And the same feeling of independence pervaded, also, the smaller divisions, even the smallest. Each affirmed that in the election of its ministers and teachers it was guided by the Holy Ghost, and that they, therefore, were truly chosen by the Lord; and that it was not to be supposed that He would by any immediate act of authority appoint others. Such an exercise of His prerogative, as unnecessary, would be incredible, and no intimation of it is given in the Scripture.*

Thus the Head is practically shut out from the government of His Church, at least so far as regards any external and visible exercise of His authority. There is, indeed, no absolute denial of His right to appoint immediately His ministers as at the first; but a feeling amounting to a certainty that He will never

---

* To this there is one remarkable exception. It is the sending of Elijah the prophet before the great day of the Lord. (Mal. iv, 5-6.) This prophecy commentators, Roman, Greek, and Protestant, have recognized as pointing to a work of reformation to be done by a special messenger from God before the coming of the Lord to judge the world. As in the Jewish Church John the Baptist was sent to prepare the Lord's way at His first advent, and thus do what the then existing ministers were not able to do; so would it be again in the Christian Church before His second coming. Again must God send a special messenger and prepare the people for His Son. Also Matt. xxi, 34;

exercise it. Thus of Him it may be said, as of a constitutional monarch whose ministers are chosen by the people, " He reigns, but does not govern."

Thirdly, the effect of popular election on the religious life of the Church, and on its righteous administration. The experience of all republics has shown that rulers and legislators, chosen by general suffrage, represent the average mental and moral status of the electors. And it cannot well be otherwise. Nor can we expect it to be far otherwise in the Church. As with the Jews; "like people, like priest." Our observation to-day shows that spiritual rulers and teachers will, in general, represent the beliefs and opinions of those who elect them. Whatever religious ideas may become popular, they speedily find clerical representatives. However powerful the Spirit of truth has been in guiding into truth, and in dictating Creeds and Confessions of Faith, yet Church history shows us that almost every possible form of error has had its advocates amongst those set in the Church to guard against it. What a long array from the second century onward of conflicting schools and sects, almost always under clerical leadership, and how greatly multiplied within the present century! The words of the Apostle have been fulfiled (2 Tim. iv, 3—): Many, having itching ears, and not enduring sound doctrine, have heaped to themselves teachers, and turned to fables. Assuredly, if the Lord had chosen His teachers, the history of the Church, as regarding doctrines, would be greatly unlike what it has been, and what her present condition is.

The same may be said as to its righteous administration. How little of brotherly love, of forbearance, of impartiality, of compassion, has marked the proceedings of ecclesiastical tribunals. What persecutions, what cruelties stain the annals of all the centuries. How intense the spirit of hate among conflicting sects, carried out by their leaders when able to use the sword of the State, in bloody acts, the earth defiled with the blood of the saints and of the martyrs of Jesus, shed by those professing to be His servants, and to be carrying out His will. The bishop added to his pastoral staff the sword; under his palace he built the dungeon. Unity must be maintained, if necessary, by force; and the truth, by the death of heretics. There is no more painful reading than large portions of Church history. But prophecy teaches us that the full fruits of popular election are yet to be seen, when the falling away shall come to the full measure of its extent and intensity, and find expression in the acts of the Christian nations when they shall be called upon to choose who shall reign over them.

II. The bearing of the loss of the first love on the work of the Holy Ghost in the Church.

We are here to keep clearly in mind the distinction of the offices of the Head and of the Holy Ghost, and yet the unity of their work in the Church. It belongs to the Head to appoint His ministers, either personally or through the Holy Ghost; and to the Holy Ghost to endow those thus appointed with His grace and gifts, and thus prepare them for their several ministries. But He assumes no headship; He appoints no ministers. As the Spirit of Christ, His work is to do His will. . . "He shall glorify me, for He shall take of mine, and declare it unto you."

It need not be said that if the loss of love works an estrangement between the Church and the Head, the Holy Ghost is hindered in the exercise of His office. As we are taught by the Apostle Paul (1 Cor. xii and xiii), spiritual gifts can be given to those only who love the Lord, and who through this love will use their gifts to His honour, and to the good of the Church. If given to the unloving, they will be misused, and serve to spiritual pride and selfishness. We can thus understand why love is the indispensable condition of spiritual gifts; and that also without these no full witness can be borne by the Holy Ghost to the Head.

But we are here especially to do with that form of witness which is termed prophecy, since of spiritual gifts in general the world can know nothing. It was said by the Lord: "He shall testify of Me." And how is this testimony to be borne? Not by a secret influence upon the spirits of individual disciples influencing their lives, but by His speaking through their lips, by vocal utterance of which the whole Church could have knowledge. (Acts x, 44—; xix, 6.) As the Apostles were to bear their audible witness, so should the Holy Ghost, and this was "the double witness" by which the truth was to be established. "He will show—declare—you things to come... He shall receive of mine and shall declare it unto you." Though spoken to the Apostles, these words were not meant for them alone, and assuredly were not to have their complete fulfilment in the apostolic age. Sent to dwell in the Church unto the end, the Lord's ever present witness, the work of the Holy Ghost in guiding into truth, and of testifying to the absent Head, and of making known things to come, must continue to the Lord's return. If His voice was silenced, there was no more the double witness — the witness of God and of men — the full witness to His Son and to His work.

We are not concerned here to speak of all the workings of the Holy Spirit in the Church, in its sacraments, ordinances, and in the preaching of the Gospel; but only of the ends to be effected by His utterances through the mouths of His children for their common instruction. And of these ends we may mention:

First, His designation of those whom the Head would have to serve Him in the ministries of His Church. This point has already been incidentally considered. The Holy Ghost Himself appoints none. He makes known through His organs, the prophets, the will of the Head, and endows with His gifts and powers the chosen ones.

Secondly, His work in making known to the Church her own spiritual condition as seen by the Head, especially as to life and practical godliness.

That the estimate which the Church has of herself at any period of her history, like the estimate which the Jews had of themselves, may be very unlike that of her Lord, is shown in the seven Epistles to the seven Churches. And this inability to know herself becomes greatest at the time of the end, as shown by the Epistle to Laodicea. This Church, full of pride and self-exaltation, says: "I am rich, and increased with goods, and have need of nothing," and knew not that in the eye of the Lord she was " wretched, and miserable, and poor, and blind, and naked." Such ignorance of her real spiritual condition is possible to the Church only when the Holy Ghost has been grieved, and His voice silenced. When the Lord can speak to His people by those whom He inspires, as Jehovah spake to the Jews of old, He can make known to them how they appear in His eyes, and dispel the delusions begotten of ignorance and self-sufficiency. If He cannot so speak, they cherish their delusions, and become more and more the children of pride, and are most boastful when the judgments of God are about to break upon them.

Thirdly, His work in warning the Church against approaching dangers, and treacherous enemies. It is His office to declare things to come, and the silencing of His voice deprives the Church of her chief safeguard and defence. So long as He lifts it up in warning she cannot be taken unawares. His words give discernment so that she can detect the wiles of her great enemy, his falsehoods, his murderous purpose, even though he come in the guise of an angel of light. Having ears to hear what the Spirit saith to the churches, His children may know what the Lord is about to do, and be ready to take part with Him. But if they have no ears to hear, the Holy Ghost must cease to speak, and thus the Church knows not the place to which she has come in the progress of the Divine purpose; knows neither her present duties nor her dangers. Evil is called good, and good evil. Twilight rests upon the present, and deep darkness upon the future. The Divine voice no longer heard, the voices of false prophets are heard on every side, crying in the deepening gloom as if it were the dawn of day, " Peace and safety"; and crying loudest when the Antichrist is at the gates.

It is this silencing of the voice of the Holy Ghost in the Church which removes a chief hindrance in the way of Antichrist's appearing. We may safely say that the Church, in all the centuries since His voice ceased to be heard in supernatural utterance, has never seen herself as she has been seen by the Lord. The Christians of the last days especially, when the spirit of pride and self-sufficiency is most prevalent, and deeply infected by the evil influences around them, least of all can know their own spiritual condition. It is the Head only who, through the Spirit of truth, can teach them to discern and to reject the Antichristian falsehoods so subtly mingled with His truth. He only can reveal to them their departure from His right ways, their blindness, their poverty, and their nakedness. The Church, left to herself, and confident in her own wisdom and strength, cannot protect her children from the plausible errors and delusions of the great teacher of lies.

Under the guidance of her self-elected leaders, and without the warning and guiding voice of the Holy Ghost, the Church early entered on her perilous way. The Lord, indeed, has most graciously fulfilled His promise: "Lo, I am with you alway, even unto the end of the world"; and has made her in a measure "the light of the world, and the salt of the earth." But as said by one, "His work has been rather to over-rule than to rule." He has brought good out of evil. He has made the Church to be the channel of inestimable blessings to men; but He has never been able through her to attest Himself before the world in the fulness of His grace and power, either in her order, obedience, peace, truth, or holiness, or in the greater works done by Him through her before the nations.

III. The bearing of the loss of the first love on the relation of the Church to the world, and especially as to her place and work preparatory to the establishment of the Kingdom of God.

The wide and deep distinction which the Lord made between His Church and the world, we have seen in His own teachings. This distinction would continue till His return, when the prince of this world would be cast out, and all nations be subject to the King from heaven. Till this time the Church would be in the world, as He was, a pilgrim and stranger, looking upon her mission of preaching the Gospel and educating her members, as only preparatory to His return. But with the loss of the first love which subordinated all things to His honour and prayed for His return, doubting thoughts arose in her heart; she ceased to feel herself an espoused virgin waiting for the coming of the Bridegroom and the marriage, which alone could give her the right to sit with Him on His throne. She would take the kingdom in her own name, and before the time.

That we may understand the full significance of this changed attitude of the Church, let us consider the conception of the kingdom of God or of heaven, and the modifications through which it has passed.

The main element in the conception of the kingdom of God on the earth, is that of a perfectly righteous rule, embracing all the nations; under which rule all injustice, oppression, and strife will cease, the evils of poverty be known no more, and all men dwell in peace together as brethren. We have no reason to believe that the Oriental peoples, or, later, the Greeks and Romans, looked forward to any such universal kingdom of righteousness, either in the earlier or remoter future. They knew nothing of the social perfectibility of man, or of human brotherhood, and saw no goal Divinely appointed toward which the race is tending. Perhaps there was in Stoic philosophy, with its cycles of change and periodic conflagrations, some conception of the unity of the race; but scarcely of any continuous progress. The golden age was at the beginning of a cycle, not at the end. It was said by Lucretius, the philosophic Roman poet:

"All things by degrees must fail,
Worn out by age, and doomed to certain death!"

It is among the Hebrews, a monotheistic people, and through revelation, that we find the origin of the conception of a kingdom of God. Let us note the elements that entered into it, and its subsequent modifications.

Hebrew Conception. This conception had as its basis a belief in one God, supreme, righteous, and directing all movements in nature and humanity towards a definite end, and that end, the establishment of His visible authority over all nations. Under His rule, all discord and strife would cease, and peace and prosperity everywhere prevail. All peoples would honour and worship Him, and the world come to its golden age. Thus the Hebrews were made to look forward rather than backward. In the past, indeed, as declared in their sacred books, was Eden and innocence, but very early came the serpent, and sin, and death; and not till these were overcome could the kingdom of God come. Then there would be more than restitution of the old Edenic order; all would be made new. (Is. lxv, 17.)

Two things are to be noted in this Hebrew conception: that the kingdom was not to be established by a gradual, moral progress of the nations, but by God's supernatural actings; and that, while it is His kingdom, and He is the supreme ruler, it is to be administered by one of the lineage of David, whom He would send. It would be universal. All nations would obey His king, and without end. This blessed Messianic period was the great theme of Old Testament prophecy, and the Messiah its central figure. The distinction taken, as we shall later see, by the Apostles between the Messianic kingdom as redemptive, and the eternal rule of the Messiah after redemption is completed, is not brought out in the old prophets. They speak of His dominion as "an everlasting dominion," not discriminating its two successive phases, redemptive and post-redemptive, as is done by St. Paul * (1 Cor. xv, 24).

Apostolic Conception. This, though in its main elements the same as the Hebrew, was far higher, since the Apostles saw in the supernatural Person of the King a foreshadowing of the greatness and glory of His kingdom. (2 Peter i, 16.) As the Incarnate Son of God, and having all power in heaven and earth, His kingdom, though on earth, could not be classed with earthly kingdoms. Its symbol was the Holy City, the new Jerusalem coming down from God out of heaven. And, as the King was a man raised from the dead and made immortal, and so could be

---

* The apostle does not deny the eternal duration of the Son's rule, when he speaks of His giving up the Kingdom to the Father, but affirms that the mediatorial or redemptive form of it will come to an end, because its purpose will have been accomplished; all things having been brought into subjection under Him.

106   INITIAL STAGE OF THE FALLING AWAY.

God's perfect Ruler through all ages, so must all those be who would be His helpers in the administration of His rule. His kings and priests must be made like unto Him; and under such a heavenly government a perfect social order could be established, and all nations dwell in peace under His sway.

The Apostles always distinguished clearly between the Lord's present priestly work in heaven, beginning at His ascension, and His future kingly work on earth. He had gone to the Father to be made the great High Priest, ever interceding in the Most Holy place. When this work of intercession should be finished, and the Church, His body, gathered and perfected, then would He come forth to seat Himself upon the throne of His glory, and begin His work as Judge and King. (Matt. xxv, 31.) He was, indeed, at His ascension invested with all authority, but His present exercise of it is providential and unseen. The world has not yet known or recognized Him as the King. The sphere of His visible rule is now in the Church itself, where His will is made known in the choice of its ministers, and in its whole administration, and is supreme. Not till He returns and takes the kingdom, is His rule over the nations made manifest, and all human rulers recognize Him as the source of all their authority. Then He " takes to Himself His great power, and reigns." Till that time the Church must be in the world as He was in it, its Divine claims not recognized, and exposed to enmity and reproach. Not till He enters upon His kingly office can the Church reign with Him.*

> * The distinction taken by theologians between "the kingdom of grace" and "the kingdom of glory," is a just one, rightly understood; the first, *regnum gratiæ quod ad ecclesiam in his terris*

Post-Apostolic Conception. This differs from that of the Apostles in the fundamental point of affirming that the Lord, at His ascension, took upon Himself His kingly as well as His priestly functions. Abiding Himself in heaven as High Priest, it is said that He commissioned the Church to administer the kingdom during His absence, and to bring all nations under obedience. When He should return, it would be to a world in which all enemies had already been put under His feet, and be for final judgment, and to deliver up the kingdom to the Father. (1 Cor. xv, 24—.) Thus there are not two periods chronologically successive, and each with its special work, a Church period and a kingdom period; the one beginning at His Ascension, and embracing the time of His priesthood in Heaven; and the other beginning at His return, when He enters upon His work as Judge and King, and continuing to the time when all enemies have been put under His feet. There is but one period, it is said, beginning at the Ascension and ending at His return. During all this period He abides in heaven, acting as the High Priest, and the Church, ruling for Him on earth, fulfils all the promises made to men of the blessedness and glory of the heavenly kingdom. Before He returns all the predictions of the prophets are to be accomplished,

militantem spectat, and the second, *regnum gloriæ quod ad ecclesiam in coelis triumphantem spectat*. These refer to the two differing spheres and times of His rule — that in the Church through His Spirit during His absence, and that over the nations when He returns in glory, and the Church is glorified with Him.

The error of not a few is in identifying the two, and thus making the kingdom of glory to be either the blessedness of the disembodied saints, or that later condition of things when He has given up the kingdom to the Father.

all nations will believe on Him, and righteousness
and peace fill the earth. To accomplish this many
centuries may be needed.

This conception of the reign of Christ through the
Church during His own absence in Heaven, so radically unlike the teachings of the Apostles, was of
slow growth. It was not till after some centuries
that it was fully developed. Passing through several
modifications, its essential principle, as formulated by
Augustine in his "City of God," found its final
embodiment in the Church of Rome with its infallible head. Great stress was early laid by Rome upon
the kingly character of the Church as representing
the King; and its claims to rule for Him in the earth
became more and more positive and definite as His
return was delayed. The Eastern Church also
affirmed that the Church is the Kingdom; and almost
all Protestant bodies affirm the same; but Rome only
has carried the principle to its logical conclusions by
affirming the absolute supremacy of its bishop, as
Christ's vicar, over all secular rulers; and teaching
that all princes should kiss his feet, that he may
dethrone Emperors, that he is able to release subjects from their allegiance to evil men, and the like
prerogatives.*

We have now to enquire how this conception of the
kingdom of God as to be realized through the rule of
the Church, grew up, and to note some of the consequences following its acceptance; its relations to the
principles of Evolution, and to Socialism, and consequent modifications, will be later spoken of.

In the apostolic days the distinction between the

---

*See these stated *Dict. Papæ*, Greg. vii.

Church and the world was continually emphasized as fundamental and permanent. It was in the world, but not of it. We have seen in our examination of the Lord's words spoken to the disciples respecting the future of the Church, how often He declared that it would meet the same reception in the world He Himself had met, and for the same cause. He had been rejected by it because He came to convict it of sin: "Me it hateth, because I testify of it that the works thereof are evil." And of the Holy Ghost whom He would send He said: "When He is come He will convince ("convict" R. V.) the world of sin, of righteousness, and of judgment." What He had done when on earth, His disciples must continue to do in the power of the Holy Ghost,— preach the Gospel. But the Gospel is always a calling to repentance, and therefore always offensive to human pride. It had stirred up among the Jews the deepest hostility, and it would do so in the world at large. That this hostility would be gradually overcome, and the Gospel everywhere be welcome, He never said; but on the contrary, expressly affirmed that His disciples would be called to suffer as He had suffered. "I have given them Thy word; and the world hath hated them, because they are not of the world, even as I am not of the world." "Ye shall be hated of all men for My name's sake," and this down to the time of His return. During the whole period of His absence they would be "as sheep among wolves," exposed to reproaches, persecution, and even death.

The truth of the Lord's words the Apostles proved in their own experience. What St. Paul said of himself, was true in its measure of them all: "I think that God hath set forth us the Apostles last, as it were appointed to death: . . We are made as the filth of the world, and are as the offscouring of all things unto this day." (1 Cor. iv, 9–13.) It is believed that most of the Apostles died as martyrs. It was the law of the dispensation that "through much tribulation must men enter into the kingdom of God." The cross, not ornamented and gilded — a symbol of honour,—but with its bloody cords and nails, must be borne by all.

It was very natural, as the first love grew cold, and the return of the Lord seemed indefinitely delayed, that the disciples should become weary of cross-bearing, and begin to ask: "Are not these disheartening words of the Lord and of the Apostles to be limited to their own day? Is this hostility of the world to the Church to continue to the end? How is this consistent with its heavenly mission, and its gospel of love? Has He not said that the gospel should be as leaven leavening the meal, and as a mustard seed growing up into a tree? Did He not say that "All power is now His"? Does He not call Himself " the Prince of the kings of the earth?" Must not the strong man, Satan, be bound before we can spoil his goods? And when in the fourth century the Roman emperor became a believer, and Christianity had the imperial power behind it, it became almost the universal belief that the day of suffering and persecution was past. From all Christian quarters the jubilant cry went up, " Satan is bound, the day of triumph is come, Christ is reigning through His Church." Now the prophesies can have their fulfilment: " All nations will come to her light, and kings to the brightness of her rising."

This change as to the time of the establishment of

the kingdom, and the belief in its administration by the Church during the Lord's absence, was most momentous, and brought with it many other changes both as to belief and action. Some of these may be mentioned.

First, The gradual forgetfulness of the promises of the Lord as to His speedy return; and the loss of faith in their fulfilment. In all His words to the disciples respecting His departure He had encouraged them by this promise; and warned them not to be ensnared with worldliness, and forget to watch and pray for Him. But all His commands, and His admonitions to stand "with loins girded, and lamps burning, as servants waiting for their master," and the like admonitions of the Apostles, were forgotten in their newly awakened expectation of the speedy triumph of the Church. Gradually His return, instead of being an object of desire, and thought of as near at hand, began to be regarded as far distant. If the Church was commissioned by Him to convert all nations, and everywhere establish Christianity, a long period must necessarily elapse; and He would not come to cut short her work. As it was her commission, not simply to preach the gospel of the kingdom, but to administer it, and to extend her authority over all nations, she must, therefore, address herself with all her powers to this work; and not until the world had been brought by her unto obedience to Christ could He return to final judgment. Thus, instead of being kept always before the eye of the Church as her Head and Lord, guiding and directing all her activities, and whose return might be at any moment expected, He was withdrawn in good measure from her attention as Himself personally inactive. Having transferred authority to the Church to set up the kingdom, it was inevitable that not what He was doing, but what the Church was doing, should become the matter of chief interest to her members.

Secondly, Another consequence of this change of belief was, that the Church, in her effort to subdue the world, neglected her own spiritual culture and growth. The preparation of her children for her Lord's return, that they might " be found of Him in peace, without spot, and blameless," and enter with Him into His glory, practically became of little moment, since that return was in the remote future. The great present interest, the paramount duty, was external, not internal — to gather new members, and make the nations Christian. As regarded individuals, the important thing was preparation for death, which must come soon and to all. Readiness for the change that would take place suddenly, in the twinkling of an eye, from mortality to immortality — a change that concerned the whole Church — was no more thought of; the great point was not through fulness of spiritual life to hasten the coming of the Lord, and thus to escape death by translation, but to die individually in peace. Thus eschatology was narrowed to the act of death, and the state of the disembodied.

Thirdly, Another consequence of the change of belief was the need early felt by the Church of a human head. As has been said, the belief that the Lord had set one man as His vicar to rule for Him, was of slow growth, but naturally followed the loss of the expectation of His speedy return. In order that there might be unity of action in the great work of converting the nations, there must be unity of will in the Church; and this could be best attained, not under many bishops, but under one made ruler over all. The Church, to administer the kingdom of the Lord effectually, must have an earthly head as His representative, one clothed with His authority. This idea, gradually taking possession of the mind of the Church, found its realization in the bishop of Rome. As Christ's vicar, the sphere of his rule must be as large as that of Christ, embracing not only those within the Church, but all without it. His authority must also be higher than that of any earthly ruler, for as Christ is "the King of Kings and Lord of Lords," so must be His vicar. This claim of the Roman bishop was, indeed, in some parts of the Church, long and strenuously resisted, and especially by kings and princes; but, nevertheless, a large part of Christendom early saw in him the earthly head of the Church, holding his place by Divine appointment.

Fourthly, Still another consequence of this change of belief was the practical denial of the power of Satan as "the prince of this world." The Church could not deny his existence, for it had been most clearly testified to by the Lord, and afterward by the Apostles. Nor could it be said that his power had been overthrown, and that he was no longer to be feared. St. Paul had called him "the god of this world" (2 Cor. iv, 4), and St. John had said: "The world lieth in the wicked one." (1 John v, 19, R. V.) In the Revelation (xii, 3—) he appears under the symbol of the dragon as the active enemy of God and of His Christ, and this down to the overthrow of the Antichrist, and till he himself is bound. (Rev. xix, 20—.) But notwithstanding these explicit declarations, and the continued recognition of various forms of Satanic activity as regards individuals, the Church early began to say: "Satan no longer reigns, he is bound, he can offer no effectual opposition to our missionary activity, and to our administration of the kingdom." There was little agreement, indeed, as to the time when he was bound, whether at the Ascension of the Lord, or after the Empire became Christian; but the fact itself was accepted, for how could the kingdom of God be said to come, and Christ to reign, so long as Satan and his angels continued to have their former power in the earth?

As no longer exposed to the attacks of this subtle and powerful adversary, no need was felt of special watchfulness. The strong man being bound, the Church could securely spoil his goods; being cast out of the earth, the Church could take possession of it.

Fifthly, Another consequence of this change of belief was that, as the earthly head of the Church was exalted above all secular rulers, her bishops could take their places among the princes of the earth. The Church had ceased to be a pilgrim and stranger, she was the bride of the Ruler in heaven; exalted to sit with Him in His throne, the world was to be subject to her, and, therefore, all distinctions and honours belonged to her leaders as the nobles of the King.

Looking backward, we see how powerfully this conception of the present Church-period as the kingdom-period,—the time of Christ's rule administered by the Church — has affected her whole internal history, and her relations to the world. The Lord has passed gradually out of sight, hidden behind her ministers and leaders elected by her, and practically deprived of His rule within her; and of His honour among the nations through the elevation of her Roman head. It may be said that no statesman of to-day thinks of taking the Lord personally into account in his plans for the future. Rulers ask in regard to their political movements, what will the bishop of Rome or the clergy do, but who asks, what will Jesus Christ do? It is everywhere taken for granted among the nations that, if indeed He exists and has all power, He has practically withdrawn from any active part in the government of the world. It need fear no interference on His part. He may come again in some remote future to be our Judge, but now men are dealing with Christianity as an ethical system only. As to all practical matters of government, He is as if He personally did not exist. We may put into the mouths of most rulers of our day the words of the Israelites respecting Moses absent in the mount: "As for this man, we wot not what is become of Him."

PART III.

TENDENCIES IN OUR DAY PREPARING THE WAY OF THE ANTICHRIST.

MODERN PANTHEISTIC PHILOSOPHY.
MODERN PHILOSOPHY AND THE NEW CHRISTIANITY.
DEIFICATION OF HUMANITY.
TENDENCIES OF MODERN BIBLICAL CRITICISM.
TENDENCIES OF MODERN SCIENCE.
TENDENCIES OF MODERN LITERATURE AND THE PERIODICAL PRESS.
CHRISTIAN SOCIALISM AND THE KINGDOM OF GOD.

PART III.

TENDENCIES IN OUR DAY PREPARING THE WAY OF THE ANTICHRIST.

MODERN PANTHEISTIC PHILOSOPHY.

We can readily see in the early departure of the Church from the primitive order through the loss of the first love, what the line of subsequent development must be if there were no repentance and return. The Head unable to exercise the full prerogatives of His Headship; the Holy Ghost unable to lift up His voice to warn and instruct; the Church thinking to build up a kingdom in this world, and to rule in it; here are all the elements of a history full of peril and struggle. Of this history for eighteen centuries we are not now to speak. Looking backward, we may see its winding course, its mingled good and evil, the growth of the tares and wheat. But passing over the time intervening, we fix our attention upon the present tendencies and movements in the Church and in Christendom, and ask, To what goal are they leading? To know this, we must consider the new conceptions of God, of Creation, of the Incarnation, of the Person and work of Christ, of the relation of the Church to the world, and of the coming of the kingdom of God. As the marked tendency in our day is in Philosophy and Theology to spiritual Monism, we begin with Philosophy, that through it we may better understand the principles underlying and directing modern religious thought, and determining its outward expression.

The relation of philosophy to religion is in itself a very close one; and in modern Germany philosophy is equivalent to speculative theology. Philosophy has for its problem to bring all existence into unity, to find some first principle which is the ground of all, and embraces all. It looks behind phenomena to learn their causes; through the ever changing to find the unchanging; through the many to the One. The object of its search is the first great Cause, the ultimate Essence, the Absolute Being, or God; and thus get rid of all dualism. As philosophy necessarily affects the conception of men respecting God, and therefore the conception of their relations to Him, and of His actings toward them, it must affect their religion; hence we see the importance of our present inquiry: What does the most recent and current philosophy teach us of God?

It will hardly be questioned by any one competent to judge, that the tendency of modern philosophical thought is to undermine the faith of men in a personal God; and, in general, in all that system of religious doctrine which has the Incarnate Son as its centre, and is embodied in the Catholic Creeds. It needs scarcely be said that, so far as this is done, the way is being prepared for him who "exalts himself above all that is called God, or that is worshipped." So long as men have faith in a personal God, the Creator of the worlds and of man, One who governs all things according to His will, and exists apart from all, no man can seat himself in the temple of God " shewing himself that he is God"; such a claim would be instantly rejected as both blasphemous and absurd. Before such a claim could be listened to, there must be wrought in many minds such a change in their conception of God that this claim of Divinity would not offend them as something strange and incredible, but be accepted as wholly consistent with what they believe of the Divine nature, and of its relations to humanity.

The purpose of this enquiry, therefore, is to ascertain how far the orthodox Christian conception of God as personal, the Creator and Ruler of all, is being effaced, and that of an impersonal God substituted for it. So far as this is done, the conception also of the Incarnation of the Son of God as held by the Church, is radically changed. Instead of the union of "the two natures in one Person," the essential unity of the Divine and human natures is asserted, and the way thus opened for the deified man. Our enquiry relates chiefly to the tendencies toward the denial of the Father and the Son as seen in Agnosticism and Pantheism, but a few words must be said also of Atheism.

Atheism: The term Atheist is often applied to those who deny any supreme Being with intelligence and will, the Creator of the world, and distinct from it. It is often also applied to those who say that, if such a Being exists, we can have no knowledge of Him. But this is to confound Atheism with Pantheism, on the one side, and with Agnosticism, on the other. We can, strictly speaking, call only those atheists who deny any design or order in the universe, any first principle or cause, personal or impersonal. These may be classed as idealistic and materialistic atheists ; the idealistic, who affirm God to be an idealistic fiction, an idea of their own minds ; the materialistic, who affirm that all that exists is matter and motion, "atoms and empty space"; and that we need only atoms and their properties to explain the universe.

Atheism has never had any great number of advocates, for it is repugnant to the laws of our intellectual nature, and to all noble moral aspirations. Yet, in recent times, a good many scientific men have professed themselves materialists, finding support for their belief in the newly-discovered properties of atoms, and the supposed fact of the conservation of energy. Tyndall defines matter as "that mysterious thing which accomplishes all the phenomena of the universe," and in which is "the potency of all life." Huxley says, though his utterances are often inconsistent, that "the physiology of the future will gradually enlarge the realm of matter and law until it is coexistent with knowledge, with feeling, and with action." The materialistic school in Germany has been, of late years, especially aggressive, and has largely affected the popular mind. Probably the number of those who affirm matter to be self-existent, and find in it the substance of all being, is now considerable. The atoms are their God, and for a Creator and moral Ruler they have no need.

Atheism thus sets aside, not only the Christian religion, but all religion. As it has no ultimate spiritual principle, nothing but physical forces, there is nothing to worship. And, as there is no future life, as much as possible must be made of the present. According as it prevails among the people there must be seen increased devotion to material interests, with growing disregard of the intellectual and spiritual. Science, because it craves absolute and unchangeable law, is favorably inclined to materialism. It dislikes any Divine interposition ; its aim is physical, not moral.

Agnosticism: This term, claimed by Professor Huxley as a word of his coinage, is used to express man's necessary ignorance of God. In itself it is a negative rather than positive term. Agnostics do not, like atheists, deny absolutely that there is a God, but say, we cannot know whether He exists or not; and, if He exists, we do not know that we have any true knowledge of Him. The central principle of Agnosticism is thus the unknowability of God arising from the limitations of our minds. As this is a mode of thought already quite general, and bears directly upon the main point of our enquiry, we must briefly consider it; first, in its philosophical principle, secondly, in its religious applications.

Going no further back than to Hume (d. 1776), who has been called the father of modern Agnosticism, we find him denying that we have any true knowledge of the attributes of God, whose existence, however, he did not deny. But all our ideas of Him are, and must be, anthropomorphic. "The whole is a riddle, an enigma, an inexplicable mystery."

This Agnosticism was the logical result of the philosophical principle then generally accepted, that all knowledge is based upon experience.

It was reserved to Kant (d. 1804) to make Agnosticism an integral part of his philosophy. He affirmed that all we can know of things external to us is their phenomena; of what is back of these phenomena, and underlying them, we are, and must be, ignorant. Of the three great objects of knowledge, God, Nature, and Man, we can affirm nothing certain. Kant gives three antinomies — contradictory propositions — which, he affirms, can neither be proved nor disproved. 1. "There exists, either as a part of the world or as the cause of it, an absolutely necessary Being; *Contra,* An absolutely necessary Being does not exist." 2. "The cosmos had a beginning, and is limited in space; *Contra,* The cosmos had no beginning, and is not limited but infinite." 3. "The soul is an indissoluble and indestructible unity; *Contra*, The soul is dissoluble and transitory." (Critique of Pure Reason. Meiklejohn's Trans.)

Thus, according to the Kantian philosophy, reason is unable to attain any certainty as to these vital points; "it is hemmed in by a press of opposite and contradictory conclusions." It is true that Kant attempted in another way to prove the existence of a God, but only as a postulate or pre-supposition, made necessary in order that man may keep the moral law, which is imperative. God exists because a necessary means to enable man to gain the victory over evil. It is generally admitted that this attempt is unsuccessful, and that any positive affirmation of God's existence is inconsistent with the leading idea of his philosophical system. Dorner says of this system that "it leaves to the Divine, as compared with the Human, merely the semblance of existence." Professor Seth ("Scottish Philosophy") remarks: "Kant is the *fons et origo* of the most cultured agnosticism of the day." Religion with Kant is simply morality, and Christ's significance is only that of a moral Ideal; and, therefore, our faith in Him is moral, not historical. "A rational theology must be founded upon the laws of morality." Humanity is the true Son of God. Whether the Scriptures are historically true or not, is a matter of no real importance, since the ideal of reason alone has validity.

Thus Kant, by denying that we can have any true knowledge of God, of the world, or of man, laid the foundation of an universal skepticism. As the mind can think only under its limitations, our conception of God must be anthropomorphic, and, therefore, both unreal and unworthy. Nevertheless, "the notion of a Supreme Being is in many respects a highly useful idea."

As bearing upon this point of Agnosticism, two later writers should be mentioned, Hamilton and Mansel. The purpose of Hamilton, in opposition to the German pantheists, was to show that the Infinite and the Absolute are beyond the limits of our knowledge. He affirms that "All we immediately know, or can know, is the conditioned, the relative, the phenomenal, the finite." "We cannot know the Infinite through a finite notion, or have a finite knowledge of an Infinite object of knowledge." Hamilton thus placed himself in direct opposition to all who think that they can define and understand the nature of God. In this sense he was an agnostic; but he also affirmed that, "through faith we apprehend what is beyond our knowledge." "When I deny that the Infinite can by us be known, I am far from denying that it must, and ought to be believed."

Mansel ("Limits of Religious Thought") takes in substance the same ground. "The conception of the Absolute and the Infinite, from whatever side we view it, appears encompassed with contradictions." "To speak of an absolute or infinite Person, is simply to use language to which, however true it may be in a superhuman sense, no mode of human thought can possibly attach itself." Yet Mansel believed in such an absolute and infinite Person. "We are compelled by the constitution of our minds to believe in the existence of an absolute and infinite Being." And this being is personal. "The highest existence is still the highest personalty; and the source of all being reveals Himself by His name, 'I am.'" Thus Mansel agrees with Hamilton that "Belief cannot be solely determined by reason." The seeming contradictions between reason and belief may exist only in our minds, and prove simply the limitations of thought.

But, however good in themselves the motives of these philosophers, it cannot be denied that their affirmations of the necessary ignorance of men in regard to God have given a strong impulse to Agnosticism.* The inference is

---

* It is said by Pfleiderer ("Development of Theology") that "in the course of the next decade, upon this agnosticism Mat-

that, as we can know so little of Him because of our mental limitations, it is useless to carry on the search. And, it is also objected, that to affirm faith without knowledge is credulity. Let us, then, they say, resign ourselves to ignorance. Some of those who thus speak are, doubtless, willing to be ignorant, and glad to find some philosophic grounds on which to stand; but there are others, in their hearts seekers after God, who are burdened and perplexed by the intellectual difficulties which all questions connected with the Infinite and Eternal must present.*

Pantheism: As to know rightly this form of error is of the highest importance in our enquiry, it is necessary to state as clearly as possible its leading principle and to illustrate it; this will be best done by a brief outline of its modern historical development.

The essential element of Pantheism, as stated by Saisset ("Pantheism"), "is the unity of God and nature, of the Infinite and the finite, in one single substance." The Infinite is not swallowed up in the finite, nor the finite in the Infinite, but both co-exist; and this co-existence is necessary and eternal. Thus we have the One and the many, the Absolute, the All. It will have no dualism, it will

thew Arnold based his ethical idealism, Seeley his æsthetical idealism, and Spencer his evolutionism; three theories which, with all their dissimilarities, have this in common, that they all regard the impossibility of a Divine revelation, and of a revealed religion, to be the necessary consequences of the incognizability of God."

* It should be observed that many who call themselves agnostics, are not really such. The real agnostic simply affirms that he does not know about God, he is in doubt; this is a purely negative position. But to affirm or to deny a God is a positive act. The true agnostic neither affirms nor denies, he has no belief one way or the other; he simply doubts. How far from this position, for example, is Mr. Leslie Stephen in his recent book, "An Agnostic's Apology." He affirms that the limits of human intelligence exclude all knowledge that transcends the narrow limits of experience. Theology is thus excluded, God is un-

unify nature, man, and God. Let us trace the development of this principle, and for this purpose it is necessary to speak of Spinoza.

Descartes (d. 1650), the founder of modern philosophy, who distinguished God from nature as its Creator, divided nature into the two created substances, extension and thought. But these have nothing in common, and thus arose a dualism that he was not able to reconcile. Spinoza (d. 1677) attempted to set this dualism aside by affirming one Substance, embracing both thought and extension, both God and nature. This Substance, infinite and absolute, has an infinity of attributes; but of these we know only the two, thought and extension, each of which has an infinity of finite modes. This Substance, the permanent reality under all transient phenomena, is ever changing ; all finite things are only passing modes of its being, transient manifestations of its essence, coming out of it and again absorbed into it. Spinoza called this substance God. Man, as to his body, is simply a mode of the Divine extension ; as to his soul, of the Divine thought. Both are individualizations of the Infinite.

If this Substance be God, embracing in Himself all existence — the Absolute, the All in all — we ask, Has He

knowable, the universe is a dark riddle. There is no revelation, no miracle, nothing supernatural, no future life. These are not negative, but positive affirmations; not those of an agnostic, but of a gnostic, of one who knows. The old Creeds, all statements in the Church symbols as to the nature of God, the Trinity, the Incarnation, he affirms can now "produce nothing but the laughter of skeptics, and the contempt of the healthy human intellect." And he affirms that " Agnosticism is the frame of mind which summarily rejects these imbecilities." Mr. Matthew Arnold is equally positive. He affirms that we cannot believe in God or angels, because "we absolutely have no experience of one or the other." He knows that God is not a Person, but merely a Force or Power. And, in general, it may be said that no men are more dogmatic in their utterances than most of the professed agnostics.

consciousness, intelligence, will? No, says Spinoza. These are elements of personality, and He is impersonal. We cannot ascribe to Him purpose or design; He is without feeling; He cannot love or pity, reward or punish; of His own will He creates nothing; all things eternally exist, and are in a perpetual flow. He is the universal and impersonal principle of the universe, which has neither beginning nor end.

Thus there is one Substance in which co-exists the Infinite and finite. But here the problem meets us: How does the Infinite become the finite; the Absolute, the relative; the One, the many? How does the one impersonal Substance become personal in man? The dualism of Descartes is not set aside; God and nature, extension and thought, soul and body, remain distinct as before.

This pantheistic philosophy of Spinoza was for a time little understood, and generally regarded as atheism. That it wholly denies the Christian belief respecting God, need not be said. Man is not a creature of God made in His image, but a part of Him, a finite manifestation of His infinite essence; he has no free will, and cannot be morally responsible. No finite thing has any reality, all reality is in God.

So well satisfied was Spinoza with his philosophy that he could say: "I have explained the nature of God;" and modern German philosophers have called him, "The god-intoxicated man."

The attention of philosophers following Spinoza was chiefly given to other questions, such as the origin of our knowledge, and the nature of our mental powers. Of Kant and his teaching notice has already been taken so far as is necessary for our purpose. He left the dualism between thought and being, subject and object, phenomenon and noumenon unsolved. Indeed, his distinction between the pure and the practical Reason made it more conspicuous.

Fichte (d. 1814) took up the problem, affirming that all things must be derived from a single principle, and solved it by making the subject or the Ego supreme; it creates the object. Everything external to itself exists only in the consciousness of the Ego, a form of its productive activity. Nature is reduced to a non-entity. "The conception of a particular substance is impossible and contradictory." The universe, and even God Himself, are of the mind's creation, so that Fichte could say to his class: "Gentlemen, now we will create God." The supreme Being in his system is no more than the Moral Order of the world: "We need no other, and can comprehend no other." This moral order is what Mr. Arnold calls "the Power that makes for righteousness."

This idealism of Fichte was in its principle rather atheistic than pantheistic, but became pantheistic in its later development. For our purpose it is important to note how it tends to the exaltation of man, on the one side, and to the annihilation of God, on the other. Of his philosophy Dorner says: "Each man *per se* is immediately, not through the mediation of Christ, but by nature, God. . . God is the only reality in any one." Christ has, indeed, an unique place as the first born Son of God, but "all men are equal to Him in that which constitutes their proper reality." It is said by Morell (Hist. of Phil.), "With Fichte the idea of nature and the idea of God absolutely vanished; self became the sole existence in the universe, and from its own power and activity everything human was constructed"; and to the same effect Prof. Seth: "Self, as the eternal sustaining subject of the Universe, formed the beginning, middle, and end of the system."

In Schelling (d. 1854) the pantheistic element comes much more clearly into view. Of the two factors, subject and object, thought and being, God and nature, he will not with Fichte allow the one to swallow up the other;

but will identify them in one primary and eternal essence or first Principle, which is hardly to be distinguished from the Substance of Spinoza. This first Principle is ever developing itself, or "embodying its own infinite attributes in the finite." Thought and being cannot be separated, for thought is shown to be in all nature by the presence of law. But there are degrees of thought from unconscious matter to conscious man, and the law of the development of the infinite Essence is from lower to higher. "It developes itself sometimes with, and sometimes without self-consciousness." "Nature," says Schelling, "sleeps in the plant, dreams in the animal, wakens in man." "Mind in man is nothing else but nature gradually raised to a state of consciousness." The universal Divine life runs through a process, but can manifest itself only in finite forms, and so comes under limitations, each individual form being necessarily imperfect. But as being the Divine life in each individual, the finite is not merely finite; it is that in which God has His historical life. "It is God in his growth." The collective finite, or the world, is the Son of God. This incarnation of God in Nature is the principle of philosophy, everything is to be explained by it. But it is in man that this absolute essence, or God, comes to the full possession of itself, or to self-consciousness; and man, therefore, is the highest of beings. In him the process of the Divine development comes to its culmination. Of this development Morell remarks that "all difference between God and the universe is entirely lost. Schelling's pantheism is as complete as that of Spinoza." Of some later modifications of his philosophy it is not necessary here to speak.

It is at this point that Hegel (d. 1831) took up the problem, accepting much from his predecessors. He begins with pure undetermined being, or, what is equivalent, with Nothing, with zero; and this he calls the Idea, or God; and out of this must all things come. Creation is not an act. "Without the world God would not be God." It is, therefore, only an eternal process of becoming which he has to explain. He finds the law of this process to be the law of thought. As thoughts alone are real existences, and are creative powers, the laws of thought are those of being. Thus the two kingdoms of thought and being, or of spirit and nature, are one. In individual things there is no reality, man is a passing phenomenon; the only reality is in the first Principle, the Idea; in other words, in God. In all its determinations this first Principle determines itself; in producing differences, it produces itself in them. The Infinite becomes the finite; the Absolute, the relative. In all these determinations there is progress, but man only of finite things attains to self-consciousness. In him the self-determining Principle, or God, who is everywhere in nature, comes to know Himself, or to self-realization; as distinct from the world, He has no self-consciousness; He attains to this in man. Thus man is both one with nature and with the absolute Spirit, and, therefore, the highest of beings, the last in the chain of development; in fine, man is God.

Thus we have, according to this philosophy, a spiritual principle or essence called God, which is eternally differentiating itself, or eternally becoming. All finite, or differentiated existences are simply necessary modes of His existence,— progressive manifestations of the One Infinite Essence. The law of this progress Hegel lays down as, "The identity of contradictions." It is not necessary to our purpose here to speak of this; we are now concerned only with the nature of the relation which he makes to exist between the Infinite and the finite, between God and man. And we see here his advance upon Spinoza. With Spinoza there is no real progress, man is but one of the transient forms of finite being;

with Hegel, he is the end of the series. Only in man does God fully realize Himself.

It is true, and should be said, that there has been much dispute among the students of this philosophy whether Hegel meant to absolutely deny the personality of God, and the immortality of man, or not. But the most competent and impartial interpreters so understand his philosophy. It has been very recently said by Professor Seth ("Hegelianism and Personality"): "If the system leaves us without any self-conscious existence in the universe beyond that realized in the self-consciousness of individuals, the saying means that God, in any ordinary acceptation of the term, is eliminated from our philosophy altogether; the self-existence of God seems to disappear. . . Evidently this is to renounce the idea of anything like a separate personality or self-consciousness in the Divine Being." "As to immortality, Hegel shelves the question."

With Hegel the climax seems to be reached, the last word to be spoken. All dualism is resolved, God alone exists. He is the All, both the Infinite and the finite, the Absolute and the relative, the Eternal and the temporal. His life is an Eternal process of self-development. We know the law of His development, and that its ultimate term is man. Humanity is the consummation of Divinity.

Of the later developments of the Hegelian Philosophy in Germany it is not necessary here to speak. Its three great divisions into Right, Middle, and Left, are well known. The first attempts to reconcile this philosophy with the personality of God, and the immortality of the soul; the second holds God's personality "in a general pantheistic sense," but denies immortality, and the Christ of the Church; the last knows no God apart from the world, no immortality, and no Incarnation but that in which all men alike partake. In this school are Strauss and Feuerbach, whose position will be examined in another place.

Pessimism: The chief representatives of this philosophy are the Germans, Schopenhauer and Hartmann. The fundamental principle, as said by Professor Bowen ("Modern Philosophy"), is that "there is an universal, all-pervading Will, a blind, and incognitive, and unconscious God; coinciding in this respect with the one universal substance of Spinoza." Of this Will every individual human existence is but a transient phenomenon, and death is its annihilation. Christianity as a religion Schopenhaur wholly rejects, as, indeed, he does all religions except that of the Buddhists, which denies the existence of a God. He says (Religion and other Essays, Trans. 1893) that "Everything true in Christianity is found in Brahmanism and Buddhism." The world is the worst of all possible worlds; nothing is so good as to cease to be. "All qualities are innate, the bad as well as the good," and "a man's acts proceed from his innate and unalterable character"; they cannot be other than they are. Of Hartmann, Professor Bowen says : "He is a thorough-going monist;" his unconscious "Principle" is the equivalent of Spinoza's "Substance" and Schopenhauer's "Will." In the universe is no mark of an intelligent free-will. The world, if not the worst possible, is so bad that we are "to will the annihilation of all things, and thus get rid of the misery of existence." "The blissful repose of nothingness" is the consummation, the haven of rest, to which we look forward.

That this pessimistic philosophy is gaining an increasing hold upon the public mind, seems to be shewn by the larger circulation of its writings, both in Germany and elsewhere; but, if so, this must be ascribed chiefly to the loss of faith in God, and of the hope of a higher future life. None of its advocates openly commend suicide; but this mode of ending a miserable existence is one which must naturally suggest itself, and be more chosen as the gloom of the last days darkens over the earth.

Of the bearings of this pessimistic philosophy on morality, something will be said later.

Neo-Kantianism, or Hegelianism: Of this philosophy, which has within a recent period appeared in Scotland and England, and whose chief representatives are the late Professor T. H. Green, and the Professors E. and J. Caird, some words may be said. So far as we are here concerned with it, it does not differ in any essential point from original Hegelianism. Its central tenet, as we are told by Professor A. Seth ("Hegelianism and Personality") is "the identification of the transcendental self with a Divine or creative Self"; or, in other words, the identification of the Divine and the human self-consciousness. As regards this Divine Self, or, as it is frequently called, "Spiritual Principle," there is much vagueness of expression. Professor E. Caird ("Evolution of Religion") speaks of it as "a self-determining Principle manifesting itself in all the determinations of the finite." It is said to be "somehow present and active in each individual." Is this "Spiritual Principle" the Christian God? Does it exist for itself, with a distinct self-consciousness, and with all that constitutes personality? Apparently not. Its self-consciousness is that of the individual man, separated from which it is nothing. But this takes away the individual self-consciousness; and, as said by Professor Seth, "man's selfhood and independence are wiped out with a completeness which few systems of pantheism can rival." "There is only one self — the Universal or Divine — and this all-embracing subject manifests itself alike in the object and in the subject of human consciousness; in nature and in man. Both are God, though they appear to be somewhat on their own account."

Of the pantheistic character of this Neo-Hegelian philosophy, it is said by Professor Upton ("Bases of Religious Belief"), writing of Professor E. Caird's "Evolution of Religion": "So far as I can understand his position, it is simply unmitigated pantheism, for, according to it, every moral decision to which man comes, noble or base, is an act for which no human being but only God is responsible." "Sin, repentance, moral responsibility, become only empty words."

Evolutionary Philosophy: Of this philosophy Mr. H. Spencer is the chief representative. He must be classed among the agnostics, as affirming that no definite conception of the Infinite or Absolute is possible. For a personal God he substitutes a Force or Energy which he calls "The Unknowable," but of which, he says, we have a dim but positive consciousness. We know it "to exist," to be a "reality," "the first cause of all," "the source of power"; in a word, "an infinite and eternal Energy by which all things are created and sustained." Yet he tells us, also, that it is "utterly inscrutable," "absolutely incomprehensible," "forever inconceivable."

In what relation does this Energy stand to the universe? It is its cause. There has been no act of creation, but an eternal evolutionary process, passing in endless cycles from "the imperceptible to the perceptible, and back again from the perceptible to the imperceptible." The law of this process is "the continuous redistribution of matter and motion." Nothing that exists can be other than it is; all life, intellectual and moral, as well as animal, comes under this law.

We are here concerned with this philosophy only as it bears upon religion. Having substituted for a personal God "an infinite and eternal Energy," can we worship it? Mr. Spencer thinks that the feeling of wonder and awe which it inspires, is worship. It has, indeed, no positive attributes, it is not good, or wise, or merciful, or just; it is merely a force working unconsciously and blindly; but we are told that this is better than the Christian God, and that if we cannot pray to it, or bow down in worship, we can fear and wonder as we behold its mighty workings in the universe.

It is apparent that belief in such a dynamic force can have no more practical bearing upon the moral conduct of life than the belief in gravitation. It has in it no religious element. It not only denies the personality of God, but the personality of man also; and presents to us God, nature, and man, as under a process of Evolution which has neither beginning nor end. For immortality there is no place. Man being only one of the forms of expression of the Universal Energy, has no free will, and no moral responsibility. It need not be said that with this philosophy revealed religion has no possible points of contact, and least of all has Christianity.

Of the Hegelian philosophy a recent writer says: "In itself it is unmixed anthropotheism, not the exaltation of a creature into the place of God, but the assertion that the creature is the sole and essential God. . . Alas! Herein lies its bad excellence, that while utterly expunging from creation, as a popular representation, a present Deity; while rejecting an Incarnate Saviour, an indwelling Spirit, an inspired record, a coming day of judgment; its subtlety is such that there is no point of Christian verity, no office of the adorable Trinity, no text of Holy Writ, for which it has not an appropriate niche in its temple of lies. It contradicts nothing, it stultifies everything; it confounds, neutralizes, and eliminates all objects of present faith. It is the first truly philosophical system which, denying the life to come, eternizes the present. . . The thought of man is the fountain, the judgment of man the judge, of all things. . . And man, though as an individual born and mortal, is as man the eternal essence." A German writer says of it that it is "a paganism dressed up anew, and sublimed to a self-adoring worship of mind." A very recent writer, Professor Wenley ("Contemporary Theology and Theism") says: "The warring of the pantheistic and monotheistic tendencies, both implicitly present in Hegel, ended, unfortunately, in a complete victory for the former."

In examining the anti-Christian influences now at work, we find the current pantheistic philosophy the most fundamental and powerful. Beginning with the century, it has now penetrated all regions of human thought. Theology, Literature, Science, Art, all bear its impress. Its growing influence has been often noted. It is said by J. S. Mill (1840): "The philosophical writings of Schelling and Hegel have given pantheistic principles a complacent admission and a currency which they never before this age possessed in any part of Christendom." Buchanan (1857) says: "The grand ultimate struggle between Christianity and Atheism will resolve itself into a controversy between Christianity and Pantheism." Saisset (1863) speaks of Pantheism "as having made, and daily making, the most alarming progress." "This is the beginning and end of German philosophy, it begins with scepticism, it ends with Pantheism." It is said by E. Caird (1883): "In the scientific life of Germany there is no greater power at present than Hegelianism, especially in all that relates to metaphysics, and thus to the philosophy and history of religion."

Fairbairn observes ("Place of Christ in Modern Thought"): "It were mere folly to attempt to understand modern movements in theology without Hegel, especially those that circle around the history of Christ." Christlieb ("Modern Doubt"): "Fichte and Schelling made the idea of Divine personality to be absorbed in an all-confounding idealistic Pantheism, which received from Hegel its last development. This philosophy appears in German literature from Schiller to Heine. Hence, we meet at the present day so many educated persons whose faith in a personal Deity has resolved itself into faith in the moral order of the universe, or in some universal law or principle."

But no proof need be given of what is universally confessed. A mighty wave of Pantheism, beginning in Germany, has been sweeping over Christendom during the present century; and now finds but little to resist it. As Greek philosophy developed when the popular religions were in a process of disintegration, so is it now. It was then an attempt to replace the old faith by a new philosophic religion. So to-day, Christianity being regarded in many quarters as incapable of giving a satisfactory theory of the world and of human life, philosophy steps in and undertakes the task. It will give us a new religion based upon a new conception of God, a new Christianity based upon a new conception of Christ, a universe evolved, not created. How far the new will supplant the old, time only can show us, for we do not know how far faith in the Christian Creeds has been silently undermined. But Christianity meets a new enemy, a philosophic religion which boasts itself able to satisfy, as Christianity is not able to do, all the demands of the intellect; a religion more suitable to our advanced culture than one transmitted from an ancient and half-civilized people. It is a religion which many will gladly welcome, for it opens a wide gate and a broad way in which all men, of whatever race or belief, may walk without jostling one another.

MODERN PHILOSOPHY AND THE NEW CHRISTIANITY.

We have seen the attempt on the part of modern philosophy to get rid of all dualism, and to bring all things into unity. Regarding this philosophy as the characteristic and most potent antichristian influence of our time, we are here especially concerned with its bearings upon Christianity; but its influence is seen in all spheres of human thought, in Biblical criticism, in Science, in Literature, in Sociology, and in Art. We are now to consider only the two chief modifications of Christianity springing from this attempt to unify God and man; and which are becoming familiar to the Christian ear under the general name of the "New Christianity," though sometimes called the "New Religion," the "New Theology," the "New Reformation," the "New Orthodoxy," and other like terms.

What is this New Christianity? and who are the Neo-Christians? As yet no very clear and positive answers have been given. There is a vagueness of statement, or, perhaps, in some cases, an intentional reserve, which makes it difficult to distinguish between the new and the old. It is said by one of them: "The time has not come for writing the New Theology." But all its advocates affirm that Christianity is in a transition state. Theological knowledge, like all other knowledge, must be progressive. Thus, we are told by a recent writer, (Allen, "Continuity of Christian Thought"), that "the traditional conception of God which has come down to us through the middle ages, through the Latin Church, is undergoing a profound transformation. . . A change so fundamental involves other changes of momentous importance in every department of human thought, and, more especially, in Christian theology. There is no theological doctrine which does not undergo a change in consequence of the change in our thoughts about God." It is said by another: "We need a new theology constructed on a new foundation."

If there is such a change going on, and one so momentous, in Christian Theology, we are bound to give it the most careful consideration. We are not dealing, we are repeatedly assured, with merely verbal distinctions, old wine in new bottles; if this be all, it is not a matter of vital importance. The body is more than raiment. But it is much more than this. As was recently said by one of its representatives: "We cannot keep the new wine in old bottles: this can end only in destroying the bottles, and spilling the wine."

But when we seek to know more accurately the fundamental principles and distinctive features of the New Christianity, we find that, in fact, there are two doctrinal systems, differing widely in their conceptions of God, and in their Christologies, yet reaching substantially the same result — that Divinity and humanity are one. Let us examine them successively, and learn what is distinctive in each. We begin with that school which makes distinctive the doctrine of the Divine immanence in man.

I. The Divine immanence in man.

We are told by this school of Neo-Christians that "the idea of God as transcendent, is yielding to the idea of Deity as immanent in His creatures." It is said ("Progressive Orthodoxy"): "We add a single remark upon the general philosophical conception of God in His relation to the Universe, which underlies these Essays. It is a modification of the prevailing Latin conception of the Divine transcendence by a fuller and clearer perception of the Divine immanence. Such a doctrine of God, we believe, is more and more commending itself to the best philosophy of our time, and the fact of the Incarnation commends it to the acceptance of the Christian theologians." This Divine immanence is the fundamental fact on which this school of Neo-Christians builds its theology.

As transcendence and immanence are philosophical terms, we must note their meaning in philosophy.

It was the doctrine of the pantheist, Spinoza, that all that exists, exists in God. He is immanent in the universe, and cannot in any act pass out of Himself, or transcend Himself.* God and the universe are one. "All the energy displayed in it is His, and therein consists His immanence." "A being acting out of himself, is a finite being." Creation, being a transcendent act, is impossible.

If we may not charge this school of Neo-Christians with pantheism, we must ask in what other sense we can understand the Divine immanence in nature and man? Is there an immanence, distinct from that indwelling of God in man through the Holy Ghost of which the Bible speaks, which is not pantheistic, but preserves the essential distinction of the Divine and human natures, and of the personalities of God and

---

* *Deus est omnium rerum causa immanens, non vero transiens.*

man? It is here that we meet great vagueness of expression. It has been defined by one as "such immanence that the human mind is one in principle with the Divine mind"; and by another, as "absolute oneness with God"; by another, "that man and God and the universe are fused into one"; by another, that "humanity is consubstantial with God." Are we here taught that God and man are of the same essence or substance? Or, are we to take a distinction between unity and identity? Can we say that we are one with God in kind, and yet not identical with Him?

It may be answered by some that this unity means no more than that communion of man with God of which the Lord and the Apostles speak, such unity that "we dwell in God and God in us"; and that "in Him we live, and move, and have our being." But that this, and like expressions, are not to be taken in a pantheistic sense, is shown by the whole tenor of the Bible. Man made in the image of God, and so capable of communion with Him, is still distinct from Him; not God, but a creature of God. If this unity with God be all, the New Christianity gives us nothing new. Its immanence is only the indwelling of the Holy Spirit in man, and preserves his personality and responsibility.

We have, then, still to ask, what other meaning we are to give to the term immanence that is not pantheistic? Perhaps we may learn this by asking the meaning of other terms, in frequent use, as expressing the relation of men to God, "Divine Sonship," and "Divine Humanity." The word Divine is confessedly ambiguous; it may mean simply likeness, or it may mean identity of essence. That man was made in the image of God, affirms likeness ; and on the ground of this likeness, he may be called Divine. So man, as made by God, is His son, and this sonship may be called Divine; and the same term be used of our humanity. But neither term of itself affirms identity of essence. Man may be Godlike and not God; if a creature of God, he cannot be God.

Thus we are still left uncertain in what sense our humanity and our sonship are Divine. But we may obtain light by asking what place these Neo-Christians give the Lord Jesus — the Incarnate Son ? What was His Sonship ? in what sense was it Divine? We are told by an eminent writer of this school — Pfleiderer — that He does not differ from others "because of an unique metaphysical relation between Him and God." The peculiar and exclusive place given Him in the Creeds, as the one pre-existent and only-begotten Son, does not belong to Him. The relation of sonship is a general one; "all men having the same Divine origin and destination." As immanent in all, all are God's sons, and He is Son of God in the same sense in which all men are. The relation is an ethical one, and, therefore, universal. The Incarnation is, as said by one, "a race fact." His distinction is not one of nature, but simply that He was the first to recognize the common filial relation, and to fulfil the duties it imposes. He thus became the religious Ideal, the perfect Son, whose example others are to follow. Knowing as a Son His union with the Father, He could say: "I and my Father are one." All men, as they stand in the same filial relation, may have the same consciousness of sonship, and affirm the same unity ; and this consciousness of our Divine sonship is " the essence of Christianity."

Thus in regard to the Person of the Lord and His Divine Sonship, we reach the result that He differed from other men only so far as He was more conscious of God immanent in Him, and so could reveal Him in word and work; and that all men are in the same sense Divine, for God is immanent in all. If we speak of Deity as especially incarnated in Jesus, it is only as a larger pitcher may hold more water than a smaller, or as one star may be brighter than another.

The question returns: How is this universal immanence of God in humanity to be distinguished from Pantheism? Many attempts have been made to draw a clear line of distinction between them by those who affirm the essential unity of the Divine and human. One of the latest of these attempts, known as "Ethical Theism," is by Professor Upton (" Bases of Religious Belief "), who speaks of all rational beings as "so many differentiations of God," or as "those created by Him out of His own substance"; and yet he would preserve man's free will and substantial individuality. But if of "one substance with God," "differentiations of Him," how is it possible to maintain distinct individual existence ? *

---

* This Professor Upton does by affirming that "the universe, with its centres of energy and personal selves, is called into existence by a partial self-surrendering of His own essential being; and God thus creates a cosmos, in one aspect distinct from Himself, in which only rational souls are possessed of freedom of will. . . God is living and immanent in all; and thus a universal Self, which we can distinguish from the finite self. This is the incarnation of the eternal, present in every finite thing." This is a wide application of the doctrine of the Kenosis, or God's self-limitation. All finite things are of one substance with God, but partially sundered from Him by His own act. Man, though a part of God, is free because "God withdraws Himself

We must call any system Pantheistic which denies man's free will, and makes the individual self to be swallowed up in the universal Self. It is on this ground, as we have seen, that Professor Upton declares the philosophy of the Absolute Idealists or Neo-Hegelians to be "unmitigated Pantheism."*

It is only when the fact of the creation of nature and of man by an act of the Divine will is clearly held, that Theism can be clearly distinguished from Pantheism. Nothing that God by an act of His will brings into being, can be a part of Himself. The Creator cannot be the created. Any philosophy which makes the universe to be of the Divine Substance, or an eternal or necessary manifestation of God, and any theology based upon it, must be pantheistic. If, as said by Hegel, and repeated by many since, "God without the world would not be God," the world is an integral part of Him, without which He would be imperfect; and, therefore, if we affirm Him to be perfect, it must be co-existent and eternal.

But it is our purpose here only to state beliefs and show their bearings, not to disprove them. We are concerned only to note how the attempts to get rid of

---

from identity with his will," and thus gives him some degree of independent reality.

This attempt to make man of the substance of God and yet preserve his personality and freedom, and thus to avoid pantheism, can scarcely be called successful. It is not easy to see how "Ethical Theism," by dividing Deity into perfect and imperfect, unlimited and limited, can escape being called pantheistic.

* Professor J. Seth speaks in the same way: "Professor Caird maintains explicitly the entire immanence of God in man as well as in nature. The immanence of God precludes His transcendence; His unity with man makes impossible that separateness of being which we are accustomed to call personality."

all dualism between God, nature, and man, all tend to pantheistic identity. If the orthodox doctrine of the Incarnation be set aside, and that of a universal incarnation under the name of Immanence be substituted for it, the Neo-Christians are right in saying that " our conceptions of God, and of His relations to men, are undergoing a profound transformation." Especially this transformation is seen as regards the Person of the Son. It is said by Dorner: " The characteristic feature of all recent Christologies is the endeavour to point out the essential unity of the Divine and the human." The dualism of the two natures in Christ must be got rid of. We are told by one of this school that "the peculiar power and truth of Christ's humanity will not be reached till this anomalous division and composition of His Person be abolished."

Thus, if we accept the teachings of this new theology, the old distinction of the Divine and the human must be given up. As said by one: " We are passing over from the conception of God as another Self existing over against the human self, to the more spiritual view of God as the Self-immanent, not only in nature, but also in the worshipper's own soul"; and it is this view "which, in the present day, most commends itself to cultivated minds." It is said by another: "This idea of the Immanence of God underlies the Christian conception . . and is an idea involved in all modern philosophy and theology. It may well be called a new Christianity. At any rate it is the only religion that will fully realize the idea of religion, and so meet the wants of the new time."

The relation of this form of the New Christianity to the current pantheistic philosophy is obvious. We have seen that modern philosophical thought has spent its strength on the problem how all things may be brought into unity, and that Hegelianism professes to give it its final solution. Philosophy and theology are at one: the first affirms that God came to self-consciousness in man; the second bases on this a universal Incarnation. It is said by Professor Seth: "Hegelianism has attempted to find a unity in which God and man shall be comprehended in a more intimate union, or living interpenetration, than any philosophy had succeeded in reaching." This unity it finds by making God and man essentially one. Thus Dorner says of Hegel's Christology: "The unity of God and man is not an isolated fact once accomplished in Jesus; it is eternally and essentially characteristic of God to be, and to become, man. His true existence, or actuality, is in humanity; and man is essentially one with God." As the Divine impersonal Principle or Idea first fully realizes itself in man, man is the real God, the culmination of the Divine development.

It need not be said that between this philosophic Pantheism carried to its last results, and the Christianity of the Creeds, there is a chasm, broad, and deep, and impassable. But as always between the old and the new there are some who attempt to mediate, so is it now. Between those who hold fast to the old historic Christianity and its Creeds, and those who teach the new religion of absolute Pantheism, appears a mediating party, the Neo-Christian. To the pantheistic spirit it will make large concessions. It will not affirm boldly that man is God, but in effect effaces any real distinction between them by its doctrine of a Divine immanence, making humanity

Divine; and on this basis will reconstruct Christian theology.

Let us now briefly sum up the bearings of this new form of Christianity on the relation of men to God, and on the work of Christ as man's Saviour.

1. If God and man are not separated by any real distinction of natures, it is idle to speak of our humanity as fallen and corrupt. The Divinity in us may be obscured, but is indestructible.

Our sin and misery lie only in the unconsciousness of our Divine Sonship, and our redemption is in our awakening to a consciousness of it. It is a process within every man's own spirit, and is effected when he realizes his Sonship. There is no need of any sacrifice for sin, or of any mediator outside of our humanity. "As directly united with God, man possesses his full salvation within himself." Jesus did not redeem us from the law of sin and death by His sacrificial death; but from Him, as from all prophets and religious heroes, goes forth "a redeeming force," only in a far higher degree, because "He, among all the ethical and religious geniuses and heroes of history, occupies the central place. . . As He possessed the new and most exalted ideal of man, so He presented it in His life with impressive and educating power." His work in our salvation was not to bear our sins in His body on the tree, and by resurrection to become the source of a new life; but to furnish an ideal for men, and to educate them by His earthly example. As said by the writer last quoted: "The true redeeming and saving faith of the Christian consists in his adopting this ideal as the conviction of his heart, and the principle of his whole life."

2. As the work of Jesus was completed by giving

in His earthly life a moral and religious ideal, His relations to us since His death have no real importance. His life on earth was a historical demonstration that God and man are essentially one, and having taught men their Divine Sonship, His work was done. As to His bodily resurrection, some of the Neo-Christians are silent, but some affirm its belief to have been a hallucination of the early disciples. As an historical fact, it is not important. He is not now fulfilling any priestly functions in Heaven, or any work of mediation between God and man. He is not the second Adam, giving His resurrection life to man. The Church does not exist as His body, it has no living Head. It is the community of all the sons of God, in which He has no supreme place. It is the ethical principle of the Divine Sonship perfectly illustrated in Him, which makes church-unity; and as this Sonship embraces all men, so the Church embraces all. It is as large as humanity. We enter it by natural birth, we enter into its full communion when the consciousness of our sonship is fully awakened within us; and this not by the Spirit of Christ sent by Him, and working in any supernatural way, but by the redeeming force of His ideal. As there is no living Head of the Church whose life and grace are conveyed through sacraments and ordinances, these have only such value as a man's own spirit may give them.

3. If Christ is not now carrying on any redemptive work in Heaven, will He have any work in the future? Clearly, He Himself believed this, for He continually spoke of His return, and of His work as King and Judge; and this is affirmed in all the Creeds. But we are told that, while He was from

one point of view far above His time and surroundings, from another He was the child of His time, and of His people; and, therefore, we must not be surprised at His belief that He would return to set up His kingdom, and be the King and Judge. In this He shared the mistaken Messianic expectations of the Jews. The Church is now outgrowing this illusion, and sees in the Messianic King descending from heaven to establish His kingdom, only "a carnal conception of that spiritual-ethical kingdom" which will be realized only when all come to a consciousness of their Divine Sonship.

II. A Divine humanity in God.

Before considering this we may be reminded of the orthodox faith, that man was created by God in His own image, but is absolutely distinct in his essence from his Creator. It was this created nature which the Son took when He came into the world and became man; He came under the law of death, but rose from the dead, and in the risen and glorified form of this nature He now abides. As opposed to this faith, this school of Neo-Christians affirms that the Incarnation, as realized in Him, was not a union of two natures, but "the development or determination of the Divine in the form of the human." This has been otherwise expressed as "an eternal determination of the essence of God, by virtue of which God in so far only becomes man as He is man from eternity." Again: "The Incarnation is a revelation of the essential humanity of God, and of the potential Divinity of man."

Thus there is in the Godhead a human element, and, as the Godhead is incapable of change, it must be an eternal element; and, unless we affirm a dualism in the Godhead, this human element is itself "a determination of the Divine in the form of the human." Thus we get an eternal Divine-human element, "an uncreated humanity."

In what relation does this Divine-human element stand to Christ, the Incarnate Son? It was the teaching of F. D. Maurice* (see Haweis, Contemporary Rev., June, 1894): "That Jesus Christ was the coming forth of something that had always existed in God; it was the coming forth of the human side of God, God manifest in the flesh." In general, those of this school agree that before the Incarnation, or before any act of creation, the Divine-human element had in the Son its eternal embodiment. On this ground He is called by one, "the Archetypal man," and His humanity, "the Archetypal humanity"; by another, "the Eternal Prototype of humanity," "the Eternal Pattern of our race." It is because He was the archetypal man that humanity is what it is. "His humanity is more real and true than ours because it is the original from which ours is derived." "The Pattern of man," it is said by Bishop Brooks, "existed in the nature of Him who was to make him." "Before the clay was fashioned, this humanity existed in the Divinity; already was there union of the Divine and the human, and thus already there was the eternal Christ." The word "Christ includes to our thought such a Divinity as involves the human element... Of the two words, God and man, one de-

---

* Of Maurice's theology Dr. Martineau said: "It was an effort to oppose the pantheistic tendency, and is itself reached and touched by that tendency." "It owes its power not less to its indulgence than to its correction of the pantheistic tendency of the age."

scribes pure Deity, the other pure humanity. Christ is not a word identical with either, but including both." This special Christ-nature, the Divine-human, has existed forever; and it was because this Christ-nature existed in the Godhead that an incarnation was possible. Being already man, He could manifest Himself as man; as a Son of man, He could become the Son of Mary.

We thus reach a new conception of the Person of Christ, and a new doctrine of the Incarnation. As regards His Person, we are told that the term Christ includes, to our thought, such a Divinity as involves the human element. Is this eternal Divine-human element in the Son alone, or is it an integral part of the Godhead? The first is impossible, for then the Father and Spirit would be pure Deity, the Son Deity plus humanity. We must then believe that an eternal Divine-human element has forever existed, which, though common to all the Divine Persons, finds its embodiment in the Son. It was to reveal this humanity, and thus to teach men that it has always existed and is Divine, that the Son came into the world.

Being thus "the pre-incarnate Man," the Incarnation could not be the assumption of a new, created humanity, but merely the revelation of that which the Son already possessed. And this revelation was made by the taking of a mortal body, thus bringing His Divine humanity under certain limitations. Thus we meet the humanity of the Lord under two different conditions; as it eternally pre-existed in Him, and as it was in Him when He was on earth. What was the nature of this change from the higher condition to the lower, and how effected? We are told by one, that "possessing already an essential affinity, he enters into a flesh and blood affinity"; or "changes His condition of being by the assumption of a mere human body." How vague and superficial this is, need not be said. But it rests upon the assumption everywhere made by this school, that there was no such fall of man, no such corruption of nature, as the Church has held. The Divine humanity cannot be separated from God, and cannot become really evil; and therefore the work of the Son on earth was not to offer Himself a sacrifice for the sins of men, but "to present us with a perfected specimen, the type, the promise, the potency, of the entire race of tempted, suffering humanity." The sacrificial aspects of the Atonement vanish; no element of humiliation enters into the Incarnation. "It was the actual manifestation of God in the human, so that Jesus of Nazareth became the revelation of God in His absolute glory." A future and more glorious revelation of Him is not promised or to be expected. The world is already redeemed, He has made all things new, we are living in the new heaven and earth.

Thus the end of the Incarnation was not, by the Lord's assumption of our nature and by His death, "to condemn sin in the flesh," and to bring in through resurrection a new and immortal form of humanity, as has been always taught by the Church; but to show men that the eternal Divine-humanity possessed by the Son is theirs as their birthright, and that to regain it is the perfect life. As said by Bishop Brooks, the work of Christ was "to build a bridge on which man might walk, fearfully but safely, back into the Divinity where he belonged." As said by another: "He descended into the race to renew or recreate it after the original Divine image." He established no new Divine relation between God and man, He simply restored the old. He had, as the risen and glorified Man, no new and higher life to impart.

When the Lord left the earth, having finished His work, He regained His place as "the archetypal man," "His pre-incarnate state of fullness and immortality." His mission was ended when He had shown in his own Person the eternal Divinity of human nature, and set before men the heavenly ideal; it was now for them to realize it.

Let us now note some of the bearings of this doctrine of the Divine humanity.

1. The distinction between the Church and the world is effaced. As "the eternal Prototype," He, not Adam, is the Head of humanity. Our humanity is derived from Him, and is the same in all men; therefore, all stand in the relation of sons to God. We are told that when "He came unto His own," He came not to the Jews, or to any elect portion of men, but unto all men; when He uses the figure of the vine and the branches, He speaks of Himself and of the whole human race. In like manner, when St. Paul speaks of the Church as His body, he does not mean a part, more or less, of men, but the totality of men regarded as an organic whole. As said by one: "The Church belongs to all, and all to the Church." "The whole family in heaven and earth is the Church." "The appearance of the Son of God is the sanctification of the human race." We wrongly narrow the meaning of the term Church when we speak of it as composed of the baptized. "Every man by virtue of his birth is called. Humanity is the ecclesia, called

out and away from the old animal life from which it sprang." All are, in virtue of the Divine humanity, the sons of God; and we are told that "the belief of the Church that God has only one Son, and that all others, as fallen and sinful, must become His sons by regeneration and adoption, is no longer preachable or credible among thinking men." As all are children of God and partakers of the Divine nature, "every man must belong to the Church, and the Church to him, whether he knows it or not." It was said by Maurice: "The truth is, every man is in Christ," and if so, a sharer in His perfect humanity.

2. The distinction between the Church and the world being thus, as to its essence, effaced, we may no longer say that the Church is set to save men by gathering them out of the world, but is set "to save the world." This salvation it effects by showing men the Divinity of their nature, and by teaching them that, therefore, all human interests are heavenly and Divine; and that what is needed is their development. Christ, being immanent in the world, His life pervades humanity. Through Him all things are now holy. The kingdom of God, which began at His advent, enlarges with the development of the Divine humanity in all its manifold forms and earthly interests; or, in other words, with the progress of a Christian civilization. How directly this tends to help on, or rather to serve as a foundation for, the present sociological movement, is obvious; and also the place it gives to the Church as the leader in them. If the Church is to save the world by developing and perfecting it, then it must address itself with all its powers to the work of Christian socialism, for, as said by Maurice: "This is the assertion of God's order."

3. It ministers to the pride of man by thus making him the partaker of a Divine humanity by natural birth. As the Divine-human, our nature cannot become really corrupt, or be eternally separated from God. Sin is but the passing obscuration of the sun, the dirt upon the image of the coin: the cloud melts away, and the sun shines bright again; the dirt is washed off, the image reappears distinct. When made fully conscious of our Divine origin, we rise to a true sense of our dignity and power as men. As said by one: "The most glorious and perfect goodness is, in the deepest sense of the word, natural to man." "Christ came to help me to realize myself to be a man." "Whatever man does in his true human nature, is Divinely done." Since the Son came, "no man has a right to say, My race is a sinful, fallen race, . . because he is bound to contemplate his race in the Son of God."

4. While it claims greatly to exalt Christ, in fact it puts Him out of sight as the living, ruling Lord, and Head of the Church. If it does not deny His present Priesthood, it makes little or nothing of it; and ignores, if it does not deny, His return to earth to complete His redemptive work, and to lift up His saints into the glory of the resurrection life. All that is to be expected is the gradual awakening of men to a consciousness of their natural participation in His humanity, and thus lead to a melioration of present evils; and somewhere in the indefinite future, to a universal Church.

As the eternal Christ came to restore humanity to its original goodness, and not to give to it a new higher life through resurrection; all sacraments and ordinances appointed by Him look backward rather than forward. They restore the old, but give nothing new. "Baptism merely tells me that I am God's child." It is the acknowledgment on our part that we are already by natural birth, sons of God. (See F. W. Robertson's Sermons on Baptism.) In like manner, all sacraments are but recognitions of pre-existing relations. His incarnation reveals to us the fact of our sonship, and the acknowledgment of this fact is regeneration.

5. The doctrine of a Divine humanity in the Godhead, cannot be distinguished in its bearings upon the relation of God to man from Pantheism. If we have two essential and eternal elements in the Godhead, we have Dualism. But God is absolutely one. His personality excludes all mingling of elements. In the Eternal Word made man, the Divine and the human co-exist, but mingle not — "perfect God and perfect man." This is possible only in Him. His humanity, made immortal in the resurrection, and glorified by the Spirit of glory, is purely human, and of this we are made partakers through regeneration. To speak of humanity "as consubstantial with God," and to say that "God and man are essentially one," is pantheistic. When it is said by one (Rev. Dr. Parks' "Theology of Phillips Brooks"): that there is a sense in which the words of the Nicene Creed of the Incarnate Son, that "He is 'God of God, Light of Light, very God of very God, begotten, not made, of one substance with the Father,' may be applied to humanity"; how can the Divinity of man be more distinctly affirmed? The writer adds: "If this be not true, I do not believe that the doctrine of the Incarnation can be justified, or at least can have any vital meaning for us."

In this outline of the New Christianity we must keep in mind that, in both its forms, it attempts to hold a mediating position between the orthodox faith as represented in the great Creeds and the strong pantheistic tendencies of our time; and therefore may be presented under varying aspects as one element or the other may predominate in the mind of the writer. Doubtless, there are many who are quite unaware how far their theology is pervaded by the pantheistic leaven; but any one who reads our more recent theological literature with open eyes, will not fail to see that a doctrine of a Divine humanity, — a humanity eternally existing in God, or of a general Incarnation under the name of immanence, is rapidly supplanting the doctrine of a humanity created by God in His image, but now fallen and sinful and alienated from God, and to be redeemed only by the atoning sacrifice of His only-begotten Son, the Word made flesh. It is plain that the doctrine of the immanence of God in man, and that of a human element in God, each lays a broad basis for the deification of man, and so serves as a preparation for the Antichrist.

DEIFICATION OF HUMANITY.

In our examination of the words of St. Paul (2 Thess. ii, 4), where he speaks of the man of sin as "sitting in the temple of God, showing himself that he is God," and claiming Divine honour, we found reason to belive that the Apostle did not speak of a deification like that of the Roman emperors, but of one far higher, and resting upon a very different ground. This point we shall now consider in the light of what has been said of the current philosophical pantheism, and its influence upon the religious movements of our time.

In our examination of the tendencies of modern philosophy we have seen that all tend to deify man. As all roads were said of old to lead to Rome, so all present movements, social, political, religious, find their centre in humanity. Philosophy teaches man that he is Divine, and he is quite ready to believe it, and to act accordingly. Science, which shews the greatness of the universe, and which should teach him humility, only enlarges his conception of the greatness of the intellect which is able thus to search out Nature's mysteries. What eulogiums are daily pronounced upon the dignity and excellence of Humanity, and what unbounded possibilities of development are before it! If Science is able now to explain in large measure the universe, its origin, its laws, its evolution, what limit can be set to future possible discoveries? If Philosophy is competent to solve the problem of the Divine existence, and reconstruct the Godhead in thought, and define the law of its being, this itself gives proof of man's potential Divinity. It is upon the consciousness of this Divinity that the religion of the future must be founded.

The great obstacles to these tendencies to deify humanity lie in the facts of the creation of man with limited and defined powers; and of the Incarnation, as given in the Creeds, and held by the Church. Of creation we shall have another occasion to speak. As regards the Incarnation, it is obvious that so long as the absolute distinction between Christ and other men is held — "His two natures and one Person " — no man affirming that he is God, can be received by the Church. But this dualism of the two natures in one Person, which the Church does not attempt to reconcile, but accepts as a reality in Jesus Christ, is offensive to the philosophical pride which is not content till it has reduced all things to unity. It is willing, as we have already seen, to admit that He is Divine if all men are equally Divine. If we may say that God is incarnate in all as in Him, or that all partake of the Divine-human element manifested in the Son, then all are alike the sons of God; and the distinction of Jesus Christ is made one of degree, not of kind.

These two forms of neo-Christianity, although differing widely as to the Person of Christ, agree in the result that man is essentially one with God. In the first, Christ is Divine, not as the eternally pre-existing Son of God "made man" by His birth of the Virgin, but as simply man through the immanence of God in Him. God being immanent in all men, all are Divine in the same sense in which He was Divine. In the second, we have in the Son an eternal, "archetypal" man, of whose Divine humanity we are partakers, and are thus brought into unity with Deity. We are, as said by one, "consubstantial with Him, and so consubstantial with God."

It is the deposition of the Lord from His place as the One Incarnate Son through the assertion of the incarnation of God in the race, which removes the first great obstacle in the way of the reception of the Antichrist; for it is as the representative of our common Divine humanity that he will demand the homage of the world. By a belief in a general incarnation, as affirmed by one school of the neo-Christians, Christ is no more God-man as to His nature than all are God-men.

If one may suppose this belief to have spread widely in Christendom, the questions must arise: To whom, as the best representative of our Divine humanity, shall men pay their homage — to one who lived many centuries ago, when humanity was comparatively undeveloped, or to one of our own day, — the product of its highest culture? Why, it is now asked by not a few, should Jesus of Nazareth stand forever as the great example of the Incarnation? Can we affirm that the fulness of our Divinity has been realized in any one man, or at any past time? Are we not rather to expect a higher realization of it in some one to come? If humanity is under the law of dynamic evolution, or if a Divine Principle is ever developing itself in men, must there not be a continual upward religious progress? We cannot, therefore, believe that a man of the distant past is to be regarded as the final term of man's evolution, or the highest manifestation of God. Whether Christ or another will hold the higher place as the Divine man, is a matter which time only can decide. But the strong presumption is that we are to look forward rather than backward, and that it is unreasonable to regard any religious or moral type of the past as perfect and unsurpassable.

It is also to be remembered that in rendering homage to one who appears as the rival of Christ, men will not do homage to one who differs in his nature from themselves, and superior to them; but to their own nature as embodied in him. In exalting him, they exalt themselves. Yet the community of nature does not forbid that they recognize in him one in whom is a larger measure of Divinity, and so capable of taking the place of a supreme religious leader. While distinguished above others, yet is he in closest sympathy with them. He is not, like the Christ of the Church, a superhuman being coming down from heaven, and returning thither, but a true son of man; nor does he stand in special relations to a few, as does the Head of the Church, but is the representative of universal humanity.

It is, indeed, hard for many reared from childhood under the influence of the Christian faith, but now accepting more or less clearly the pantheistic theory of God's continuous self-development in humanity, or of its continuous evolution, to set Christ aside as its highest realization, and to believe that any one higher than He can come. Yet, this logical conclusion is more and more forcing its way, and demanding assent. Of this we may see many signs. The time may not be far distant when multitudes will say what a few now affirm: "It is a dishonour done to human nature to teach that in any man of the past it has reached its culmination." The path of humanity is upward and onward; the Divine element in it will manifest itself more and more, and we may not go back eighteen centuries to find the Ideal man.

Of the growing depreciation of Christ, and His rejection as the Ideal which we of to-day are to reverence and imitate, some proofs will be given later.

As illustrative of the present tendencies to deify humanity, and thus deny the special place of Christ, we give some extracts from representative writers; showing how rapidly these are preparing men's minds to receive the coming Antichrist. We begin with some writers who best represent logical Hegelian pantheism; and first with Strauss, taking the translations from Mill's "Mythical Interpretation":

"The infinite Spirit is alone actual when He shuts himself up in finite spirits... The union of the Divine and human natures is real in an infinitely higher sense when I apprehend the whole of humanity as its subject of operation, than when I set apart a particular man as such. Is not the incarnation of God from eternity a truer thing than one in an exclusive point of time? .. Taken as residing in an individual Godman, the properties and functions which the Church doctrine ascribes to the Christ are inconsistent and self-contradictory; but in the idea of the race of men, they harmonize together. Humanity is the union of both natures, it is God made man, the Infinite manifesting itself in the finite... Humanity is the miracle-worker... It is the sinless one... It is that which dies and rises again, and ascends toward Heaven. Through faith in this

Christ, and especially in His death and resurrection, is man justified before God. A dogmatic theology which, in handling the topic of Christ, rests in Him as an individual, is not dogmatic theology, but a sermon."

Thus, according to Strauss, the human race as a whole is the Godman — the Incarnate Son — the true Christ — its history is the Gospel. It comes from God, and returns to Him; ever dying to the old, and living to the new; making progress upward forever. Individuals die, but the race lives; this is the eternal life.

The race being thus the ideal Christ, we ask what is the significance and importance of the historical Christ? It is only this, that "by means of His personality and destiny, He became the occasion of bringing the union of the Divine and human into universal consciousness; the uncultivated mind being unable to contemplate the idea of humanity except in the concrete figure of an individual. . . In this way the Church has unconsciously made the historic Christ the full realization of the idea of humanity in its relation to God; whereas, in any individual we should see only the temporary and popular form of the doctrine."

Feuerbach is still more outspoken ("Essence of Religion," translated by Miss Evans): "Religion in its heart, its essence, believes in nothing else than the truth, the Divinity of man." "Its true object and substance is man." "Man, adoring a God, adores the goodness of his own nature." "The nature of God is nothing else but the nature of man considered as something external to man." "Man has his highest being, his God, in himself."

Renan speaks in the same strain. "There has never been in nature or in history any fact caused manifestly by an individual will superior to that of man." "The Absolute of justice and reason exhibits itself in humanity alone... The Infinite exists only as it is clothed in a finite form." What account he gives of the Lord in his "Life of Jesus," is well known. He is presented not only as a weak enthusiast, but as conniving at falsehood.

Leslie Stephen affirms that "Christ was simply man, and His character quite within the range of human possibilities. There is no need of postulating an incarnation."

Professor Clifford uses bolder language. "The allegiance of man may not be diverted from man by any Divinity... A helper of man outside of humanity, the truth will not permit us to see." "The dim and shadowy outline of the superhuman Deity fades slowly away from before us, and as the mist of His presence floats aside, we perceive with great and greater clearness the shape of a yet greater and nobler figure, of Him who made all gods, and shall unmake them. From the dim dawn of history, and from the inmost depth of every soul, the face of our father Man looks out upon us with the fire of eternal youth in his eyes, and says: 'Before Jehovah was, I am.'"

Let us listen to R. W. Emerson: "Jesus saw that God incarnates Himself in man, .. and in a jubilee of sublime emotion said, 'I am Divine, through me God acts, through me speaks. Would you see God, see me, or see thee when thou thinkest as I now think.' Jesus would absorb the race, but Tom Paine, or the coarsest blasphemer, helps humanity by resisting the exuberance of the power." This is to say that all men are equally Divine as Jesus; and that every one, even the coarsest blasphemer, who denies His exclusive claims, does a service to the race.

If we now turn to the philosophical representatives of Evolution, we see that they also give to humanity the highest possible place. Thus Mr. John Fiske says: "The Darwinian theory shows that the creation and perfecting of man is the goal toward which nature's work has all the time been tending... On earth there will never be a higher creature than man... Not the production of any higher existence, but the perfecting of humanity, is to be the glorious consummation of nature's long and tedious work... Man is the chief among God's creatures." This leaves no place for Christ as the Incarnate Son, the second Adam, and the Head of the new and glorified humanity. It is said by another that "Human history is the record of the process of the evolution of the Divinity out of the humanity." Another says: "Divinity is humanity raised to its nth power." "The individual man is partly the animal from whom we have come, and partly the God who is coming into him."

The ideal man, the consummation of the evolutionary process, is thus he in whom the primitive animal element is extinguished, and the Divine fully manifested. Let the race, as said by Tennyson,

> "Move upward, working out the beast,
> And let the ape and tiger die."

In this process upward the law of continuity is not broken; there is no place for a supernatural interposition, and a heavenly humanity of which the risen Lord is the source. There is only a simple unfolding of the natural, beginning with chaos and ending with the cosmos. Man begins a beast and ends a God.

These extracts, which might be indefinitely multiplied, serve to show that the line of distinction between the Divine and the human, God and man, if not openly denied to exist, is being rapidly effaced. The world is learning, and is quite ready to believe, that human nature has in itself, and in its own right, the possibility of many future Christs; and the world may rightly expect them.

We see how broad and deep a foundation is thus laid in the philosophical teachings of the essential unity of the Divine and human natures, for the deification of the Antichrist. The belief of this unity has not yet fully penetrated the popular mind, and most shrink from the name of pantheists; but the spirit of pride which it begets, is already everywhere manifest. A recent writer says: "A most notable sign of our time is the growing faith in man. . . For superhuman revelation we may put human discovery of the truth; and declare all religions, all Bibles, to be the outgrowth of human nature. As man takes the responsibility of evil, so also he provides the remedy. In place of supernatural grace converting the sinner, and trust in the atoning merits and sacrifice of a Redeemer, he substitutes the human ability to put away sin, and to do what is right and good. . In a word, in place of the descent of God, he puts the ascent of man."

Where this spirit of pride prevails it is idle to preach the offence of the Cross. To say that man is a sinner and needs a Saviour, is pessimism, and offensive; to say that he is a god, is optimism. Man has no confession of sin to make, he needs no atoning sacrifice, no Divine teacher, he accepts no Divine law as supreme over him; the assertion of his own Divinity is his creed, to live in the power of it is his religion. As said by one: "Man can obey the law of righteousness without any Divine interposition." No revelation that God has made of Himself and of His will in past generations, is authoritative for us; our God is within us, and our guide; no book can bind us; and no prophet can be our master. As one has sung:

> "I am the master of my fate,
> I am the captain of my soul."

Conscious of the Divinity within us, we teach and are not taught. To worship God aright, we must pay homage to man. To-day is Lord of all the past, and man is Lord of to-day.

This is the spirit that prepares the way for the Antichrist. Christ being deposed from His place as the only Godman; all men being as to nature equally with Him Godmen, the nations are prepared to welcome one who will prove to the deceived and wondering world his Divinity by his mighty acts, wrought in Satanic power; and will say, "This man is the great Power of God." As the representative of deified humanity, he will seat himself in the temple of God, and all "the children of pride" will worship Him. And thus the kingdom of Man will come, and the world will say, this is the kingdom of God, this is the King.

TENDENCIES OF MODERN BIBLICAL CRITICISM.

It is well known that biblical criticism has greatly changed its character within a few years. It is said by Pfleiderer ("Development of Theology") that the year 1835 marked an era, three works then appearing by Vatke, Strauss, and F. C. Baur, so fundamentally differing from earlier works, and showing so predominently the new element, that "we are justified in taking from these the special character of the biblical criticism of to-day."

Let us ask in what consists the special character of the biblical criticism of to-day. We find it in the attempt to adjust the statements of the Scriptures, doctrinal and historical, to certain new ruling ideas, pantheistic, agnostic, evolutionary, scientific; and to reject all that cannot be thus adjusted. We may divide the critics of whom we here speak into the two general classes, 1. Those who deny a personal God, or any knowledge of Him, if he exists; 2. Those who reject some fundamental facts or principles affirmed in the Bible, thus destroying its unity, and undermining the faith of men in it as the revelation of a Divine purpose and will.

1. It needs scarcely be said that all criticism of a book purporting to be a historical account of the actings of God with men from the earliest times, must take its character mainly from the critic's conception

of God, and of His relations to men. If the critic conceives of Him in the pantheistic way, as Absolute Spirit, impersonal, unconscious, without will or purpose, or as the unknowable Force of the Agnostics, the Bible is on the face of it incredible. No man can accept it as credible who does not believe in such a God as it sets forth,— One who is in the fullest sense personal, who has made and rules all things according to His will, who has a purpose in human history which He makes known to men, who can give them ordinances and rites of worship, and reward or punish them as they obey or disobey. If there be not such a God, making known His truth to those whom He chooses, and inspiring them to teach others, the Bible is a record of what could not possibly have taken place. Its Jehovah is a being who does not exist, and all its accounts of His dealings with men are idle fictions.

When, therefore, a critic sits in judgment on the Bible, we ask him, first of all, what he believes respecting God and His relations to men. Can these relations, as presented in it, be true? If his conception of God be such that he starts with the assumption of the necessary untruthfulness of most important points of the biblical record, it is idle to consider his criticism in detail; if, indeed, that can be called criticism which assumes the necessary falsity of the statements criticised.*

---

* In Jewish history, as presented by the pantheistic critics, we have not the dealings of God with the Jews, but the evolution of their conception of God. The historical statements have value chiefly as illustrative of the growth of spiritual ideas. God is not a Person making known to them in gradual revelation a purpose in which He calls them the workers together with Him, but an impersonal spiritual Principle developing itself in them. It

We may then exclude from the class of true biblical critics all those who, denying a personal God, make thereby the fundamental statements of the Scriptures, dogmatic and historical, impossible. And the agnostic must also be excluded, since his affirmation of the unknowability of God is, in substance, a positive assertion that the Bible, as a revelation of His character and will, cannot be true. Of its essential falsity to the atheist, it is not necessary to speak. The critics of these several classes are thus set free from any inquiry as to the reality of the great facts on which biblical history rests — the creation, the relation of Adam to the race, the fall, the redemption, the Incarnation. Its foundation truths denied in advance, the Bible ceases to be a sacred and authoritative book, and has an interest for the critic only as the sacred books of other peoples have, that he may show its origin, its gradual growth, how its statements came to be believed, and what influence they have had in moulding modern religious belief. Its study is mainly a matter of antiquarian research, and its chief value is as an illustration of one conspicuous form of religious development.

It may seem strange that pantheists, agnostics, and atheists should think it worth while to employ themselves upon such a work of supererogation as to attack the Bible in detail, when they have already condemned it in the gross; but many books of this kind

is on this ground that such histories of the Jews as given by Kuenen, Reuss, Renan, Menzies, and others, although they may have value for the critical student, tend to weaken the faith of the general reader in the Biblical history. If this does not conform to the historian's philosophy of God and of man's religious development, the conclusion is foregone that the events could not have taken place as narrated.

of pseudo-criticism are yearly written. We may take as an eminent example Strauss in his "Life of Jesus." With his pantheistic conception of God and of His relations to men, he could not accept the Gospels as possibly true. Such a man as the Incarnate Son, the Christ of the Church, could never have lived. Undoubtedly there lived the man Jesus, a super-eminent religious genius, yet in nature a man like other men, without supernatural powers, a son of His age; and the work of criticism is to separate the nucleus of historical truth in the gospel narratives from the encrustations that have grown up around it. The reader, knowing his philosophical starting point, knows from the first to what conclusion Strauss will come; and that, even if there were absolute agreement among the Evangelists as to the details of the Lord's earthly life, the more important of their statements would have been rejected all the same.

Again, let us take the agnostic, Mr. M. Arnold, with his critical pre-suppositions, as he has expressed himself in his "God and the Bible." The God of the Bible is the "Eternal Power that makes for righteousness;" not personal, not a Being who thinks and loves. All that we know of this Power we "know in the same way we know of the force of gravitation, by its effect upon us; we know no more of the nature of one than of the other."* All the miraculous

---

* Mr. Arnold is unwilling that this Power should be called the Unknowable, for he feels the absurdity of saying: "The Unknowable is our refuge and strength, a very present help in trouble." "Out of the depths have I cried unto Thee, O Unknowable." He explains the Jehovah of the Hebrews by affirming Him to be "the unconscious deification of the law of righteousness."

statements we are to regard as poetry or legend; and so, also, what he calls the materialistic features — the supernatural birth and bodily resurrection of Jesus, the expectation of a Messianic kingdom, and of a new heaven and earth. The fall of man is a legend, Satan an imaginary being. "Theology goes upon data furnished by a time of imperfect observation and boundless credulity."

There being so little of doctrinal and historical truth in the Bible, we ask with some surprise what Mr. Arnold can find in it to commend it to popular reading, for he tells us, "the world cannot be without it, and we desire to bring the masses to use it." After taking away all that it teaches of a personal God, of His Incarnate Son, of creation, of sin, of atonement, of resurrection, of judgment, we wonder to be told that we may still retain in the expurgated book "the elements of a religion more serious, potent, awe-inspiring, and profound, than any which the world has yet seen."

II. Of the critics who do not wholly deny the truthfulness of the Bible on *a priori* grounds, and yet only partially accept its statements, no classification can be made. They are of all shades of opinion, according as their criticism is determined by their philosophy, their science, or their feelings. Many, coming to the Scriptures with a philosophical theory of the order of man's religious development, will make this order the test of truth, and reject all statements that do not conform to it. It is on the principle of "a psychologically possible process of development" that much of the more recent criticism of the Old Testament is based. Some affirm that the Hebrews could not have been monotheists in Moses's days, for Monotheism must have been a later development; and that Jehovah was simply a tribal God, and the Hebrews polytheists. Nor could the Mosaic ritual have been given so early, since ritual presupposes a long period of religious development, and comes at its end, not at the beginning. We may not, therefore, speak of " the Law and the Prophets," but of the Prophets and the Law. The account of the Covenant with the Jews cannot be true, since the selection of one people would be " particularism," and make the Deity partial; and, therefore, Jewish history is no more sacred, and of no more real importance as a revelation of God, than the history of any other people. And, in general, we may not speak of any "falling away" from a Covenant relation, of any decline from a higher spiritual condition to a lower; but rather of a continual upward progress in Jewish history. In the destruction of the first temple, and the cessation of its worship, the Jews suffered no loss. It was, in fact, we are told, a religious gain. They entered thereby into a larger liberty, and a more spiritual service. So, also, in the destruction of the second temple; the synagogue was a great advance upon it.

Others base their criticism mainly upon scientific grounds, into which more or less pantheistic elements enter. We are told by some evolutionists that we must give up the Mosaic cosmogony, and the idea of a creation. The uniform persistence of Force in nature puts miracles and all Divine interpositions out of the question; and biology refutes the biblical account of man's formation, and shows his development from the lower animals. As there is a natural law of progress in humanity, the account of the fall cannot be accepted. Nor are we to accept the supernatural birth of the Lord, since nothing can come into humanity from without; all is developed from within. And the future of humanity must be in the same line as the past; no break of dynamic continuity, no resurrection, no day of judgment, no new creation.*

Others still reject the Bible on the ground that in many things it affronts their moral sense. An all-powerful God, being Love, could not have done in the treatment of the nations what He is said in the Old Testament to have done, nor does He punish individuals or nations for disobedience to His will. Redemption from sin and evil by the death of His Son, as related in the Gospels, does not satisfy their injured feeling, for why should sin and evil exist at all? We must choose, they say, between imperfect goodness and imperfect power; and, whichever taken, the Bible ceases to be authoritative.

---

* A very recent illustration of the disposition to adjust the teachings of the Bible to modern scientific theories is seen in "The Place of Death in Evolution," by Dr. Newman Smyth, 1897. We are told by him that death had originally no moral significance, but gradually acquired one. In itself it is both useful and beneficent, and necessary in evolution. It lifts man into a higher stage of life, and, therefore, will in the end be universally welcomed. Of course there can be no bodily resurrection, and the resurrection of the Lord was an expression to His disciples of "His spiritual identity." When a man dies, death is no more; and when all are dead, death will disappear forever. Dying is "passage out of death into life." When there is "complete detachment of the soul from atomic matter, and it is brought into new and better connection with the elemental forces, the natural is completed in the spiritual." This is the resurrection. Thus the earth is made a birthplace for souls, which, transported at death into some other world, have there their growth and development.

Dr. Smyth thinks that "the coming defender of the faith once given to the saints will be a trained and accomplished biologist."

But underlying all hostile criticism, and giving it a force which it could not otherwise have over the popular mind, is the feeling which is in the air, that the Bible is a superannuated book. Transmitted to us, for the most part, from a remote past, and embodying the religious conceptions of an uncultured people, what authority has it over us? It reflects, as we are incessantly told, the crude beliefs of a people living in the early age of humanity, when men's conceptions of the Supreme Being were necessarily narrow and very anthropomorphic; a time when any scientific study of nature was unknown, when legends were everywhere received as facts, and dead heroes were magnified into gods. It is not possible for us of this century to go back to such undeveloped forms of religious belief. We have outgrown them. Our religion must be conformed to the advanced philosophy and science of our own time, to the modern ideas of man and nature. The Bible is, indeed, valuable as a record of what men have believed, but its conceptions of God are the conceptions of childhood, and must now be greatly enlarged, and our relations to Him be determined by our wider knowledge of nature and of humanity.

Many illustrations might be given of the growing disposition to regard the Old Testament as superannuated, having little historical value, and no religious authority. Thus it was said a half-century ago by Theodore Parker, who, in this matter, represents a multitude: "The Old Testament contains the opinions of from forty to fifty different men, the greater part of them living from four to ten hundred years before Jesus, and belonging to a people we should now call half-civilized. . . It, therefore, has no authority, and if an appeal is made to some command in it, we answer that nobody knows when it was given, by whom, or to whom. The physics of the Bible are shown to be a false science, its metaphysics false philosophy, its history often mistaken."

A very recent writer, Professor Goldwin Smith, in a magazine article (1895) entitled "Christianity's Millstone," affirms the Old Testament to be this millstone. The New Testament must be separated from the Old; the two should not be bound up in the same volume. "The time has surely come when, as a supernatural revelation, the Old Testament should frankly, though reverently, be laid aside, and never more allowed to cloud the vision of free enquiry, or to cast the shadow of primal religion on our modern life."*

---

*Some are now making an attempt to accredit the Bible by presenting it as a book for literary study. It is said that by "a judicious selection" of its most graphic and eloquent passages it may be made a source of literary, as well as spiritual, stimulation. As expressed by one writer: "Who shall say that it is not to be included in the curriculum of polite learning as a theme, perhaps of equal moment with Shakspeare?" This is meant to do the Bible high honour. But how could we find a more significant sign that it is ceasing to be regarded as an inspired book, unfolding to men the character and purpose of God, His mercy and grace in His Son, salvation from sin, and the terrors of judgment? Instead of being read as a book in which the voice of God is heard calling all to repentance, to obedience, and to righteousness, a voice which no man may disregard but at the peril of his soul, we are told to read it as literature, — a collection of elegant extracts, of biblical masterpieces. Doubtless the purpose is by appealing to the literary taste, the imagination, the sense of the beautiful and sublime, to obtain for the Bible a new hold upon the attention of cultivated people. But its sacred character is thus lost. It is merely a book among books — of value for intellectual culture, but no more the one book, able to make us wise unto salvation, to which we come upon the bended knee, praying for that light from the Spirit who inspired it, without which we read in vain.

It is probable that some of those who are undermining the faith of men in the Old Testament, are desirous of preserving a measure of faith in the New. But the two cannot be separated. We can explain the appearing of Jesus and His teachings only by accepting the covenant relation of the Jews, the law and ritual as Divinely appointed, and the Divine inspiration of their prophets. Taken as a whole, there is a beautiful unity, God's purpose in the Incarnation running like a golden thread through all. There is a beginning, middle, and end, but the end separated from the beginning is unintelligible.

It is a loud modern cry that we give up the traditional Christ of the Church, and go back to the historical Christ. We must rediscover the long-lost Jesus. We must by criticism of the gospels learn who He was, and how much of what He is reported in them to have said and done, He did, in fact, say and do. We can regard nothing as settled; all must be examined anew. Endless questions here arise: who the writers of the several Gospels, the time of their composition, their relations to one another, their accuracy, the rule of interpretation, and the like. The same questions arise as to the Epistles. The discussions of learned scholars have been minute and long drawn out, and, we may add, almost fruitless, because without any agreement of results as to the one point in question, the person of the Lord.*

---

* It is to be noted that those who reject the personality of God make the knowledge of Him to be intellectual only. As said by one: "Theology is not a matter of faith, but of intellectual grasp and careful scholarship." And this is necessarily the case if, as we are told, we must study all forms of religion to learn "the self-evolution of the Idea" in them, and thus come to

It is a striking illustration of the separation between the Head and the Church, that after eighteen centuries its scholars are going back to the records of His earthly life to find out who He was! If it had continued in the heavenly fellowship to which He exalted it, it would be able to tell the world with one voice both what He was and what He is.

There is another school of critics who come to the Gospels in the Kantian spirit, and who make very little of facts; the idea is all. Having the ideal Christ, we need no more. It is unimportant whether there was a real man corresponding to the ideal. It is not, it is said, by His acts as a Mediator between God and us that Christ saves us, but as the representative and example of the idea of self-sacrifice. This idea once gained through Him, it must be separated from His individual person that it may become universal. He may wholly disappear from memory; but the idea remains ever active, and we need not go back to its origin.

But we may not go here into details as to the several critical schools. The critics, writing from all

the knowledge of God. If God be a Person, then can we all, learned and unlearned, come into personal communion with Him and know Him as our Father. But this approach to Him is not alike open to all without regard to spiritual character. As it is in the power of a man to make himself known to some and not to others, much more is it in the power of God. Those who dare to rush unbidden into the Most Holy to find Him, will find only thick darkness. To the weary and the heavy-laden, the meek and penitent, the Incarnate Son says: "Come unto me," and they shall see His face; but to the proud and presumptuous who say: "Bring Him to our tribunal, and we will sit in judgment on Him," He is invisible. The critic who feels no need of a Redeemer, may scan the pages of the Evangelist with his microscope, but will find no Son of God.

points of view about the Lord's person and work — historic, philosophic, scientific, agnostic, evolutionary — each determining by his own pre-accepted criterion what measure of truth there may be in the gospel narratives, have filled the minds of their readers with confusion and perplexity. Almost any modern commentary is an illustration of the critical spirit of the times, and of the perplexity which it brings to the common reader.*

Nor in saying this do we disparage the service which genuine criticism may give to the better understanding of the Biblical records. Every kind of knowledge, geological, archeological, historical, scientific, linguistic, is valuable for the light it may cast on these records, and let there be no suppression of the light; but it is to be remembered that the real point at issue between Christianity and anti-Christianity is not the verbal accuracy, or the general infallibility of the Bible.

We can suppose the possibility of the destruction of every copy of the Bible now in existence, but this would not be the destruction of Christianity. It lives in the living Head of the Church: and however valuable the sacred records of the past, their loss would bring no limitation of His prerogatives, or of His ability to manifest Himself to men. Whilst, therefore, gladly acknowledging the aid which criti-

---

* We may take, as an instance, Godet on the Gospel of John (English Trans.) In the first volume of five hundred closely printed pages we find two hundred and fifty-five occupied in preliminary discussions quite beyond the reach of one not especially versed in such themes. The natural effect is to awaken doubts in our minds, for those must be very serious objections which demand such elaborate replies.

cism, the higher and lower, may furnish to the elucidation of the Bible, we remember that the book is only a means to an end; and that its value is in opening to our knowledge the purpose of God in His Son so far as it has been accomplished, and preparing us to be His helpers in what remains to be done. To one whose eyes are steadily fixed upon the risen Lord, a great deal of the current biblical criticism will seem trifling, if not wholly useless. In the multitude of details unity is lost, the goal is not seen; men's hearts are set upon the past while God desires present action. Only one question is of supreme interest to us: Is the Virgin's Son, raised from the dead, now at God's right hand, having all power in heaven and earth? If the critic says, "He is not, He sleeps in some unknown grave," of what value are his laboured and wearisome efforts to prove small contradictions or errors in a book which can have for us only an antiquarian interest? If the critic says, "He is now living and Lord of all," why trouble himself to refute what, in the nature of the case, is of very small importance, and which the Lord may at any moment refute by His acts?

Can any one think that honest and earnest men will long remain in this state of doubt as to the truthfulness of the Scriptures, or profess to believe what they do not in fact believe? Most will say: "The Bible must be taken as a whole, or rejected as a whole. We will take it as the Church has received it, in its entirety, or we will cast it away altogether." No protestations of biblical critics that they can tear out a page here and a page there, that they can substitute abstractions for Persons, "Eternal Verities" for Father and Son and Spirit, legends for facts, speculations for prophecy, and still keep all that their spiritual needs demand, will satisfy him who will have realities, not idle words. He will say: "I will put the book away, I will not perplex and weary myself in attempting to separate the truth from the error. When biblical scholars have come to some fixed conclusion as to what the Bible is, and what it teaches, and the Church has put the finally ascertained truth into her rewritten Creeds; then I can read it with some assurance that I am not deceiving myself with empty beliefs."

No building can long stand when the foundation is undermined; the first rude shock makes it fall. Many, indeed, may continue to profess great reverence for the Scriptures, as did the Jews of the Lord's day, and study them much, simply because they interpret them in the spirit of the time, and find in them what they wish to find. And we have reason to believe that there are many who, like Mr. Arnold, sing the praises of the Bible long after it has ceased to have for them any authority, or any theological value. They think that it has for the masses an ethical value, and fancy that, while scholars and cultivated people like themselves find much of it out of date, its ideas of moral order and right will keep their hold upon the popular mind, and help to preserve social peace.

Looking to the future, we may not attempt to conceal from ourselves the real character of much of the current biblical criticism. Formerly, accepting the Scriptures as a revelation from God, showing His purpose in nature and man, it limited itself to pointing out some discrepancies, or apparent contradictions; errors affecting particular points, historic or dogmatic, but leaving their general truthfulness unimpeached. The special criticism of our day is far more aggressive and destructive. It affirms on *a priori* grounds, philosophical and scientific, that very considerable parts of the Bible cannot be true.

It would, of course, be unjust to say that all, or even most, of our biblical critics go to this extent. Not a few attempt to stay the destructive work; but that this work goes steadily on, becoming more and more aggressive, no one acquainted with the more recent critical literature can doubt. Nor can we doubt that it has more and more the tide of popular feeling with it. One of these critics, well qualified to judge, has very lately said: " We rise from the survey of this exegetical literature with the feeling that we have only begun the critical history of the biblical writings." Even now the process of biblical disintegration has gone so far that we see in the "Polychrome Bible" all the colours of the rainbow.

This overthrow of the faith of men in the Bible is a great step forward in preparing the way for the Antichrist. It is of comparatively less importance in the Roman Catholic than in the Protestant communion, since the former makes the Church itself to be an infallible teacher; and to those thus believing, what the biblical critics may say is a matter of indifference. Still it is abundantly manifest that in the Roman communion the loss of faith in the Scriptures is greatly weakening the faith of many in the Church. But to the Protestant, the loss of faith in the Bible points to a great religious change. It leaves him without any guide or teacher, for his choice must be between the biblical teachings of God and of His relations to the Universe and to man, and the teachings of Pantheism. Men are too nobly constituted to be atheists, nor can they long be agnostics. They cannot remain in the pains of doubt, or emptiness of unbelief.

To reject or ignore the Bible on whatever grounds is to be ignorant of God and of His purpose in man and thus to be exposed to the most dangerous form of delusion, that of self-deification. In proportion as unbelief in the Scriptures increases, the Person of the Incarnate Son, who, as the First and Last, the Beginning and the End, alone gives it unity and meaning, recedes from our sight; and, as He recedes, darkness deepens over both present and future. For years the most unobservant has seen how within the Church the study of prophecy has been greatly disparaged,—a sure sign of that decay of faith which, beginning here, extends itself to history and doctrine and ends in their final rejection.

Thus the Bible, made up, as we are told, of disconnected and discordant parts, emptied of all historical unity, revealing no Divine purpose, neither explains the past nor casts light upon the future. Why retain it? Put it among other sacred books, call it literature, keep it for its teachings of ethics, and as illustrating the evolution of religion; but the new age must have its new Bible, one reflecting its advanced knowledge of God and man and nature. It was said by Thomas Carlyle ("Essays"): "A Bible is the authentic biography of noble souls." "To each nation its believed history is its Bible; not in Judæa alone, or Hellas, or Latium, but in all lands and in all times." We may, therefore, look for a new Bible which will not narrow its records to the life of one covenant people, but be the history of the evolution of the idea of God in all the noble spirits of the race; and thus be the sacred book of a universal religion!

TENDENCIES OF MODERN SCIENCE.

How greatly the conceptions of men as to the vastness of the universe, and how long existent, have been enlarged in our day, need not be said; and a like enlargement has taken place in our knowledge of the smallness of atoms, and the molecular constitution of material bodies. But we are here only concerned to ask: First, What is the bearing of this enlarged knowledge upon our faith in God as the Creator? Secondly, What its bearing upon our faith as to the place given in the Scriptures to the earth and to man, and particularly to the fact of the Incarnation? Thirdly, What is the effect of scientific study upon the mind as regards its reception of spiritual truth?

I. Its bearing upon our belief in the statements of the Scriptures respecting the creation of the world, and thus upon our conception of God.

So far as regards the vastness of the universe, there seems to be no good reason why it should be harder for us to believe in the creation of many worlds than in the creation of a few, or even of one. The bringing of something into existence that did not exist before, is the proof of creative power put forth; and it is this which is in question, rather than its degree. Yet there is a vague feeling in many minds that the vast extent of the universe as now known to us, tends strongly to disprove the fact of a creation, and to confirm the idea of its eternal existence.

It may be admitted that if the universe were known to be absolutely limitless or infinite, the idea of a creation would be much harder to realize; but here Science is silent. It may, perhaps, be said that a limited or finite universe would tend to prove a creative act; and an unlimited or infinite one tend to prove its co-existence with God, and an unceasing manifestation of Him; and, therefore, uncreated and eternal. But our ignorance here is too great to furnish ground for any valid judgment.

The real difficulty which not a few have found in the Scripture doctrine of a creation, and in the faith of the Church respecting it, does not arise from any teachings of Science as to the immensity of the universe, or as to its origin, for of this origin it knows and can know nothing; but rests upon a metaphysical ground — the inconceivability of creation. It is affirmed that we cannot think an absolute beginning, only a change in that which already exists. Nor can we think of an absolute end. This leads to the conclusion that the universe has always existed, and that any affirmation of its creation, or beginning, must be rejected. But this belief that creation is unthinkable, is held but by a few. It is said (J. S. Mill, "Examination of Hamilton's Philosophy"): "We can conceive both a beginning and an end to all physical existence." But even if inconceivable, yet "there are many things inconceivable to us which not only may, but must, be true." The fact of a creation is not disproved, even if we are not able to think it; but if it were not a fact, this would vitally affect our conception of God. If the universe did not come into being by any act of His will, but was co-existent with Him, we must say with Hegel, that "God without the world would not be God." But this is to say that without the world He would be incomplete, imperfect. The world is necessary for His self-development, His self-perfecting. It follows that that without which He is not perfect God, is necessarily a part of Him. The universe co-eternal with Him is essentially one with Him and indivisible. Thus the dualism of God and nature is set aside, and we have unity; but the unity of Pantheism.*

If we now ask, what does the modern hypothesis of evolution say as to the matter of creation, we are told by Martineau ("Study of Religion") that "we are passing over to the idea of evolution rather than of creation." But the most prominent evolutionists tell us that with the origin of the universe evolution has nothing to do. It deals only with the changes which take place among existing things, and does not concern itself with the question how or when these things began to be. Darwin affirms that "the beginning of the universe is an insoluble mystery." In like way Professor Tyndall says: "Evolution does not solve, does not profess to solve, the ultimate mystery of the universe." Professor Clifford bluntly says: "Of the beginning of the universe we know nothing at all." It need not be said that, as evolution

* It was said by Goethe: "Everything which exists necessarily pertains to the essence of God; therefore, God is the one being whose existence includes all things." He sings:
"God dwells within, and moves the world and moulds,
Himself and nature in one form enfolds."

A recent writer, Rev. L. Abbott, says: "Creation will be recognized as a continuous process, eternal as God is eternal, and because God is eternal."

is a process by which A becomes B, or one known thing becomes another known thing, to speak of an evolution of which we know neither the beginning nor end, or, in other words, of an eternal process, is absurd. It is a phrase without meaning. The mind demands a starting point and a goal; and any theory of the universe which does not present them, gives nothing for the mind to grasp.

But, notwithstanding the declared ignorance of the evolutionists as to the beginning of the universe, or an act of creation, the general tendency is to deny it. It is said by Professor Huxley: "It is clear that the doctrine of evolution is directly antagonistic to that of creation. . . As applied to the formation of the world as a whole, it is opposed to that of direct creative volition." There are probably many who have a confused notion that evolution in some way takes the place of creation. As stated by Mr. H. Spencer, it has a marked affinity with pantheism. Pantheism begins with the Infinite which eternally determines itself in finite forms. In evolution the absolute Power works eternal " change from indeterminate uniformity to determinate multiformity." The Power which effects the change is a dynamic one, without consciousness, intelligence, or will, the law of its activity being " the continuous redistribution of matter and motion." As there is no Creator, there has been no creation, but an eternal becoming.*

* Mr. Spencer, who affirms a creation to be unthinkable, and yet must have a starting-point for his evolutionary process, finds an imaginary one in a primitive homogeneity or homogeneous mass, which becomes during the ages heterogeneous, and again in the succeeding ages becomes homogeneous. Thus, to avoid the difficulty of evolution in a straight line, or without any continuous movement, he chooses a circle which allows him to

It has been said (Draper, " Conflict between Religion and Science "), " Philosophy has never proposed but two hypotheses to explain the system of the world: first, a personal God existing apart, and a human soul called into existence or created, and thenceforth immortal; second, an impersonal intelligence, or indeterminate God, and a soul emerging from and returning to him. . . . The theory of creation belongs to the first of these hypotheses, that of evolution to the last."

Professor E. Haeckel, the chief representative of material Monism, finds his God in the Cosmic Ether: " All forces have foundations in a simple, primal principle pervading infinite space — the Cosmic Ether; we can regard this as all-comprehending Divinity; and thus belief in God is reconcilable with Science." There is no personal God or Creator. " This notion is rendered quite untenable by the advancement of monistic science. It is already antiquated, and is destined before the present century is ended to drop out of currency throughout the entire domain of purely scientific philosophy."

pass "in an endless cycle from indeterminate uniformity to determinate multiformity, and from multiformity to uniformity." All this gives no explanation of the origin of his homogeneous mass, atoms, ether, or what not; nor does it explain how Mr. Spencer came to the knowledge of it in its condition of uniformity, or how he knows what it will be when it comes into its condition of multiformity. A man who should walk a few rods on a railway of a thousand miles, of whose changing course and termini he knows nothing, and can tell us from his observation what the course and termini are, would be a wise man; but only a babe as compared with Mr. Spencer, who from the few years of man's existence on the earth is able to look backward and forward a few hundred millions of years and tell us the order of the ever-recurring cycles of the great universe.

If a creation by God is denied, can we find in the universe any intelligible purpose? If we reject the pantheistic theory that it is a part of God, and so coming under the law of His self-evolution, we can simply say that it exists. We can speak with certainty only of the present. But as we cannot believe that the universe brought itself into being, or can annihilate itself, we must affirm not only that it exists, but that it has always existed, and always will exist. There is thus an eternal series of changes, but is there also progress? Is there any goal to which they lead? If, as said by one of this school, "the present visible universe is a phase, only a phase, in the unrolling of an infinite panorama," what will be the next phase? There are many who talk of the teleology of evolution, and who find its final term and culmination in man. This is done by Professor John Fiske; and Darwin asserts that "in the distant future man will be a far more perfect creature than he now is." There is no ground for such assertions. Belief in progress through evolution can rest only on one's knowledge of the purpose of an intelligent and beneficent Being, who is also omnipotent and eternal, and who directs all the movements of nature. If there be no such Being and no purpose, the universe drifts forever aimlessly on. The brief limits of human life on earth furnish no sufficient data whereby to judge of the character of the future ages. We may believe that to-morrow will be as to-day, but this is only a blind belief of which we can give no account. What to-morrow will bring, only to-morrow can tell. It may be a partial repetition of the past, it may bring something absolutely new.*

* We may remark here the fallacy of much which is said of

A personal Creator of the universe being thus, on one ground or another, set aside, the Christian can no longer say: "I believe in one God, maker of heaven and earth." He can no longer sing: "The heavens declare the glory of God, and the firmament sheweth His handiwork." The earth is an infinitesimal part of a vast system of worlds, ever moving on without guide or lord. If the whole human race should at once cease to exist, it would not be an appreciable incident in the life of the universe. Science can with its telescopic eye fill the immensities of space with material orbs, and in an imperfect way compute their sizes and distances, and guess at the manner of their formation, and what forces are acting in them ; but of all that has any high significance for us, — whether inhabited by rational beings or not, beings who stand, or ever will stand, in any moral relations to us, it can tell us nothing.

With the Father, the Creator, disappears also from the heavens the Son, the Word. According to the apostolic teaching, the Son, pre-existent, was the instrument of the Father in the creation of the worlds. "He was in the beginning with God. All things were made by Him, and without Him was not any thing made that was made." "In Him were all things created, in the heavens and upon the earth . . all

the reign of inflexible and unchangeable law. The only permanent law we know, is that of change — a perpetual flux. Of the universe at large we know neither what it has been nor what it will be ; the blackness of darkness rests upon both its beginning and end. And of our earth, without revelation, we know only of a continued series of changes, of whose goal, if there be any, we are absolutely ignorant. Only through a Divine purpose can we find unity in these changes.

things have been created through Him, and unto Him; and He is before all things, and in Him all things consist," or, as in the margin, "hold together." It is His person which binds all worlds into unity. The universe is what it is because made for Him; and separated from the Divine purpose in Him, its history and destiny cannot be read aright. As seen by Science, we behold only immense masses of matter rolling through space; as seen by the eye of faith, we behold orbs preparing for the habitation of intelligent and spiritual beings made in the likeness of their glorified Lord; orbs into which sin and death can never enter, and from which holy worship, offered in the name of the Son, shall go up forever to the Father of all.

It is plain that the character of one thus looking upon the universe as without a Creator, a Ruler, or a purpose, must take upon itself a peculiar impress; and of this we shall soon speak.

II. The bearing of our enlarged knowledge of the Universe upon our faith as to the place given in the Scriptures to the earth and to man, and particularly to the fact of the Incarnation.

The opening sentence of the Bible is sublime in its brevity. "In the beginning God created the heavens and the earth." Nothing more is said of the formation of the heavens except incidentally; but that the Hebrew prophets and poets had noble conceptions of the greatness, and of the fixed order of the Universe, is abundantly evident. The formation of the earth is given in some detail. Its importance, however, is not physical but moral. It is the one among the worlds chosen by God to be the place of events which affect in their results all intelligent creatures, and so are of universal significance. It is the moral centre of all worlds, because God has manifested here His moral character as nowhere else in the Universe. If the early generations of men, in their astronomical ignorance, made it the physical centre, this does not affect its real importance, which is in no way dependent upon material greatness. If, then, the recent revelations of astronomy show us the vastness of creation, the countless number and almost measureless size of its suns, making the earth in comparison to be most insignificant; this, in itself, gives us no sufficient ground for rejecting the statements of the Bible as to the great events which have taken place upon it. It is well for us to remember that in our own solar system the mighty sun has value only as ministering to the needs of those who dwell in the small and dark planets around it; and of these it is most probable that only our own is inhabited by intelligent and moral beings. And only the same value seems to belong to all the vastly larger suns which shine in space. The greater is for the less, the sun for the planet, the planet for man; the physical exists only for the moral.*

---

*It is very generally taken for granted that there is such likeness between the sun of our system and the solar suns, that we may legitimately infer that they also are surrounded with opaque bodies, or planets, to which they give light and heat. But the later astronomers find so many points of unlikeness that this inference has little support. As such opaque orbs can never be seen, astronomy is unable to make any positive assertions respecting their existence. It may be, for aught that can be proved to the contrary, that our system is one unique in the Universe, and has its special character from the special part it plays in the Divine purpose of the Incarnation. When this purpose is accomplished here, other suns and worlds may be filled with the immortal and perfect form of life which now exists in the Son.

Accepting the truth taught in the Scriptures, that it was the purpose of God in creation to reveal Himself through the Incarnation of His Son in some form of creature being, this revelation must be, not only at some time, but also in some place. If the nature to be assumed by His Son is that of man, the inhabitant of the earth, here He must be born, and live, and die. Viewed in the light of His Incarnation as taking place here, the physical greatness of our orb has nothing to do with its real importance. The relative smallness of the earth may rather give us the reason for its choice, since for the purpose of human trial and redemption, a world where all the inhabitants may be brought into near intercourse, the gospel preached to all, the Church gathered from all, and a system of worship established for all, may better answer the Divine intent than one as large as our own sun, or as Sirius. But without doubt the material insignificance of the earth leads not a few to question whether anything that has taken place upon it can be a matter of real importance to the rest of the Universe.

As to the place of man in the Divine economy, the question is asked: Why should it be the human nature which the Son of God assumes? It is easier, many say, to believe that it was the ignorance and conceit of the Hebrew writers, not the Spirit of God, which declares the whole Universe to be interested through the Incarnation in the destiny of man. But one who believes that the Son of God was born here upon our earth, will have no difficulty in believing that humanity was constituted at the first for the very end of its assumption by Him; and that, therefore, man holds the highest place in the order of intelligent beings. The earth, as the place where the Word was made flesh, and lived, and died, and to which He is to return, is the moral centre of all the worlds. We may not infer from its physical insignificance that the Incarnation, as taking place upon it, was of little moment; but rather the religious importance of the earth as chosen to be the theatre of that event in view of which all worlds were made. We may in the choice of this orb see the first example of that principle of election so often afterward exhibited in the Divine actings. The earth was chosen from among all orbs, man from among all intelligent beings, the Jews from among the peoples, the tribe of Judah from among the tribes, the family of David from among the families, Mary from among all the royal daughters, the little city of Bethlehem from among all the cities. In all this there is nothing derogatory to the greatness of God. However vast the Universe, all the creatures in it must come under the limitations of time and space; and He deals with them as under these limitations.

If, as has been said, we put away from the Universe a Creator and a purpose, it can have no meaning for us, no intelligible history; so is it with our own earth, which is so small a part of the great whole. It may be said that we do know a progress here in the past, and may legitimately infer a progress in the future. A passing from a lower to a higher condition is taught us by Geology; and Biology assures us that from lowest beginnings man with his wonderful capacities has come. We may, therefore, rightly conclude that the earth will be better and better fitted for man's habitation, and he himself rise higher and higher in the scale of being. Having this testimony of experience, we may look forward with confidence to the future, and expect a steady and continuous progress of humanity.

It is not to be questioned that evolution as thus presented has great power over many. Here, they say, we are building upon facts, we are dealing with realities. It is better to rest upon the certainties of Science than upon the uncertainties of Revelation. Nature herself tells us of a great and glorious future for man, and this should fill us with courage and hope.

But this reasoning will not bear examination. The earth cannot be separated from the rest of the Universe, and be put under a law of its own. It moves on in the general movement. As a part of the great whole, it is under the law of perpetual change. Its present phase is simply the last of the numberless ones through which it has passed. How long will the present phase continue? How will it end? No one can say that the lifeless and desolate moon may not be a prophetic type of the earth's history. At what stage of the endless process we now are, Science cannot tell us. But seen in the light of God's purpose in His Son, we have the assurance of a future for the earth most glorious, and of which we know no end. "In the regeneration, when the Son of Man shall sit on the throne of His glory," it shall be made "new." It will be known and reverenced forever as the birthplace of the Lord of all, and the place of His triumph over sin and death, a place most holy.

III. We ask as to the effect of modern scientific culture upon the spiritual receptivity of the mind.

It is said by Martineau: "The general tendency in modern natural science is to foster habits of thought embarrassing to religious conviction." The reason for this is obvious. To live habitually in a region of thought where a personal God is not found, where physical law is supreme, a miracle impossible, prayer unheard, where sin is disobedience to a natural law, and repentance only the sense of pain, is to make such a chasm between Science and Christianity, that Christian truth becomes intellectually as well as morally unintelligible. The supersensible doctrines of the Trinity and the Incarnation, the gospel history with its miracles, the resurrection and ascension of Jesus, and His return to judge the world, all seem illusions, — the dreams of those who have not entered into the realm of scientific realities.

One who believes the Universe to be ruled by invariable law to which all men are subject, will naturally be disposed to apply this rule in all human affairs. Human conduct must be conformed to natural law. If there is a Power working through laws, and hidden behind them, as said by Professor Huxley, which stands to us as our moral governor, "the great chess-player of the Universe, who never makes a mistake or makes the slightest allowance for ignorance," the same habit of mind will be found in us. As the Power treats us, so may we treat our fellows. If the man who plays with this Player, and plays ill, "is checkmated without haste, but without remorse," he may bear his defeat with a stoical equanimity; but his brethren who play with him the game of life will scarce expect any sympathy or compassion from him if they lose. It is shown very clearly by Professor

Shairp ("A Scientific Theory of Culture") that selfishness would be ten-fold more concentrated if we believed ourselves to be under the rule of inflexible law only. There being no God to sympathize with us, why should we sympathize with one another? All things take place according to an eternal and inexorable order. He who sins must reap the full consequence of his sins; there is no forgiveness, no remission. Nothing can be changed. Let each man bear his own burden in silence.* Among the forces that rule the Universe is found no Divine will, but, it is said, we have suffered no loss. For a changeable personal will, is now substituted invariable sequence; and thus the knowledge of nature becomes to us the matter of chief interest and value.

It is impossible that men can live habitually in the contemplation of a universe governed by physical law, without their minds taking upon them a peculiar character. They are in a region where they see only the changes of nature through the action of eternal forces, with which no personal will ever interferes. The line separating the natural and the supernatural, creation and its Creator, is effaced. A Force rules the world. But man, thus dealing with natural things only, feels the superiority of his humanity. He knows that there is nothing really great but mind; and if he knows no God of whose will Law is the expression, he must look upon himself as the head of the world; the creature of nature, and yet its lord. For him there is no moral Governor, no Judge, no feeling of dependence, no sense of responsibility.

* It is said by J. C. Morison ("The Science of Man") that "the Christian doctrine of forgiveness of sins is most injurious to morality." The sinner must pay the uttermost farthing.

No Christian man can open his eyes and not see that a new class has sprung up, such as Christendom has never before seen; highly cultured men who explore the heights and depths of the Universe, seeking knowledge of its laws and forces, but who acknowledge no Divine will or purpose, contemptuous of theology, without any object of worship, confident in the boundless development of science, and boastful of the glorious future of humanity. These are pre-eminently "the children of pride," who say, "We have explored the Universe, and find neither God, nor angel, nor devil." In them we may find the realization of "the scoffers of the last days," as described by the prophetic Spirit. Of any purpose of God in the world as bearing on its origin or destiny, they take no account. Of Jesus Christ they know nothing, except as a religious teacher who died long ago, and whose ethical teachings are still to be mentioned with respect. But His atonement for sin, His resurrection, His ascension, His return to judge the world, these are beliefs which people fettered by tradition continue to cherish, but which will fade away with the growing light of the years.*

Need it be said that to men of this spirit the Gospel of the Cross is a sore offense; and the call to bow down before the Crucified One, and to cry, "Christ

---

* It will be noted that what is here said applies only to a part, and, it is to be hoped, a very small part of the students of physical science. There is what some one has called an "atrophy of faith," through an all-absorbing study of nature and its laws, which seems to render it impossible for the mind to understand and appreciate higher spiritual truths. Of the moral character of this state of mind God alone is the Judge, but all can see how injurious are its effects upon the religious faith of the unscientific who look to Science for light.

have mercy upon us," is heard by them with smiling indifference or contempt. Who is He, that we should bow down before Him? Sin and atonement, these are outgrown beliefs. All that has been said of Christ's coming to judgment must be put away as a Messianic error of His time, into which He fell, and not worthy of our thought. An Antichrist is a creature of pessimistic imagination, no more real or to be feared than the symbolic dragon of the Apocalypse. Thus, men of this class are pre-eminently fitted to become, first the votaries, and then the slaves of the lawless one. So far as this proud and unbelieving scientific spirit extends, and takes hold of men, is his way prepared.

It is becoming more and more evident that Science without Revelation is wholly unable to solve any of the great problems of life. It gives us no explanation of the origin of the Universe; it cannot find in it any purpose or ruling idea; all things are under an irresistible law of change, each step being determined by its immediate antecedent. The Universe is "a vast autocratic machine," in which we can find no assurance as to its future, or as to the future of man as a race, or as to his personal immortality. Science is essentially pessimistic, since it reaches no results which answer the questions and satisfy the higher longings and aspirations of the human soul, but rather leaves them in deeper darkness. Of the service of Science, so far as regards the material interests of man and the physical well-being of society, we have no occasion here to speak. All this only makes more striking the contrast between its material riches and its spiritual poverty.

TENDENCIES OF MODERN LITERATURE.

This term Literature is here used in its larger sense, and not confined strictly to works of the imagination. For the sake of clearness, periodical literature will be treated of by itself.

We may note three stages in the history of ideas. First, their origin in the minds of individual thinkers, or as results of scientific discoveries. In this stage they are confined to a few leading minds, and may for considerable periods of time be little known and without influence.

Secondly, their popularization and general diffusion. As the rough nuggets of gold must be tested and purified before they are made into coins and can enter into general circulation, so is it with the new ideas of philosophy and science. There is a time of critical discussion, and then in modified forms, freed from technical language, they appear in literature, and begin to exert their influence on the popular mind in its beliefs and modes of thought.

Thirdly, when generally diffused, these ideas find their embodiment in laws and institutions. Of this last stage we shall have another occasion to speak.

The period in which we live is one in which new ideas, religious, scientific, political, social, moral, are struggling to get possession of the popular mind.

To this end they must be popularized, and put into intelligible and attractive forms; and this is done through literature. It stands as a medium through which the abstract and far-removed ideas of the few may be made intelligible to the many. But there is necessarily a contest between the new and the old, and the literature of our time clearly shows the marks of this contest, both in its substance and its expression. We see a want of clearness of thought, of accurate definition, of logical sequence, of positive standards of judgment. The subjective element is predominant, and with much of excitement and passion, there is also great vagueness of expression. In few writers do we find the calm, clear utterance of matured and assured convictions.

But before considering that which more particularly concerns us, — the religious character of our modern literature, — a few words may be said upon literature as affected by the democratic spirit.

The essential and distinctive element of this literature we find to be, that it deals with man as man. It is disposed to look with dislike or indifference upon all adventitious distinctions, as of rank, or class, or wealth. These are often not deserved, and have little to do with the real worthiness of men. In monarchies and aristocracies individual men are prominent, and to them history devotes itself, and the poets sing their deeds; in a democracy it is the race, the universal humanity. Affirming the equality of man with man, it affirms equal rights to all; and attacks all political conditions and social institutions which serve to make or preserve inequalities. In the past, humanity has not had its right and sovereign place; it must now cast off its manacles, and assert its real prerogatives. As the race is ever progressing, there can be but little reverence for the past. Humanity is far more than its great men; no age can exhaust its riches; its last products are its best.

With these democratic pre-suppositions it necessarily follows that the past cannot give us a literary standard. Each generation must be a law to itself. Every man should speak out that which is in him, and not follow the models of the past. An author should not seek the cultivated few, but the unlettered many; and find in their sympathy and approval his highest praise. Regarding the race as one, we should put away all narrow or provincial lines, and even national limitations, and look forward to a literature which shall be the expression of the universal humanity. And this humanity should have full expression. All its capacities should be unfolded, all that is in it find utterance,—its hopes, its fears, its miseries, its desires, its passions, its aspirations. Nothing human is to be regarded as low or vulgar, or to be hidden out of sight. What is needed is not self-concealment, but self-expression.

As it is the tendency of democracy to make humanity the centre of all thought, this tendency is seen in its literature. It is said by De Tocqueville: "There is one thought full of vigour and poetry. All that belongs to the existence of the human race taken as a whole, to its vicissitudes, and to its future, becomes an abundant mine of poetry. The poet will cease to deal with supernatural beings, but man remains, and the poet needs no more. He will become himself the chief theme of poetry."* We may thus

* Of these tendencies to glorify all that is human, man's aspirations, passions, and appetites, Algernon Swinburne and Walt

expect to find in democratic literature only humanitarian ideals. Outside of humanity we need not look. We must rise into higher conceptions of its goodness and dignity, and of the possibilities of the future. A religion that degrades it by its doctrines of sin and atonement, is to be put away.

I. We now come to consider recent literature as affected by the agnostic and pantheistic spirit.

Of this spirit traces may be found in the literature of all ages; but in Christendom it appears most visibly in that of the present century. It was said by De Tocqueville: "The Germans introduced pantheism into philosophy, and the French into litera-

---

Whitman may be regarded as truest representatives. Swinburne has been called "a neo-pagan." His attitude toward Christ may be judged of by the following lines:

> "Though before thee the throned Cytherean
> Be fallen, and hidden her head,
> Yet thy kingdom shall pass, Galilean,
> Thy dead shall go down to the dead."

His attitude toward naturalism is seen in his "Poems and Ballads," afterwards suppressed by the publisher because of their erotic character, but reprinted in New York under the title, *Laus Veneris*.

The same naturalistic spirit is seen in Whitman in even greater degree. He is a defender of the rights of nature. If a human being is to be honoured, let him be honoured in every part of his being, in every organ and function and natural act of the body. Our age wants real men who act out what is in them, and are not ruled by conventionalities. The humanity of to-day cannot be bound by any restrictions, religious, social, political, of the past. The ideal of Whitman is the naked natural man. He has no fear of vulgarity, he cherishes no aristocratic modesty. As partaking of a Divine nature, let man show himself as he is; let him gratify its impulses, higher and lower, its aspirations, its appetites. Thus only do we see the real man in place of the artificial. The true hero is he who dares to follow nature, and assert his Divinity.

ture. Most of the works of imagination published in France contained some opinions, or some tinges, caught from pantheistic doctrines, or they disclose some tendency to such doctrines." But the same tendency was seen earlier in the German Goethe (1749-1832), of whom Heine says: "All his works were saturated with the same spirit that breathes in the works of Spinoza." For Goethe Thomas Carlyle had a great admiration, regarding him "as by far the notablest of all literary men for a hundred years." Expressions respecting nature, and man's relations to it, may be found in the early poems of Coleridge and Wordsworth, which may be interpreted as pantheistic, though both repudiated pantheism and were firm believers in the Christian faith. Shelley was an avowed atheist, but many of his poems are pantheistic.

Without mentioning earlier writers, no names are more prominent in the literature of the last few years than those of Thomas Carlyle, R. W. Emerson, and Matthew Arnold. The influence of Thomas Carlyle in literature has been very great. What is the religious character of this influence? Carlyle does not avow himself a pantheist, and may perhaps be more fitly classed as an agnostic. Whether he wholly disbelieved in a personal God, it is hard to say; since his early religious training continued to the last to have much power over him, and his language is so indefinite. The distinguished and impartial critic, R. H. Hutton, ("Contemporary Thought and Thinkers,") speaks of "his ambiguous religious jargon, the meaning of which it was impossible to define"; but he adds that "the effect of his pantheistic practice of substituting 'the Immensities' and 'the Eternities' in place of Almighty God, was even more disastrous to his numerous devotees than a blank assertion that He was 'unknown and unknowable.'" All his writings make the impression that he saw no personal God ruling in the universe, and no Divine purpose founded on the Incarnation, but only a Force omnipresent and omnipotent. He asks, changing the words of the Psalmist: "Knowest thou any corner of the world where Force is not?" Personal immortality he seems to have denied or ignored.* Of Jesus Christ he makes little mention, and apparently regarded Him only as an ethical teacher, whose work was ended at His death. That He lives, and will come again to earth to judge the quick and dead, he regarded as a dream, believed only by visionaries. Religion is communion with "the mysterious, invisible Power visibly seen at work in the world." Of his heroes ("Heroes and Hero Worship") as incarnations of Force, we shall later have occasion to speak.

What has been said of the pantheism of Carlyle may be said in fuller measure of R. W. Emerson's pantheism. It lies at the basis of all his essays and poems, and finds frequent and undisguised expression; but he does not state it in any clear and definite terms. But as has been said by Mr. Manning ("Half Truths and The Truth"): "When he uses the words soul, spirit, mind, intellect, we shall find that he does not refer to anything individual or personal, but to an all-surrounding, all-filling substance, which he calls Divine, and regards as constituting the whole of reality." This seems a right inference

---

* In the Life of Tennyson he is reported as saying to the poet in regard to immortality: "Eh! Old Jewish rags, you must get clear of all that."

from Emerson's words: "The ultimate fact we reach on every topic is the resolution of the All into the ever-blessed One." "There is one mind common to all individual men. . . . This universal mind is the only and sovereign agent." "One blood rolls uninterruptedly in endless circulation through all men; as the water of the globe is all one sea, and, truly seen, its tide is one."

These quotations, and those before made in another relation, sufficiently show the spirit which breathes in all his writings. It is not we as pure personalities who live and act, but the great "Over-soul," the "World-soul," the "Universal-mind," which lives and acts in us. This unity of nature with the Divine World-soul makes us Divine. In his own words: "Empedocles undoubtedly speaks a truth of thought when he said: 'I am God.'" Jesus could use the same words of Himself, but was no more God than we all are gods; and the highest conduct of life is always to speak and act in the consciousness of our Divinity. It is said by R. H. Hutton that "Emerson is contemptuous of the pretensions of special access to God, and this when he speaks of Christ and Christianity." All men have equal access to the Universal Spirit, and the Christian religion and its Founder have no advantage over others. All religions are equally Divine; "all the necessary and structural action of the human mind." The same pantheistic spirit appears in his poems.

The religious position of Mr. Arnold is well known. He asserts ("Literature and Dogma," "God and the Bible,") that "the world cannot do without Christianity, but cannot do with it as it is." What modifications then does he propose? He will retain the word "God," but he means by it, "the Eternal not ourselves, that makes for righteousness;" not a person, but a Power, impersonal, unconscious, unintelligent. Having thus set aside the Christian God, the Lord Christ must also be set aside, "His magical birth and resurrection and ascension." So also all miracles. "In miracles we are dealing with the unreal world of fairy-tale." The Bible, deprived of all its supernatural elements, and of a large part of its historical truth, has still, in his eyes, a literary value, and may have a good moral influence upon the masses, especially the Gospels, which contain the Lord's ethical teachings. But of such beliefs as of the fall of man, the existence of angels, good or evil, of the resurrection, and apparently, also, of any life after death, we must rid ourselves.

Turning now to the poets of our day: Of Tennyson it is said by Mr. Van Dyke ("The Poetry of Tennyson"): "His theology has been accused of a pantheistic tendency, and it cannot be denied that there are expressions in his poems which seem to look in that direction." But Mr. Van Dyke affirms that the poet "believed in a living, personal, spiritual God, immanent in the universe, but not confused with it." This seems to be a fair judgment. He also believed in the personality and free will of man, as he expresses himself in the line —

"Our wills are ours, to make them Thine" —

and in personal immortality. But while Tennyson held these high truths, his position as to the great distinctive fact of Christianity — the Incarnation — and to the Person of the living Lord, and to His future work, is not clear. His belief as to the future of humanity seems to be based rather on evolution than on the

Divine purpose in Jesus Christ, in whom the creation will find its perfection and glory.

> "The one far-off, divine event
> To which the whole creation moves,"

is rather the old creation gradually developed, than the work of the Son when, sitting on His throne, He makes all things new. When he speaks of "bringing in the Christ that is to be," he apparently speaks of the wider diffusion of a Christian spirit, and not of His return and kingdom.

In Browning we meet so much obscurity of expression as to leave the reader in doubt as to his religious belief. Prof. Dowden calls him "a Christian pantheist." Mrs. Orr, author of a "Life of Robert Browning," says in "The Contemporary" (Dec., 1891): "Mr. B. neither was nor could be at the time of which I speak" (the later years of his life), "a Christian in the orthodox sense of the word, for he rejected the antithesis of good and evil, which orthodox Christianity holds; he held in common with the pantheists, though without reference to them, that every form of moral existence is required for a complete human world. . . . He spurned the doctrine of eternal damnation with his whole being as incompatible with the attributes of God; and since inexorable Divine judgment had no part in his creed, the official Mediator or Redeemer was also excluded from it. . . But he never ceased to believe in Christ as, mystically or by Divine miracle, a manifestation of Divine love. . . . The one consistent part of his heterodoxy was its exclusion of any belief in Revelation." As to immortality, "his habitual condition was that of simple hope," and as to its nature, "it was simply a continuance of the life begun on earth, and involved neither conditions of fitness, nor possibility of exclusion. But it clearly borrowed nothing from the words of Christ."*

We see in Browning, as in Carlyle, the influence of his early religious training continuing though a great change in his dogmatic beliefs had taken place; and also, what is little seen in Carlyle, and still less in Emerson, the need felt of a Christ to stand as the Image and Representative of a far-removed Supreme Being, and sorrow that He lives no longer in his faith.

Of lesser modern poets it is said by Miss Vida Scudder ("Life of the Spirit") that Clough was "intellectually an agnostic, though with a dim hope that there is a God." Rosetti "never questioned, but never believed." "He had a solemn sense of a vast encompassing mystery, but lacked all conviction." In Morris is "no religious element." She adds, "To many modern imaginations the two thousand years of Christianity seem a parenthesis in the world's story, a dream that is passing away."

We pass now to the novelists. One of the marked literary features of our day is the great multiplication of works of fiction. They constitute a very large part of the popular reading, and have great influence since there are presented in them under imaginative forms the current ideas of the day as they enter into the thoughts and feelings of daily life, and so affect

* We may conclude with Mrs. Orr, that "Mr. Browning's Theism was more definite than his Christianity;" but his God was at best "a colourless omnipotence or a power combined with will." It need not be said that while he speaks of Christ as showing forth love, he rejects Him as a sacrifice for sin, and a Mediator between God and man. Of the living Christ, and of the future life as dependent upon resurrection, he knows nothing.

moral conduct. Whilst some portray the past, most deal with the present, and reflect in their pages its agitations and strifes, its longings and hopes, its doubts and fears. In many we find discussions of leading topics, economical, social, religious, — the relations of the rich and poor, of the sexes, of marriage and divorce, of woman suffrage, of the inspiration of the Bible, of the nature and future of religion. Some treat of occult forces, of the unseen world, of eastern pantheism, of theosophy, of spiritism, of hypnotism, of re-incarnation. Others still present their theories as to the relation of mind and body, of mental healing, of Christian science, of heredity; and some give vivid pictures of the present social evils, and of a future perfected society.

Amidst such a variety of themes, presented from many points of view, we find no principle of unity, unless it be that of the progress of the race. Whilst there is seen in most discontent with the present conditions of human life, it is assumed that if these conditions can be changed, human nature will develop itself in such richness and beauty as the world has not yet seen.

In this department of literature, as in those already spoken of, we find dominant the humanitarian element; man's duties to God are summed up in his duties to his fellow man. Beneficence is Christianity. Of this form of humanitarianism Dickens is a leading representative. In not a few, when Christianity is alluded to, it is only as a hard, narrow, exclusive religion, from which men must be emancipated if they would be truly free. Its restraints are burdensome, its morality is ascetic.

With this humanitarianism agnosticism is often

combined. The most eminent instance of this is George Eliot. Of her writings she herself says: "My books have for their main bearing or conclusion, that the fellowship between man and man, which has been the principle of development, social and moral, is not dependent upon conceptions of what is not God; and that the idea of God, so far as it has been a high spiritual influence, is the idea of a goodness purely human, *i.e.*, an exaltation of the human." Her biographer, G. W. Cook (Sterling edition of her works, 1887), says of her: "The speculative part of religion she did not believe in, and it was only the humanitarian and emotional side of it which interested her. . . . The elevation of humanity was what she sought for as the meaning of all religion." But it was not in any work of Christ, past or future, that she looked for this elevation. He was to her as nonexistent.*

Of other individual novelists we have no space to speak. That many have great literary merit, and are good and wholesome in their influence, need not be denied; but the question before us is whether, taken

---

*Some extracts from her biography will give a clearer idea of George Eliot's religious position. Of herself she says: "For years of my youth I dwelt in dreams of a pantheistic sort, but I have travelled far away from that." But if she gave up her pantheism, she did not come into any clear belief of a personal Deity. It is said by Mr. Cook that "she had not gained a more distinct and positive idea of God. . . . The moral sanctions for her did not grow out of belief, and she did not find it essential for any of the higher purposes of life." "In her emotions she found the sanctions for religion." It is said also by Mr. Cook that she did not believe in any personal existence in the future. Of the three terms, God, Immortality, Duty, she pronounced the first to be "inconceivable"; the second, "unbelievable"; the third, "peremptory and absolute."

as a whole, their influence is friendly or hostile to biblical Christianity. Does their perusal tend to deepen, or to efface the sense of sin; to elevate Christ as the Redeemer, or to make the work of redemption on the cross unnecessary and unmeaning, and to loosen the bonds of a sound morality? Do they enforce Christian views of life, exalt the homely virtues of contentment, patience, forgiveness? Are their highest types of character those having in highest degree the likeness of Jesus? Do they foster the spirit of self-deification in man, or awaken in him earnest desires for that condition of immortality and glory into which the Lord would exalt him? It is these, and the like questions, which must determine the bearing of this form of literature upon the Christian faith.

II. We will now turn to the Periodical Press. Great as is the power of the periodical press, including under this term all magazines and newspapers, there seems good reason to believe that it will be still greater in the days to come. The number of periodicals continually increases, reaching all classes, and necessarily affecting in greater or less degree their opinions and beliefs. Noting the present tendencies, we may ask what part this periodical literature will probably play in the great contest between Christianity and anti-Christianity.

In considering the matter, there are some points which are to be kept in mind. One of these is that most of these periodicals are printed to be sold; and that to be sold, their matter must be suited to the popular taste. Large sums of money are often invested in them; and it is very rare that their owners will maintain them at a pecuniary loss. This is sometimes done by religious or other organizations in order to have an organ; and occasionally by individuals who are zealous to diffuse some special opinions. But in general it is true that a periodical, whether its circle of readers be small or large, to be pecuniarily successful, must reflect their beliefs and opinions. In this respect it stands upon the same footing as any kind of manufacture which must meet the tastes of its purchasers.

An exemption from the law of supply and demand is often claimed for the press on the ground that it ministers to mental, not to physical needs; and that its high function is to enlighten the public mind by the diffusion of truth. It is obvious of what great benefit the periodical press might be if it fulfilled this high function. But to do this it must be in the hands of truth-loving, unprejudiced, and able men; men who value the true and the good above their pecuniary interests, and of such men only. This, all know, is not the case. Any man who is able to provide himself with type and press and to hire writers and helpers, can set up himself as a popular teacher, no matter what his motives, or principles, or personal character may be. There is no limit to the multiplication of periodicals but that of pecuniary inability to print, or want of readers. As there are in every community varying degrees of culture, intellectual and moral, we may expect to see a corresponding variety of periodicals. Unprincipled men will be found who will print what the lowest and vilest ask for, caring nothing for morality or the interests of society. The only restraint upon them is the law, and its penalties are little feared.

It needs no argument to show that periodicals are very efficient means of both good and evil, but we may not overrate this efficiency. There is a popular current of thought and feeling—the spontaneous judgment of the multitude—which they must follow. The press cannot create the spirit of an age, it can only give it utterance. Its power lies in its ability to give publicity to principles and movements, or to withhold it. According to its position it may proclaim or may ignore vital truths and facts; may give prominence to events and to men, or pass them by in silence.*

We may note, also, that the periodical press regards all subjects as coming within its sphere,—sacred and secular,—everything which affects humanity. Nothing is too high or too low. It sits in judgment upon all men, upon all questions; and its judgments are often uttered in a very dogmatic way as irreversible.

With these general observations upon the character and position of the periodical press, we reach the point of especial interest to us, on what side, judging from present indications, will its influence be cast in the coming contest of Christ with His great enemy. Those who believe that Christian principles are gradually to take possession of the mind of the race

---

*How far the publicity given by the newspapers to crimes of all kinds tends to increase them, is a question often discussed; but the fact can scarcely be denied. We are thus made acquainted with things of which we were better ignorant, and the knowledge of which leaves a moral stain which we may strive in vain to wash out. This is true in highest degree of children, who through the daily or weekly newspaper are made familiar with forms of vice which should be known to those only who have some right to the knowledge. This publicity is beyond doubt a powerful factor in the increase of crime; and likely to become still more powerful in the future, as the depraved appetite grows by what it feeds upon.

will naturally regard the press as an important, and indeed, indispensable means to this end; and as now taking upon itself more and more a Christian character. But those who accept the teachings of the Lord and of His Apostles respecting the apostasy, as they have been already stated, can hardly fail to see in it a very powerful means of helping on the apostasy by its diffusion of antichristian teachings. It must be borne in mind that this teaching will not be acknowledged by its teachers, at least for a time, as antichristian. It will be presented as in fact the true Christianity, only those doctrines and forms being put aside which our age has outgrown; a modified Christianity suited to the nineteenth century. In the interest of truth and of religion we are bid to leave the old and press on to the new.

The first step is thus the free utterance of the new; and to this end the pages of our periodicals must be open to all, and this is now in good measure the case. Almost any man who has a certain degree of literary ability, can present in them his special opinion or belief upon any subject, including religion. It is thought true liberalism to give largest freedom in discussing and even controverting the cardinal doctrines of Christianity. Of course there are some fixed beliefs as to morality which may not be controverted. It is not yet permitted to defend free love, or to advocate theft. But as regards religion there seems to be no restriction to the liberty of utterance. The columns of not a few of our magazines and newspapers are open to those who deny any God, any revelation of a Divine will, any life after death. Principles are continually defended which subvert Christianity; and it seems to be generally accepted that, as this is the day of free thought, whatever a man thinks he may express; and, therefore, should have a place for its expression.

The significance of all this we may not underestimate. It is practically saying that as to religion, nothing is to be regarded as settled. We have not yet attained to the perfect truth, but are seeking, after it. Christianity, like other religions, is under trial. But this negative position is not long tenable, and is gradually changing to one more positively hostile to Christianity. The effect of such discussion upon the popular mind must be to breed doubts, and to lead, if not to absolute unbelief, to agnosticism and spiritual apathy.

We can easily see from present tendencies how the periodical press may become a very powerful instrument in preparing the way of the Antichrist. Some may think that this will be counteracted by the Christian press.* But we have seen that secular periodicals must in general, upon pecuniary grounds, adapt themselves to the changes in public opinion; and this is the case also with the religious. To this there will be some exceptions, but as a whole they cannot be relied upon to defend "the faith once for all delivered to the saints." We see already in not a few, illustrations how this change of posi-

* Of the newspapers called religious, most are organs of sects or parties, and play a chief part in perpetuating the divisions of the Church. As their pecuniary success depends on the maintenance of the sectarian spirit, their readers learn from them very little of truth in regard to other sects, and often have their minds set against their brethren by misrepresentation of their principles and action. There is thus fostered in the readers of these journals a narrowness of spirit which forbids that unity of doctrine, of action, and of worship, which is the duty of the Church as Catholic under its one Head.

tion from the defense to the denial of Christianity,—first to its modification, and then to its rejection,—can be effected, and yet be almost unperceived. Some old Christian doctrine is seen to be in contradiction to some new, popular philosophic or scientific teaching, and to be losing its hold upon the faith of men; shall it be re-affirmed and defended? But this involves unpopularity, and perhaps pecuniary loss. The easier way is to give the offensive doctrine some new interpretation, and so better adapt it to other current thought; or to keep silence respecting it, and let it quietly die out of men's beliefs. Illustrations of this process may be seen in regard to the doctrines of Satan and evil spirits, of the resurrection of the body, and of the personal return of the Lord, which are already more and more ignored. To these, other doctrines may be gradually added, as that of human sinfulness, of Christ's virgin birth, of atonement, of His resurrection, of His priesthood, till finally little more than the shell of Christianity is retained; and the Church suddenly awakes to find itself antichristian, as the Church in the fourth century suddenly awoke to find itself Arian. Thus the very journals which have been relied on as defenders of the faith, may become efficient instruments in preparing the minds of many for him who will claim to be the representative of a better religion.

As regards that portion of the press which now proposes to hold a position of neutrality in religious matters, and to treat Christianity only as one of many religions, and needing many modifications, we may expect that it will so affect popular opinion that it will be prepared to hail Antichrist as he in whom the religious spirit finds its highest embodiment.

And if he attains such power as the Scriptures foretell, and none may buy or sell but with his permission, he will surely not leave the press uncontrolled. It will be permitted to say only what he wishes to have said, and any utterances against him will be followed by swift and severe punishment.

Without mentioning other forms of modern literature, we may say in general that we see in them all the marks of a transition period. Modern Science has made prominent the questions, whether the Universe is not eternal, whether we are not to substitute inflexible and universal Law in place of a Divine personal Will, whether the chief study of man is not that of the forces of the universe, and their bearing upon human conduct, and what the antiquity of man, and his future, and the future of the earth. Modern Philosophy asks whether man must not be a part of God, and without personal freedom, and to be swallowed up again in the Divine substance. Thus Science and Philosophy have opened to Literature a new world. How shall its writers interpret life in the light of the new ideas?— what its meaning?—what its value? Doubts and questions arise on every hand. Few are assured of their position, and positive in their utterances. Some attempt to harmonize the old and new. Most hesitate and waver. Belief in a Divine Providence stands in contrast with a gloomy fatalism, the hope of a blessed immortality with dark forebodings of annihilation.

With the spread of the new ideas, which dethrone God and His Christ, literature must take on itself more and more an antichristian character. Its prophets and its poets will unite in their jubilations on the speedy coming of the new age, when the superstitious and narrow beliefs of the past will give place to a rational and comprehensive religion based on science and glorifying the Divinity of man. Then will literature as the interpeter of life, find in humanity its noblest theme, and reach the full measure of its capacity and power.

Though mention has been made only of English literature, it is believed that its general character represents that of all the nations of Christendom. We see in them all the same influences at work, though in different degrees, and modified by national characteristics. Readers of Tolstoi, of Tourgenieff, of Auerbach, of Ibsen, of George Sand, of Zola, to speak of no others, find themselves in a region which has little in common with Christianity.

CHRISTIAN SOCIALISM AND THE KINGDOM OF GOD.

The term "Socialism," now on all lips, is a new one; what does it mean? As used by many, it means no more than philanthropy or beneficence directed to the removal or melioration of social evils; and particularly of poverty. But in the mouths of its leading representatives it means much more than this; it means a new social order, or radical reconstruction of society, the chief features of which are the enlargement of the functions of the State, and the legal equalization of property. Government is to take upon itself the control both of the production and distribution of wealth. In technical phrase, "Collectivism," or ownership of land and capital by the State, is substituted for "Individualism," or individual ownership. It is said by an accredited authority (Schäffle, "Social Democracy,") that "the Alpha and Omega of Socialism is the transformation of private and competing capital into a united and collective capital." As a preliminary step, the State must become democratic, for "Socialism is the economic side of Democracy." And not only are governments to become democratic, but all peoples are to become economically one, since the industrial interests of all are identical. Socialism looks beyond any single state or nation; it talks much of "the solidarity of the nations."

Socialism is thus a term of wide and deep import. It marks a new movement in human history, which, if carried out, will subvert most existing social institutions, and replace them by new ones; or at least greatly modify them. And what is the motive of this change? It is that the present social system is incompetent to attain the ends for which society exists. It has been tried for centuries, and now the burdens under which we are labouring are unbearable. We can get rid of poverty with its attendant evils, and of oppression, and injustice, and war, only by means of a new social organization, a new development of civilization. The end aimed at is a perfected society, a reign of righteousness upon the earth; in fine, the Kingdom of God.

With this general statement of its principles, and of its aims, let us consider that phase of it which is called Christian Socialism.

Its origin is easily explainable. The Church, accepting the false conception of the Kingdom of God already spoken of, and regarding as its mission the work of establishing it in the earth before the Lord's return, feels itself bound to fulfil it. We have seen that at no period of the past has this kingdom been a reality; the predictions of the prophets respecting the prosperity and peace of the nations under Messiah's rule, have never been fulfilled. The Church, therefore, is under obligation to fulfil them, and to fulfil them now, for we are confessedly come to a time of the distress and perplexity of nations as well as of individuals. Thus a Christian Socialist, Professor Ely, says: "It is believed by all competent observers in all civilized nations that this last quarter of the nineteenth century is a period of one of the greatest crises in the world's history." All see that old institutions, religious, political, social, are giving way, as unable to meet the needs of humanity, and no one knows what to put in their place. It is not strange, therefore, that Christendom is calling with great earnestness upon the Church to do what it claims to be able to do,— to save it from the perils threatening it, and to bring in that blessed condition of society of which the prophets speak. If it cannot do this, if it has no remedy for present evils, if it cannot give in the future something far better than in the past, it is weighed in the balance and found wanting. It is condemned out of its own mouth, and the world will have no more of a Christianity that has so long deceived it with idle promises.

It is in response to this imperious call that we now hear so much of Christian Socialism. It is an attempt to realize those expectations of temporal prosperity which the current conception of the mission of the Church has awakened. It is an attempt to mediate between Socialism in its more advanced form and Christianity, and thus preserve the existing Christian institutions, and the social order based upon Christianity. Christian Socialists, at least for the most part, think only of the melioration of present social evils by the infusion of a more Christian spirit into legislation, and into the administration of existing laws and institutions, without any radical political or social changes. Christianity, it is said by them, when fully applied is able to remedy all social abuses and to overcome all economic as well as moral evils. Let us, therefore, address ourselves to these problems. Let Christianity remember its high mission, and put forth its full power and bring righteousness and peace into the earth. It is, they say, to the failure of the Church to arise to the greatness of its calling, that the present evil condition of Christian society is in great part due.

Thus, Christian Socialists think to solve these social problems by enlarging the sphere of Christian activity. In all Protestant churches — the Roman Church stands in a somewhat different position — we hear the cry: We have too much regarded the purely spiritual side of Christianity, and too little the practical; we have looked too much to a future life, and too little to this; we have given too great a place to abstract doctrine, to Creeds and to Confessions of faith, and have neglected the application of Christian principles to the social and political evils around us. We have drawn too broad a line of distinction between the sacred and the secular, between the Church and the world. We must now change our mode of action. We must not ignore any question that affects human well-being. All sciences, arts, inventions, everything that aids in the culture of man or the improvement of society, comes properly within the Christian sphere.

Starting with the assumption that it is the Divinely appointed mission of the Church to make the Kingdom of God a reality before the coming of the King, this enlargement of its labours is certainly logical. Its sphere must embrace the whole range of human interests, and it has, therefore, the right to speak with authority. And herein the Church of Rome has had the courage of its convictions, and has vigorously attempted to extend its sway over all questions that affect man's welfare; seeking, indeed, the co-operation of the State, but giving it only a subordinate place. But Christian Socialists, coming chiefly from Protestant bodies, disclaim Church authority, and rely on the spirit of love manifesting itself in individual action. This spirit is to be infused into our modern civilization, and the spirit of selfishness purged out; and thus all men be brought to regard the interests of others as their own. Gradually, our present civilization will be Christianized, social discontent and discord will cease, and the Kingdom of God will come.

Practically, in this form of Christian Socialism there is little that passes beyond the teaching of the Gospel, for Christianity is the religion of love and beneficence. But, as in the present divided condition of the Church there can be no unity of action, even among Protestants, all that is done must be done by individuals singly, or through voluntary charitable organizations. No one can doubt the purity of motive or the self-sacrificing spirit of the Christian Socialist thus labouring; but it is plain that voluntary organizations in the many religious bodies, acting independently, can accomplish very little. They cannot reach the root of the evil; and charitable organizations, so-called, are more and more offensive to many whom they seek to benefit, and who say, "We are not willing to accept as alms what belongs to us as right. What we seek is not almsgiving, however liberal, but such an ordering of society as will make poverty and other like social evils impossible."

Thus, Christian Socialism, in order to effect any important and permanent results, feels itself forced to pass beyond the sphere of mere voluntary effort. How, then, shall it gain its ends?

We are told that the Christian Socialists must enlarge their conception of their mission. For the saving of individuals they must substitute "the saving of society," and to this direct their efforts. They must act upon the assumption that "society is an organism, and the individual a part of a larger whole"; and, therefore, we must consider the whole rather than the parts. In the words of Professor Tucker, (And. Rev.), "The conception of the Church is rapidly changing in the minds of those within as well as of those without. It no longer stands for the rescue of individuals; it stands, by growing consent, for the improvement, the regeneration of society. . . . The Church must be instructed in its social duties, and led out into action." It is said by another: "Concern for the social whole is the one object of religion." And by another, that "social salvation means a never-ceasing attack on every wrong institution until the earth becomes a new earth, and all its cities cities of God."

But what shall we say in respect to these social changes, of the place of the State, which by its lawmaking power controls society? Suppose the State and the Church disagree as to what constitutes "social regeneration"? Is the Church to control the State? and how shall this be done? Shall it go down into the political arena, and make its representatives the legislators, and embody its principles in laws? Here Christian Socialists are not agreed. Some wish to keep a clear distinction between the ecclesiastical and civil spheres, between the sacred and the secular. But where shall the line be drawn? Accepting the fundamental principle that it is the mission of the Church to make the earth new, and all its cities cities of God, no department of human activity can be without its sphere; and if the State do not concur in its action with the Church, it must itself be reformed or reconstructed. It is said by Canon Fremantle: "If the Church is to realize God's Kingdom in the world, it must occupy itself with all human relations; it embraces the whole social and political life; it must use the State for this purpose." This seems to be the only logical and consistent position, but it raises anew the old and never-settled question of the relation of the Church and the State. Rome affirms that the Church is to control the State, but this class of Christian Socialists seem to look forward to the identification of the Church and the State. The aims of both are the same — the highest welfare of man — and no distinction of sacred and secular is to be taken, either as to work or to office.

Some go further in this direction than others. It is said by one, Professor Ely: "All legislators, magistrates, and governors are as truly ministers in God's Church as any bishop or archbishop."*

It will be well for us at this point to keep in mind the four chief theories as to the relations of the Church and the State which have found advocates.

1. That each is of Divine appointment, having the same end, the preparation of men for the Kingdom of God, but with separate and distinct spheres of action, and corresponding ministries; and neither should in-

---

*It is to be noted that Mr. Maurice, who may be regarded as the father of modern Christian Socialism, through a series of tracts published by him in 1850, made the Church to embrace all men without exception. He does not deny orders of ministry in it distinct from those of the State, but by his fundamental principle he effaces the distinction between the two, the religious and the secular, and so makes the ministers of each to have substantially the same sphere and duties. He could, therefore, say: "Christian Socialism seems to me the assertion of God's order." (Life, Vol. I.) This order when realized makes Church and State one.

trude into the sphere of the other. This is the doctrine of the Lord and of His Apostles.

2. That the Church, now representing the King in heaven, and Divinely commissioned by Him to rule for Him on earth, has authority over all secular rulers in all matters of faith and morals. The Church is to the State what the soul is to the body. This is the doctrine of the Roman Catholic Church.

3. That the State has supreme jurisdiction in all matters pertaining to the social and political life of a nation, and recognizes religion only as personal and individual. The Church, if organized as a distinct community, must be wholly subordinate to the State, and teach and act only as the State shall judge conducive to the public welfare. This is the doctrine of the advanced Socialists.

4. That the objects aimed at by the Church and the State being one, the training of men in righteousness, and both being instruments of God to this end, they are to be identified and regarded as one. When this is realized the Kingdom of God has fully come. This is the doctrine of the Christian Socialists.

We are here concerned with the last. Assuming that the identity of Church and State, as to the end aimed at by each — the establishment of a kingdom of righteousness — is of God, and that this end cannot be attained till this identity of action is reached; the question arises, how it can be reached. If the State refuse to co-operate with the Church in its proposed measures, what will the Christian Socialists do? Some affirm that they must reconstitute the State, and put it upon a Christian and Socialistic basis. Thus it is said by one that " the gospel of the kingdom is to be realized on earth in the reconstruction of human society." And by another: "The present order and Christianity are enemies... This order, like the natural heart, is enmity against God." The Church must, therefore, give itself to the work of bringing the State into harmony with it, or of establishing a new social order.

But most Christian Socialists do not take this extreme position. They regard it as their duty to Christianize the State, so that it will carry out all social reforms. And as this can be done only by moral suasion, it is their duty continually to teach that the sphere of the Church embraces the secular as well as the spiritual life. As said by one: "It comes within the province of the Church to rectify and adjust all the relations of men with men." This is plainly opening a very large field of labour, and draws the attention of Christians to matters of great practical difficulty, both secular and religious. Applied Christianity, it is said, must take charge of such problems as these: the duties of States to one another; peace or war; the reciprocal obligations of governments and citizens; the rights of property; the relations of the rich and the poor, and of labour and capital; taxation; rate of wages; rights of women, and extension of suffrage; marriage and divorce; the State in its duties to children; religious or secular education, — and many other problems of like kind. And to these we may add all which concern the health of a community, sanitary and dietetic.

This enlargement of the sphere of the Church to take in almost all earthly interests, and her occupation of it, is held by the more progressive Christian Socialists as sure to be followed by such a period of peace and righteousness as Christendom has never yet seen. We are told by some that "the whole creation travails in pain together with the birth of a new Era." "We have reached the period when all conditions are prepared for the perfecting of society." "In the order of human progress, we have passed through three stages: first, Theology, or knowledge of God; second, Anthropology, or knowledge of man; third, Soteriology, or relation of man to God. We have now come to the fourth, or relation of man to man." This, therefore, is distinctly "the Sociological age"; the last and highest.

The Church of Rome, as we have said, has always affirmed that the moral relations of men to men were under her charge by Divine appointment, and, therefore, she has the right in this respect to control the State. The novelty of Rome's present position is, that it stands face to face with a proposed new social order, in which all Church authority, if not absolutely set aside, is greatly limited. Rome accepts, or rather tolerates, popular supremacy and democratic institutions; it remains to be seen how far it will give countenance to the new socialistic theories which assign to it a wholly subordinate place. But it is plain that, if Rome will hold the leadership of the peoples, it must present some solution of the problems now everywhere agitating the public mind. Thus far its policy is mediating, as shown by the late papal Encyclicals; and this policy will doubtless be held till some event forces it to a decided step. It is, however, to be noted that Rome, by its numerical superiority, its antiquity, its unity, its past supremacy, and present authority, is not obliged to propitiate popular favour in the same degree as the Protestant churches. It is still such a spiritual and ethical power in Christendom that Socialism, in its most advanced forms, is forced to listen to its utterances with respect.

If we turn to the Protestant churches, they live so much in the breath of popular opinion that, if they hope to reform society, they must yield more or less to the prevalent socialistic tendencies, even if antichristian in spirit; and this is seen to be the case in an increasing degree. Concessions are made more and more to the hostile spirit of the time. Obnoxious doctrines are given up or put in the background, and the Church is popularized by minimizing its claims as a Divine institution, and by effacing in a great degree its distinction from the world. The outer walls are given up, that the citadel may be preserved. By these concessions Christian Socialism thinks to save Christianity from the attacks of its enemies, and by its enlarging beneficent labours to draw to it universal popular support.

We now ask, What is the attitude which the Socialists *par excellence* take toward the Christian Socialists? It is, for the most part, one of hostility or of a half-contemptuous indifference. They see clearly that Christianity, as a religion for the salvation of men from sin and their spiritual preparation for a future life, and Socialism, which looks only to the improvement of earthly conditions, have wholly different aims and are essentially antagonistic. They speak of the establishment of chairs of Sociology in theological seminaries as a weak effort to meet social evils, and an attempt to perpetuate Christianity under the guise of philanthropy. What they wish is to put away the Church, and its teachings of sin and judgment, of heaven and hell, altogether; and to centre the thoughts of men on the improvement of the world and melioration of its present social condition. A few extracts from leading socialistic writers will sufficiently show this.

"Christian socialism has for its basis trade cooperation, and presupposes the prevailing industrial anarchy, and is in fact anti-socialistic." "Christian socialism mutilates Christianity, emptying it of all its original and obvious meaning." "Socialism utterly despises the other world. . . . It brings back religion from heaven to earth. . . . It looks to a higher social life in this world. . . . The social creed is the only religion of the socialist." "Socialism has no sympathy with the morbid and transcendent morality of the Gospel. A family or a nation is far more sacred than any church." It is said by Bax ("The Religion of Socialism"): "The establishment of society on a socialistic basis would imply the definite abandonment of all theological cults." And by Tolstoi ("My Religion"): "The Church has fulfilled its mission, and is useless."

It is true, indeed, that the name of Jesus is mentioned by some Socialists with honour, but it is because He is looked upon as having been a friend of the poor, a Jewish social reformer.* One writer says: "As centuries roll on, the name of Jesus will be more and more venerated precisely on account of His social teaching. . . . He proclaimed the Kingdom of Heaven, and Secularism will bring it in." But the true Socialists, those who best represent the sociological spirit of to-day, see clearly that this pre-

* We are told that some French Socialists have placed upon the wall of their assembly-room a picture of Christ, with the inscription, "Jesus of Nazareth, the first representative of the People."

sentation of Him cannot be maintained; and that His teachings are, in fact, an obstacle in their way rather than a help. It is plain upon the face of the Gospel that He came, first of all, to save men from their sins, and to call all to repentance; but genuine Socialism acknowledges no sinfulness, and needs no Divine Saviour. Says one: "Socialism sees in Him at best a weak and impulsive personality. Higher types are now to be found on earth." It does not find in Him the socialistic ideal. We need not quote in detail. Every one familiar with socialistic writings knows that to set aside His authority is a necessary step to the diffusion of genuine socialistic ideas. That He lives, and has anything to do personally with the development of society and the progress of nations, would seem to most Socialists the idlest of fancies. We may be sure that Socialism, if triumphant, will have no place for One who taught the sinfulness of humanity, the need of atonement, and affirmed that all men must stand before His judgment-seat.

While Christian Socialists affirm that through the application of Christian principles, society will be reconstructed and perfected, the real socialistic leaders regard it as a part of their mission to emancipate men from their long bondage to religious systems of every kind; and especially from the fear of the Christian God, which prevents the true development of humanity. Socialism is itself held up as a religion, based upon the second great commandment, "love to men." It does not regard it necessary to obey the first commandment in order to obey the second. Indeed, any obedience of the first, any love to God, is impossible. If a God is admitted to exist, it is for the most part only in a pantheistic or evolutionary sense; and He cannot be an object of love.

Socialism borrows from Christianity its conception of a happy future for man on earth, but eliminates from it all distinctively Christian elements. There is to be a perfected society, a kingdom of righteousness, but it is to be a kingdom of man, not of God. Humanity, not through any Divine interposition or help but in virtue of its natural goodness, steadily developes itself, and advances from lower to higher planes. While Rome thinks to bring all the world to a recognition of its authority, and Protestantism to convert it by the preaching of the Gospel, Socialism affirms that it will bring in the golden age by the establishment of a new social order, when all men will be equal, and which shall embrace all nations. As said by one of them: "When the socialistic Commonwealth is fully evolved, it is equality that will establish the kingdom of heaven in the earth."

In this belief as to the future of man, the leading Evolutionists are at one with the Socialists, though they may in part reject the idea of social reconstruction, and look chiefly to the gradual evolution of humanity under the law of the survival of the fittest. The evolutionary process may be slow, but the result is sure; only the best survive. The perfecting of man is, as we are told by Mr. John Fiske, to be "the glorious consummation of nature's long and tedious work." And Science also looks forward to the same consummation by bringing man into harmony with nature through knowledge of its laws. As said by one: "The future happiness of the race, which the prophets hardly ventured to hope for, Science boldly predicts." If this be the attitude of Socialism towards

Christianity and the Church, its increase in Christendom is a matter of highest moment.

The Christian Socialists attempt to hold a mediating position; ready to give up much that the Church has held as to the distinction of the sacred and secular, of the natural and the supernatural, of the Church and the world; and yet are desirous to retain its fundamental doctrines as to the Trinity, the Incarnation, sin, atonement, and final judgment. But this is a position in which they cannot long stand. Some will doubtless give up their Christianity altogether, for the Kingdom of God substituting the kingdom of humanity, and finally join themselves to the Antichrist; others, seeing where they are tending, will draw back, and giving up their own plans of establishing the kingdom of God, will look for His return who alone can establish it.

It is obvious, without special remark, that the socialistic ideal of a kingdom of perfected humanity through a new social order, will greatly help Antichrist in the establishment of his rule over the nations. The eyes of all are now turned forward, their minds are full of vague but ardent expectations; there is a golden age in the future, and not far distant. Nothing supernatural, indeed, is to be looked for, no returning Jesus, no resurrection from the dead, no glorified and immortal humanity. Antichrist appears; he will fulfil these expectations. He will reconstruct society, he will give to all their rights. And men see in him one who can realize their hopes. It is not to be expected that the new order will peacefully triumph; the roots of the old run too deep. Such radical changes as Socialism proposes can be carried through only by force; there must be a stormy transition period. But Socialism will serve as a powerful lever by which Antichrist may overthrow the existing political governments, and the field be cleared for the final contest. When the tempest of war now darkening the heavens has passed over Christendom, it needs no prophetic light to see that it will be another Christendom than ours.

"The look of England is to me abundantly ominous; the question of labour and capital growing ever more anarchical, insoluble by the notions hitherto applied to it, pretty certain to issue in petroleum some day, unless some other gospel than that of the Dismal Science comes to illuminate it." (T. Carlyle.)

There are some who refuse the name of Christian Socialists as implying that they are Collectivists — which they deny. For these no distinctive term can easily be found. In a large sense all may be called Christian Socialists who think it the mission and duty of the Church to perfect society, and so establish the Kingdom of God.

PART IV.

THE REIGN OF THE ANTICHRIST.

THE PERSONAL CHRIST IN THE FIRST AND IN THE NINETEENTH CENTURY.

THE PANTHEISTIC REVOLUTION.

ANTICHRIST AS HEAD OF THE NATIONS.

THE MORALITY OF THE FUTURE.

THE CHURCH OF THE FUTURE.

THE CHURCH OF THE BEAST AND THE FALSE PROPHET.

PART IV.

THE REIGN OF THE ANTICHRIST.

THE PERSONAL CHRIST IN THE FIRST AND IN THE NINETEENTH CENTURY.

Counted in years, the period from the Lord's birth to the present day is not a very long one; yet how changed the religious condition of the world within that period! Looking backward we admiringly say, What wonderful progress! We are here concerned only with the progress of Christianity. We must ask, in what it consists, and by what standard we are to measure the Christianity of to-day.

That Christianity, from very small beginnings, has become a dominant power in the earth, all know. But do we find in the numerical increase of its believers, or in the mighty influence of the Church upon the civilization of the nations, or in the honour paid it by the world, or even in the holy lives of its children, the standard of measurement we seek? We may not say this. We cannot separate Christianity from the living Christ; it lives only in Him. We can find Christian progress in the highest and truest sense only when He, the Founder of Christianity, the Head of the Church, is both better known and more honoured among those who bear His name. The questions,

"What think ye of the Christ? Whose Son is He?" are still the questions which must prove whether Christianity has made progress with the centuries. Does the Church of to-day better understand the mystery of the Person of the Incarnate Son, His teachings and His work, and more exalt and honour Him as her living Head, than did the Church of the apostolic age? Here is the standard by which we must test the Christianity of to-day.

We need not speak at any length of the place which the risen Christ held in the thought and affection of the early Church. How diligently the Apostles laboured to keep His Person, no less than His teachings, always before the eyes of the disciples, their Epistles attest. He was the centre of all their love, and hope, and labour. Although personally absent, He was still carrying on through the Holy Ghost in the Church His redemptive work; and all that was done by it, was done not only in His name and by His authority, but was in a true sense His own personal action. And His Person filled the future as well as the present with its transfiguring light. The prayer for His speedy return, for the glorious hour when they should be made like Him, was upon all lips. All eyes were fixed upon Him. They endured persecution "as seeing Him who is invisible." He was the Alpha and the Omega, the First and the Last, the Beginning and the End.

We turn to the Church of to-day and ask, "What think ye of the Christ? Whose Son is He?" Is He now as highly exalted, as truly reverenced, as devoutly worshipped, as at the first? Is He now, as the living Lord and Head of the Church, the centre of all Christian thought, and love, and hope? Are the eyes of those who bear His name continually fastened upon Him to know what is His will? Do they long for their perfected likeness to Him at His return, as the consummation of their hopes? Do they, in the full assurance of His supreme power, proclaim Him before the world as its Judge "who standeth at the door"; and admonish all kings and rulers to rule in righteousness as those who must give account to Him?

It will hardly be denied by any that the risen and living Christ does not hold the same exalted place in the thought and affection of the Church of to-day that He held in the Church of the apostolic age. This is not to say that multitudes of faithful souls do not live in personal communion with Him, and make His present existence a great reality to themselves. But there are, also, multitudes who bear His name to whom He is little more than a myth. His person, so clearly seen in the beginning although in heaven, has become dimmed and shadowy in the ages of the past. We hear much of the principles and of the spirit of Christ, but little of Himself. But while the Church is more and more silent, we hear many voices crying: He has been too much exalted, too much honoured; He must be brought to His proper level. Let us briefly note the steps by which this change has been made; and the goal of final rejection to which they lead.

The Church early embodied in her Creeds the great central and vital truth that Jesus is the only-begotten Son, "in whom dwelleth all the fulness of the Godhead bodily." The significance of this truth is infinite, no one generation can comprehend it. Under the teaching of the Holy Ghost it should have unfolded itself more and more as the centuries passed, and His Person have risen before the Church in ever increasing glory and majesty. If, then, we find to-day His Divinity disparaged or denied, and He Himself brought into the rank of common men, what shall we say? Has He not fallen from the supreme place which the early Church gave Him? And has not Christianity, which cannot be separated from Him, fallen from its original and distinctive character?

Let us briefly trace the steps of this fall, beginning with the denial of His Divinity.

If Jesus was not the one Incarnate Son of God, as affirmed by the Apostolic Church, what place could be assigned Him? Who was He? Arius (318 A.D.) early thought to answer this question by affirming that, though He was not God, He was more than man. He was, indeed, a creature, brought into existence by God, yet was absolutely separated from men by a prior and distinct act of creation. He was made before the worlds to be God's instrument in their creation, and His representative in all His relations to men; the one Mediator, and an object of worship. He was the one Divinely commissioned Teacher, having miraculous powers, and His death had an expiatory value. Rising from the dead, He now fulfils the office of High Priest in heaven; and will come again to judge the quick and the dead.

Thus Jesus, though His Divinity was denied, was kept by the Arians distinct from all men and angels, and held a unique place; below God, indeed, but above all created beings.* But this intermediate

---

* To shew the radical nature of the change which has taken place in the minds of some, it is to be noted that the Nicene

position could not long satisfy the speculative intellect craving for unity. If not one with God, He must be made one with man. And this was done by taking from Him some of the personal attributes and official prerogatives which Arius had left Him. Passing over other deniers of the truth in the earlier centuries, we find this done by Socinus (1550 A. D.) who taught that He was a man in nature like other men, not created before the world, but distinguished by His supernatural birth, His sinless life, His Divine commission as a teacher, and His power to work miracles. He arose from the dead and ascended into Heaven, and is now to be adored and worshipped, though not in the same sense as the Father.

Being thus brought down from the unique and high place given Him by Arius, His pre-existence and creat-

Creed, which was so worded as to declare without possibility of misinterpretation the Divinity of Christ, and of Him alone, is now made to affirm, that all men are Divine, all of one substance with the Father. Thus it is said by Dr. Hedge ("The Ways of the Spirit") that all without distinction can use this Creed, and confess that Jesus was of the substance of the Father, for this is true of all. "It was well for the Church, and well for humanity, that the Athanasian view prevailed against the Arian, and the Monophysite. The Arians saw no God-man, but a hypothetical Being, neither God nor man. The Nicene Creed permits us to behold that man partakes of the substance of God." "In declaring Him to be consubstantial, One with God in substance, the Creed of Nicæa dates a new era in the history of human thought." But its error was in the limitation of Divinity to Jesus. "To say that God incarnated Himself in a single individual of all the multitudes of the human family, is a proposition which cannot satisfy, if it does not shock, the unprejudiced mind." According to this, every man who repeats the Nicene Creed says of himself that he is "of one substance with the Father, God of God, Light of Light, very God of very God." What more can Antichrist say of himself, or ask of his worshippers ?

ive activity denied, though still regarded as a mediator
between God and man, it was inevitable that the distinction between Him and others should in time be
effaced. The whole tendency since Socinus has been
not only to take from His Person its Divinity, and
bring Him as to His nature into unity with the common humanity, but also to deny to Him all special
mediatorial offices. For a considerable time, indeed,
the supernatural features of His life — the Virgin
birth, His resurrection and ascension, His priestly
work in Heaven, and His return to be Judge of the
world — were retained as taught in the Gospels; but
with a growing sense of their inconsistency with His
pure humanity. Why, if only one of the sons of God,
should He be so exalted above all the rest, and set
apart by Himself? Since all in virtue of their Divine
sonship may draw near to God the Father, what need
of a mediator? Why must He bear the sins of men,
and offer an expiatory sacrifice? Why must He
stand as a High Priest offering continual intercession? Why should He return to judge the world?
Is not the omniscient God alone the Judge?

This tendency to take from the Lord's Person all its
supernatural features, and from Him all mediatorial
offices, though clearly seen in the last century, received a new impulse in the present through the
growing prevalence of the pantheistic philosophy. It
is among the Unitarians, the theological successors of
Socinus, that we most clearly trace the progress of
this tendency. At first, Jesus was denied to be Divine
on the ground of the absolute distinction of the Divine and human natures, the impassable gulf between
Godhead and humanity. When this distinction was
set aside by philosophy, it followed that He must

be recognized as Divine in common with all men; but for a time a unique place was assigned Him. But the question arose, Why should His consciousness of God be the measure of the consciousness of all men down to the last generation? Granted, that He was distinguished above all of His day by His spiritual and ethical endowments, and His teachings, therefore, to have been full of light and authority, has He, only one of the Sons of God, revealed all that the Father would have us know? Logical consistency requires that, if purely human, He should come under the laws controlling human development. Why should His teachings be regarded as absolute truth, and not be judged of by the moral and intellectual character of His age, and of the people among whom he lived? Unless we separate Him from all other men, it would be a psychological impossibility that He should not partake of the limitations of His time. We, therefore, of a much later generation, and with a far larger knowledge, it is said, cannot receive His teachings as without error; nor can we regard Him as giving the most perfect possible example of our humanity in all its manifold aspects. A perfect moral character demands a corresponding intellectual development, and this we cannot find in one whose life was so limited in its opportunities and relations. Thus it is said of Him by Miss Cobbe ("Broken Lights"): "The greatness of the sovereign, of the statesman, of the economist, the metaphysician, the poet, the artist, the historian, was not His."

In regard to His teachings it is said by Theodore Parker that "the theology of Jesus seems to have had many Jewish notions in it wholly untenable in our day. If correctly represented in the Gospels, His theology contained a considerable mixture of error." "It is absurd to maintain that He entertained no theological error in matters of importance." "Popular theology is the greatest evil of our time, and this rests on two columns, one of which is the idea of a supernatural Christ. This popular theology is in a process of dissolution."

It is said by another (Rev. S. Longfellow): "No authority is to be given to the teachings of Jesus but what each man's own mind, or heart, or conscience, can give them. In displacing Him from the place given Him by the Church, we see only another idol shattered that the true God may be revealed." And as His teachings are without authority, so His personal mediatorship is to be taken from Him. "Jesus is not the way to God, He is not needed. Go direct to the Father." "The prevalent doctrine of Christ as Mediator, Lord, and King, is a hindrance rather than a help to man's spiritual growth." And another, Rev. Mr. Chadwick ("Old and New Unitarian Beliefs"), tells us that "it is impious to specialize Jesus, and isolate Him as He has been specialized and isolated and worshipped by the Church."

But great as is this disparagement of the Lord, both as to His Person, and His place and authority, yet few have hitherto been bold enough to deny Him as a man moral perfection. Now, this is openly said: "That Jesus was a perfect man, it is impossible to prove. There are things about Him in the New Testament which are not helpful to the character of His impeccability. We know enough about Him to know that He was not intellectually infallible, yet without this He could not be absolutely free from actual wrong." "To speak of God's perfect revelation through Him, if confined to the moral revelation, is unworthy and irrational." A prominent Socialist writer says, "Socialism sees in Jesus but a weak and impulsive personality at best. Higher types are now to be found on earth."

It may be said these utterances impugning the Lord's intellectual and moral character are those of a few extreme men, and find little or no response in Christendom. But what shall we say of the recent "Lives of Jesus" which plainly declare Him to be a Son of His time, moulded by its influences, and not able to rise above its traditional and superstitious beliefs, e. g. in angels and devils? As subject to these influences, He encouraged the Messianic expectations of the day, which had no foundation except in some misinterpreted prophecies. What shall we say of Renan's Life of Him, not to mention any others of kindred spirit, passing through many editions in many languages, in which His moral character is openly assailed, and He is charged with premeditated imposture? That heathen enemies should have said like things in the first days of the Church, does not surprise us; but that these things should be said in Christendom after so many centuries, by learned and accomplished scholars, and have been welcomed by many thousands of all classes, high and low, shows the workings of a spirit of hostility to Christ which, like a smouldering fire, is getting ready to burst into a fierce flame.

Having thus seen the growing depreciation of the Lord, both as to His Person and offices, what are we to expect in the future? Will He as the living and ruling Head pass more and more out of the thought and life of the Church and of the nations? This is believed by many. As humanity rises to its destined greatness, new and brighter stars will appear in its sky, and He will gradually sink from sight. They see, therefore, no cause why any hostility should be awakened against Him. Christianity is now silently and peacefully being transmuted into a new and higher form, with its new teachers and leaders.

But we know that Christ is not thus to pass from the knowledge and obedience of men. He will by His actings affirm His supreme prerogatives as the anointed King to whom God has given all power in heaven and earth. We know that in due time He will reappear before the world in the immediate personal exercise of His headship and rule. As the Lord of the earth, He will come and take possession of it, and the nations then awake to a full consciousness of His existence and prerogatives. So long as He is regarded as a mere religious teacher, living only in the truths He taught, there is nothing to call forth any active hostility; but so soon as He shall assert His royal supremacy, and the Church shall reaffirm it and begin the preparation for Him, the latent hate will break forth in acts of violence and blood against all who abide faithful to Him, and who refuse to take upon them the mark of the Beast and worship him.

We may now sum up the successive downward steps by which the faith of the Church at the beginning in Jesus Christ as the one Incarnate Son, the Saviour of men by His cross, now High Priest and Head over all unto the Church, and to come again to be the Judge and King of the nations, has gradually decayed, and the way thus been prepared for the Antichrist.

1. The denial of His Divinity by Arius and others in very early times, but who still affirmed His unique place as the highest of created beings, His pre-existence and creative activity, His supernatural birth, His offices as the one Mediator, the Teacher of perfect truth, and our future Judge and King; thus drawing a broad and absolute line of distinction between Him and all other beings both as to His Person and offices. Although not God, He was more than man.

2. This absolute distinction between Him and other men set aside, but still a distinction of rank and office preserved. He is presented as specially chosen and commissioned by God, the one Mediator, His teacher, a worker of miracles, a present High Priest, and the future Judge, and to be worshipped with a secondary worship.

3. Through the teaching of a general Incarnation, and that all men are alike the sons of God, the need of a Mediator, either as a Sacrifice or Intercessor, is done away. Christ is to be distinguished from others only as the first to become fully conscious of His Divine Sonship, and so made our moral and spiritual Ideal. But His personal mission ended with His death, and He is not now our Priest, nor will He come to be our Judge. He is to be honoured, but not worshipped.

To this stage many have come.

4. As purely man, and one of a race ever progressing, although possessing pre-eminent spiritual endowments, He must be judged of by the standard of His age, and cannot be regarded as the teacher of the absolute truth; or even as intellectually and morally perfect when measured by the standard of

our day. His teachings are erroneous in many points, and His example not always to be followed.

It is to this stage that some, the more advanced, have already come.

5. As He is set forth in the Creeds of the Church, and made a representative of the doctrine of a sinful humanity needing atonement, and of a personal God who rules all things according to His own will, faith in Him and in His teachings is an obstacle in the way of a true and universal religion based on Divine and human unity. His yoke, both as Teacher and Ruler, must be cast off before men can come to absolute freedom of thought and action.

This is the stage to which we are approaching.

6. Presented before the world by His disciples as now living, and claiming a present personal dominion over all men, thus awakening delusive expectations on the part of many of His return and Kingdom, and so making them indifferent to the important secular interests of this time, and hostile to the worship of humanity in its great representative who seats himself in the temple of God,— He must be regarded as a hinderer of human progress, and a disturber of the public peace; and those who recognize and uphold His asserted authority, must be dealt with as enemies of the State and of religion. His worship must be suppressed, and His adherents suffer the extreme penalties of disobedience.

This stage will not come till the man of sin attains to the fulness of his power.

Thus in the end is the Christ fully deposed, and the world enthrones the Antichrist as the highest representative of a perfected humanity, of the public order, and of a universal religion.

THE PANTHEISTIC REVOLUTION.

The battle of ideas, of the old and new, though often long protracted and fierce, is bloodless. It is not till the new seeks to be embodied in laws and institutions, and thus rule human conduct, that the battle comes to its final, and often bloody, stage. And the strife is bitter in proportion as the old is entrenched in the affections of a people through long usage, and intertwined with its traditions and hallowed memories. When the new presents itself in radical antagonism to the old, claiming higher authority for its representatives, the strife becomes one of life and death. Then the change is not a Reformation, but a Revolution. Of several such political revolutions history makes mention.

A change of principles necessarily brings with it a change of the institutions based upon them. The present institutions of Christendom were built upon Christian principles, the foundation of all being the recognition of one God, whose will when expressed is to be obeyed; and the authority of Christ's teachings. The three great institutions of the Family, the State, and the Church, have taken upon them in Christendom a distinctive religious character. Sanctified by the Spirit of God, and recognized as of Divine authority, they have been made the means of the highest blessings to men. In them, through His operations, have been preserved three unities, parental, governmental, and ecclesiastical, which are all essential to the good order of society, and to true individual development; and which must be preserved. Divested of Divine authority, regarded as merely natural institutions without spiritual life and power, these unities cannot be preserved. These several relations ceasing to be regarded as having a Divine sanction, and therefore permanent, become changeable at the will of the State, and finally at the will of the individual parties. Marriage becomes a contract for two to dwell together as husband and wife so long as is agreeable to them. Subjects obey their rulers so long as their administration pleases them; and members of the Church follow their leaders if they think it expedient. Without the Spirit of God, as the spirit of cohesion, all human unities dissolve into their individual elements.*

* If it be objected to this that the Family, the State, and the Church have always existed, and will continue to exist though the Christian Faith shall become extinct, it is to be noted that Christianity regards them as more than mere natural institutions. For man, put under a redemptive system from the first, these have always had in them a measure of spiritual power and grace. They have been the means, each in its degree, whereby God has kept men from that lowest depth of wickedness and misery into which they must have come had He wholly withdrawn His Spirit. The Holy Spirit is to all natural institutions what life is to the body, the living principle which keeps them from disintegration.

It may be added here that the primal Unity, and the foundation of all other unities, is that of the Trinity — the Three in One. Of the manifested unities, the first is that of the Father and the Incarnate Son; the second, that of the risen Lord and His body the Church, embracing the unity of its members with one another. If this is not preserved, the lower unities of the Family and the State cannot be. The dissolution of bonds in all the relations of life inevitably follows if the Holy Ghost, the Spirit of life, is grieved and hindered in the Church.

For many centuries Christianity has moulded the legislation of Christendom, and continues so to do. In only one Christian State has there been an attempt to set it wholly aside, and to establish institutions upon other principles. In France the existence of God was denied, the name of Christ dishonoured, the Christian Era abolished, new feasts appointed to supplant the old religious festivals, and no worship sanctioned but that of "Liberty, Equality, and Eternal Truth." It was boasted that France had in one instant annihilated eighteen centuries of error. This madness was shortlived. The National Assembly soon declared a national recognition of a Supreme Being to be useful to the State, and decreed to Him a religious festival. A few years later Napoleon made the Concordat with the Pope, whereby Christianity became again the religion of France.

Remembering this disastrous failure to build permanent institutions upon the principles of a materialistic atheism, it will seem incredible to many that the experiment should be ever tried anew by the Christian nations, to find a foundation other than that which Christianity gives. Yet it may be affirmed in the light both of Scripture prophecy, and of the movements and tendencies of the times, that there will be another attempt in Christendom to establish new institutions upon new principles. We may designate it as the Pantheistic revolution, as distinguished from the earlier Atheistic revolution.

In considering this matter two points present themselves: First, the prevalence of pantheistic principles; secondly, their revolutionary power.

First. As to the former, some proofs have already been given showing that Pantheism, in some of its forms, not only pervades the current modern philosophy, but is more and more penetrating religion, science, literature, and all the departments of human thought. The multitude is made familiar with its principles through magazines and newspapers, through lectures and the pulpit. Its prevalence is shown in the rapidity with which such systems as those of Christian Science, Mental Science, Theosophy, and others kindred to them, have spread in Christian communities, for all have a Pantheistic basis. The moral atmosphere is full of its spirit, and many are affected by it unawares.* What shall we say of its diffusion in the future? To judge of this we must look upon its spread from another point of view, and consider its affinity with Democracy.

It is not to be questioned that social and political conditions have much influence in moulding religious opinions, and we assume that the democratic spirit will rule the future. What kind of religious influence is Democracy adapted to exert? In what direction does the democratic current run? According to De Tocqueville, it runs in the direction of very general ideas, and therefore to Pantheism. The idea of the unity of the people as a whole, as one, preponderates, and this extends itself to the world, and to the universe. God and the universe make one whole. This unity has charms for men living in democracies, and prepares them for Pantheistic beliefs. "Among the different systems, by whose aid philosophy endeavours to explain the universe, I believe Pantheism to be one of those most fitted to seduce the human

* It is said by a very recent writer, Külpe ("Introduction to Philosophy." Trans. 1897), "Pantheism is very widely held at the present day."

mind in democratic ages; and against it all who abide in their attachment to the true greatness of man, should struggle and combine."*

If these remarks of this very acute political observer are true, we may expect to see Pantheism enlarging its influence in Christendom as Democracy extends. It is not, however, necessary to suppose that the number of its advocates should become greater than that of its opposers. We are to bear in mind that, as France was by no means generally atheistic at the time of the Revolution, yet was controlled by Atheists, so Christendom need not be generally pantheistic. The leaders of revolutions are always in advance of their followers. The boldest and most logical in carrying out their principles control the hesitating and wavering masses.

Secondly. The revolutionary power of Pantheistic principles. Many who see political danger in the spread of Atheism, see none in the spread of Pantheism. We must, therefore, examine what destructive social forces lie hid in this system of belief; and to this end let us contrast Atheism and Pantheism. These are practically at one in denying the Father and the Son, but in their teaching in regard to man

---

* That Pantheism is in its nature vague and obscure, presenting little to the intellect that is definite, may rather help than hinder its general diffusion, and make it more powerful. It is remarked by Coleridge, "The Friend," Essay xiv: "The truth of the assertion that deep feeling has a tendency to combine with obscure ideas in preference to distinct and clear notions, may be proved by the history of fanatics and fanaticism in all ages and countries." All students of the French Revolution know how the most abstract principles of human right and of government were themes for heated and angry discussions in the clubs and on the streets.

they widely differ; and, therefore, affect very differently individual character. Atheism, by making man the product of material forces, degrades him; there is nothing in him spiritual or Divine. Pantheism, by making him a part of the Infinite Spirit, exalts him; he is in his own right Divine. These two antipodal conceptions of humanity must, each in its own way, powerfully affect human character and action. In the French Revolution, inspired by the teaching of Rousseau and others, the primary object was the elevation of all to the true dignity of manhood; and, therefore, all the old oppressive and degrading distinctions, political, social, religious, must be effaced. The natural rights of all must be acknowledged. But as God did not exist, men could stand in no relation to Him; all was human. Atheism makes life bare and empty. But in Pantheism, the relation of man to God gives a religious tone to all his life, and profoundly affects his relations to others. Because of the common Divinity there is established a more absolute equality between man and man than Democracy can give; and which, while in one way it favours democratic institutions, in another fosters a spirit which tends to make any voluntary form of social unity difficult if not impossible. This will be seen more clearly if we note in some detail the effect of the pantheistic conception on individual character.

1. Although based on universalism — the presence of the one Infinite Spirit in all men — it tends to produce an intense individualism or egoism, and a self-exaltation which contemns and resists all legal restraints. Every man, being Divine, is a law to himself. The Divinity in him rules and guides him. He asks nothing from others, he will not be ruled by

others, he is sufficient for himself. He owes nothing to the past, no thanks, no reverence. As said by Emerson, who continually presents this type of character for our admiration: "Nothing is sacred but the integrity of our own mind. What have I to do with the sacredness of traditions if I live wholly from within? . . . No law can be sacred to me but that of my nature. . . . If I am the devil's child, I will then live from the devil. . . . I shun father and mother, and wife and brother, when my genius calls me." "Jesus was better than others because He refused to listen to others, and listened at home." It follows that what Jesus did, all who are conscious of the Divinity within them should do; listen to and obey the inward voice. Why hearken to the voices of the past? Why listen to the utterances of an old Bible? "If a man claims to know and to speak of God, and carries you backward to the phraseology of some old mouldered nation in another country, in another world, believe him not." In other words, it is nothing to me what God has said by Moses or Paul; I am concerned only with what He says to me to-day.*

Of the effect of the belief in man's Divinity upon his individual character and action, we have seen some illustrations in what has been said of the Deification of humanity. This effect is pointed out by Mr. H. R. Hutton: "The difference between Panthe-

* Mr. Emerson gives an illustration in his own person how he made his feelings to be the guide of his action. He said in reference to the administration of the Lord's supper: "If I believed that it was enjoined by Jesus on His disciples, and that he even contemplated making permanent this mode of commemoration as in every way agreeable to an Eastern mind, and yet on trial it was disagreeable to my own feelings, I should not adopt it."

ism and Theism is this, that genuine Theism humbles the mind, while Pantheism inflates it. . . . Pantheism is an inebriating faith, of which vanity or sensationalism is apt to be the first word, though not the last." . . . "When you put the Unities, and Immensities, and Abysses in the place of God, you are very apt indeed to feel what a wonderful fellow you must be to front the World and the Eternities in that grand way."

The pantheistic man, as here described, has the characteristic features of the lawless one of St. Paul; and lawlessness must reign in all pantheistic communities. If every man has his own oracle within him, there can be no imposed obedience to a common law. No law can be sacred to any man, but that of his own nature. Let every man obey his own Divine impulses. Pantheism and lawlessness have thus a very close relation. But always, even among the lawless, the strongest will must rule when supported by an intellect of surpassing ability, an energy which never tires, and a courage which fears neither heaven, nor earth, nor hell. As the lawless one *par excellence*, the man of sin is able to rule the lawless.

2. Pantheism gives a deeper foundation for the demand of human rights. Atheism in France made much of the rights of man as man, but Pantheism demands the rights of man as Divine. The practical effect of this distinction was seen by Heine: " Bread is the people's right," now becomes, " Bread is man's Divine right." This Divine right extends to all human relations; and Divine rights are not to be asked for, they are to be taken, and by force if necessary.

This possession of a Divine humanity gives to all

who would reform or reconstruct society, a high vantage ground. The many evils which now afflict our humanity are unworthy of it, and ought not to exist. The old, with its many burdens, has no right to bind us. Why bear longer with inherited imperfection? The present voice of the Divinity in man is to decide his present action; not ancestral traditions, not transmitted customs, not legal precedents. The God in humanity cannot be bound; and, therefore, to-day is better than any day before it; it is supreme.

The effect of this is to bring in radical changes by making an almost total breach with the past. In this respect Pantheism is more revolutionary than Evolution, or even Atheism. Reformation holds to the past, but modifies it; Revolution breaks with it. Philosophical evolutionism affirms continual progress upward; but the new comes out of the old, is a development of it, and may, therefore, be called reformatory rather than revolutionary. Atheism breaks, indeed, with the past, and yet retains it, or goes back to it, because it has no creative principle in itself. Pantheism is revolutionary in its very nature. It repudiates the authority of the past, because the voice of God speaking to-day must overrule all His earlier utterances. His present word is all-controlling. It is, therefore, of no importance what men have said or done in the past; what their laws, their customs, their institutions. The way is open for new political institutions, a new social order. We may make all things new.

3. Thus while Pantheism puts away old religions, it presents a new. This Atheism could not do. When the atheistic movement in France had affirmed its negations of God, of immortality, of worship,

there was only blank nothingness before it. Between these negations and the restoration of Christianity there was no alternative. Men must go back, they could not go forward. Napoleon could not build a church on new foundations, he must rebuild on the old. The Church, therefore, with its doctrines of sin, redemption, and judgment, must be restored to its place.

In estimating the power of Pantheism over men, and its possibilities of future action, we must remember that it is far more than a religious philosophy. It is a faith—faith in the guidance of humanity through the Divinity dwelling in it. No great deeds are done except by those who have faith in their cause, and, therefore, in themselves. We find an illustration of this in the wars of the French Revolution when the semi-religious worship of Democracy, as establishing the rights of man, filled its armies with marvelous endurance and a terrible energy. Pantheism is a faith, and can serve as an impulse to mighty deeds. Its mission is to bring in a condition of things worthy of our Divine humanity; and its first step is to uproot and destroy all that stands in its way. Nothing is to be spared which hinders the realization of its great end. Religious systems in conflict with it, and especially Christianity which teaches the sinfulness of man, are doomed to destruction. It will be satisfied with nothing less than the submission of Christendom to its authority, and with its homage paid to its great representative.

Turning to the revolutionary forces of Pantheism; these are found in its radical and irreconcilable antagonism to the fundamental facts and principles of the Christian Faith. Christianity affirms a personal God; a Supreme Lawgiver; the sinfulness of man; the necessity for a Mediator; the sending of such a Mediator; and salvation through His cross. Pantheism denies all this. God is not personal; man is not sinful; there is no need of any mediatorship; nor is there any Mediator; human nature is itself Divine. It is plain that just so far as the facts and principles of Christianity have affected the laws and institutions of Christendom, Pantheism must recast them, and fill them with its own spirit. The two cannot exist together in peace.

We have already seen in speaking of Christendom as set forth under the symbol of Babylon in The Revelation, that the Christian Church, as connected with the State, and the Christian State fall together. New principles must express themselves in corresponding institutions, and the old must give place to the new. Nor is this change to be effected without violence. Of the symbol we are told (Rev. xviii, 21), "With violence shall that great city, Babylon, be thrown down." It is not that all rejoice in this overthrow; on the contrary, there is much wailing and weeping over it. But the Lawless One, and those with him, prevail. The ground is cleared for the erection of a new kingdom and a new church, to be united under one head.

It is in the rejection of all authority over him by the individual man, that we find the political and social bearing of Pantheism. Not being under God but a part of God, why submit himself to the will of another? The kingdom of the Lawless One must be in its nature a kingdom of violence, in which the strongest will and strongest arm will be master. It is this sufficiency of each man for himself that gives impulse and power to the revolutionary forces of Pantheism. This was clearly seen by Mr. R. W. Emerson.

"It is easy to see that a greater self-reliance, a new respect for the Divinity in man, must work a revolution in all the offices and relations of men; in their religion, in their education, in their pursuits, their modes of living, their associations, in their property, in their speculative views." "Let a Stoic arise who shall reveal the resources of man, and tell men that with the exercise of self-trust new powers shall appear; that a man is the word made flesh, born to shed healing to the nations, . . . and at the moment he acts for himself, tossing the laws, the books, and customs out of the window, we thank and revere him; and that teacher shall restore the life of man to splendour, and make his name dear to all history."

This bearing of Pantheism, when fully developed in individual men, upon the destiny of Christendom through its revolutionary forces, was clearly seen by Heine, who in his "Germany" (Trans.) thus expresses himself: "These doctrines have developed revolutionary forces which only await the day to break forth and fill the world with terror, and with punishment." Speaking particularly of Germany, he says: "Should that subduing talisman, the Cross, break, then will come crashing and roaring forth the world-madness of the old champions, the insane Berseker rage. . . . That talisman is brittle, and the day will come when it will pitifully break. . . . Thought goes before the deed, and lightning precedes thunder. German thunder will come, and ye will hear it crash as naught ever crashed before in the whole history of the world. . . . Then will be played in Germany a drama, compared to which the French Revolution will be only an innocent idyl. Just now all is tolerably quiet. The great actors have not yet appeared upon the stage, the great army of gladiators. The hour will come."

How far these predictions of Heine will be realized in any particular country, time must show, but that they will be realized in Christendom we see already the most significant signs. History never repeats itself; we shall see no repetition of the French Revolution. Atheistic materialism is out of date. Men are not now tempted to deny a God. On the contrary, humanity is Divine, and the first step is to make this real to ourselves. It is faith in this humanity which is the impulse to establish a new order of things that shall be worthy of it.

ANTICHRIST AS HEAD OF THE NATIONS.

St. Paul does not speak of the political power of "the Lawless One," but in The Revelation (xiii, 7) the Beast from the sea is spoken of as one to whom "authority is given over all kindreds, and tongues, and nations." That the Beast and the Lawless One are the same person, we have already seen. We have, therefore, here only to enquire how far the political and social tendencies and movements of the time are preparing the way for this universal kingdom. Of these may be mentioned, Democracy, Socialism, Anarchy, and the Unity or Solidarity of nations.

Democracy. No one is ignorant of the rapid progress of democratic principles in all parts of Christendom during the present century, and especially during the last half of it. It may be said in general of the Christian States, that the popular will is supreme in them all, even in those where universal suffrage does not exist. More and more all sovereigns and rulers are eager to learn what the wishes of their people are, and careful not to set themselves in direct opposition to them. Whether in the existing monarchies hereditary succession will give place to popular election, is not certain, though it seems probable; but all rulers, hereditary or elected, are made more and more to feel themselves the servants of the people.

This growth of Democracy serves to prepare the way of the Antichrist by making the popular will supreme, both as to the choice of the rulers and the nature and extent of their rule; and by giving legal expression to that will. When a people elects its legislators, the legislation will be what the majority of the voters demand. In the past, among all Christian nations, such legislation has, in great part, been based upon Christian principles, and involved the recognition of God's authority. So long as this authority, as declared in the Scriptures or by the Church, is recognized, the popular will is not supreme; but according as it is denied, this supremacy is more and more enlarged. If, then, the belief become general, either that there is no God, the Lawgiver, or no expression of His will which is authoritative, what principle shall determine the character and limitations of legislation? The only principle is that of the public good; whatever this demands, is right. If, for example, the law of marriage given in the Bible is set aside as without authority, what shall determine what the new law shall be? It must be what the welfare of society demands, and this is a matter of popular judgment. The same principle governs all legislation. Thus, according to the measure in which Divine authority and laws are repudiated, and governments make the popular will the supreme rule of their action, do they enter into that sphere of lawlessness which forms the fitting preparation and environment for the Antichrist.

If the authority of God over the State be rejected, it needs not to be said that the authority of Christ as His Ruler is rejected also; although His teachings as ethical may still be powerful in moulding legislation. They are, however, powerful only from their intrinsic value, not as coming from one who has a right to command. We have reason to believe that, although the practical rejection of all now recognized Divine law may be gradual, the popular supremacy, based upon the public good, will at last be affirmed as absolute in all matters pertaining to man's welfare.

As Democracy makes the popular will supreme, so it provides in general suffrage the legal means of its expression. It is possible that, as regards rulers, this may find its last and highest illustration in the choice between Christ and the Antichrist. As at the end of the Lord's earthly life the Jews were called upon, in a way which we must regard as providential (Matt. xxvii, 15), to choose between Him and Barabbas; so again will He be presented before the covenant peoples — the Christian nations — not indeed as personally present, that they may choose between Him and the Lawless One. The choice of the Antichrist is not to be the choice of the rulers only, or of the popular leaders, the multitude being unwilling, and silent, and passive; it is the act of the peoples, the direct or indirect expression of the popular will. It is the voluntary declaration of Christendom: "We will not have this man to rule over us." "Not this man, but Barabbas."

We may here note that a Democracy, looking upon its leader as its representative, willingly gives him a power even greater than the largest measure of his political prerogatives. The sovereign multitude, which sees in him not so much the ruler who commands them, as one who is the exponent and executor of their will, yields to him such a full and unreserved obedience as no mere despot can obtain. No Alaric or Tamerlane, at the head of his hordes, is so truly master as the recognized head of a Democracy, which sees its favourite beliefs embodied in his person; and to the power of modern discipline in its armies under his control, adds the zeal of a passionate, personal devotion. Democracy, headed up in one who can sway its forces, has such elements of aggression and strength as no form of government hitherto existing has had.*

Socialism. Of Socialism in general we have already spoken. It is rapidly becoming a powerful factor in political affairs; and we must enquire how it stands related to Democracy ? Does it follow it as a legitimate development? This may be affirmed. Democracy gives political equality, and the preservation of this demands social equality. But how can this social equality be effected? Socialism answers, by limiting the individual ownership of capital, and enlarging the ownership of the State; and to this end it demands the enlargement of governmental powers. But in this it goes directly counter to the democratic spirit, which seeks rather to curtail the sphere of legislation, and to give to individuals the largest liberty of action. It has been almost a democratic axiom that the best government is that which governs least. But experience has shown that, when full play is given to individualism, the natural inequalities of physical, mental, and moral endowments soon

---

* It is said by De Tocqueville, that "the notion of a sole and central power which governs the whole community by its direct influence, is natural to a Democracy. . . . To governments of this kind the nations of our age are tending. In Europe everything seems to conduce to the indefinite expansion of the prerogatives of government."

bring in corresponding social inequalities. Wealth is heaped up in the hands of the few; and society is soon divided into classes, the rich and the poor, employers and employed, the cultured and the non-cultured; and with little of fraternal feeling, or of real sympathy between them. The accumulation of property in large masses in the hands of the few, gives them extraordinary power, political and social. As there is no assignable limit to the combinations of capital, and no prevention of it by ordinary legislation, the result is to widen the chasm between the classes, and to consolidate social distinctions; thus producing alienation of feeling, and leading in the end to active hostilities, to strife and bloodshed; and, if not checked, to anarchy.

Thus Democracy, which naturally inclines to individualism, and to limit so far as possible the functions of government, is forced by experience into the opposite extreme. Individualism must be limited; the rulers made more powerful; and the State becomes more and more important as its province is enlarged. As the great end of government is the welfare of society — the common well-being — it must have the power to control in all matters bearing on this well-being, however much individual liberty may be restricted.

We may now see the bearing of Socialism in preparing the way of the Antichrist in two particulars: first, in its claims to establish a better social order; secondly, in the proposed enlargement of the powers of the State, as a means to this end.

As regards the first, Socialism affirms that its mission is to put an end to the contest now everywhere in Christendom active between the individual citizen and society, and to establish harmony, which simple Democracy is not able to do. It will, when fully carried out, bring in the Kingdom of God for which the world is waiting. Thus it awakens expectations of an age of prosperity and peace near at hand, and calls upon all to leave the old and go on to the new. It is obvious what a tempting opportunity this presents to a man of commanding ability, to appear as the representative of these hopes and expectations; and to gather around him, not only the discontented and restless, but many earnest and aspiring souls, that look forward to a great development of humanity. The ground is already prepared for him, the seed is sown, he has only to reap.

We thus see how, if socialistic ideas are received to any considerable extent in Christendom, awakening expectations of a new and better order, the Antichrist may find in these expectations the ready means of obtaining power, by presenting himself as the one by whom they can be realized. Weary of present ills, men are ever inclined to try new remedies. It is not necessary that all have a clear idea of the remedy which Socialism proposes, or fully accept its principles. It presents, at least, a flattering picture of the future; and as a swift stream carries with it much drift-wood, so many are swept onward by the prevalent spirit of the times.

Secondly, Socialism presents as the means of establishing a better social order, a great enlargement of the powers of the State. As it is a fundamental principle that government is to take charge of many interests now left wholly to personal control; it is plain that he who is able to put himself at the head of the State, will possess official powers far larger than any mere political ruler has ever possessed. As all interests are to be subordinated to the public good, and an equality of property and condition is to be established and enforced; there is scarcely any act of despotic authority which may not be defended upon the plea of the public well-being.

Anarchy. As Socialism would limit democratic individualism, Anarchy would make it absolute. The Anarchist would overthrow all government. It is said by Kropotkin ("The Nineteenth Century," Aug., 1887), "There may be order without government. . . . Humanity is trying to free itself from the bonds of any government whatsoever. . . . Social life needs no laws for its maintenance." His objection to Socialism is, that it accepts the principle of authority which he utterly repudiates. But it is not always easy to distinguish the most advanced Socialist from the Anarchist. They are agreed as to the overthrow of existing institutions, but not as to what shall follow. Though there may be many Anarchists here and there throughout Christendom, yet it is incredible that they can ever become in any country a political party of importance. The bearing of the anarchistic movement upon the establishment of the kingdom of the Antichrist is through fear. Though the number of avowed Anarchists will probably always be few, there are enough even at the present time to alarm all Christendom; since in their furious hate against existing institutions, and with the powerful means of destruction of both property and life which modern science gives them, they can keep cities in terror and agitate and perplex governments. The result of this must be a demand upon the State for protection, and a ready concession to it of all the powers necessary to repress their murderous attempts. Dreading Anarchy as the worst of all evils, if the existing governments show themselves incompetent, the cry will be for one whose iron hand can tame these wild beasts. And if we may suppose the Anarchists to continue to gain adherents, we may readily understand how welcome at last will be the strong man who can deliver society from its terror, and be its saviour; and what large powers will be willingly given him to this end.

The Unity or Solidarity of Nations. Let us now note the tendencies to unity which point to the possibility of a universal kingdom over which Antichrist can rule.

As peoples are brought through increasing knowledge of one another into friendly relations, and as their industrial interests are seen to be one, the feeling of unity strengthens itself. The old lines of division, geographical, racial, political, religious, are now more and more effaced. It is seen that all have, in a sense, a common life, and form an organic whole. But while this tendency to unity is increasingly manifest, there is also seen a development of national feeling which tends to self-assertion, and to isolation. According as this prevails, there will be a strong repulsive force which would make the union of all under one rule difficult, if not impossible. But if all cannot be brought under one government, there may be a federation of States, each retaining in good measure its autonomy, yet having a common centre and acting together in all matters of common interest.

The kingdom best entitled in the past to the name of universal was the Roman; the bond of its unity was law enforced by arms. But this unity was only external, political, and therefore imperfect. It was rather a conglomeration of nations than a homogeneous empire. To effect this there must be other bonds; not only those affecting material interests, but those affecting the religious faith and inner life of the people. If these be wanting, all that is possible is a federation of States; and even such a federation is possible only when there has been developed a strong feeling of universalism. This was made apparent in the days of the first Napoleon, who saw clearly that the interests of the several European States would be best promoted by the establishment of some central authority; yet preserving the individuality, and to a great degree the autonomy, of each. At the head of this union of the nations he would have placed France, and himself at the head of France. But the time was not then ripe for such a federation. The elements of repulsion were too strong, and a unity made by mere physical force was out of the question.

But the matter is assuming in our day a new aspect. A stronger bond of unity has been found in the great development of industrial relations, through the International Labour Associations now overspreading Christendom.*

* Of these a recent writer says : "The International Associations have held congresses for twenty-five years in various capitals. The emancipation of labour is not simply a local or a national problem, but interests the working classes of all so-called civilized countries. . . . The final aim of the party is the complete emancipation of all human beings without distinction of sex, race, or nationality." But late movements of the socialistic party indicate that it does not believe that a great international community can be formed in which the ties of blood and of

The wage-workmen of all Europe understand that they have certain common interests, and constitute one industrial community, although territorially and politically separated. And there is more than an economical unity. There are common beliefs respecting the reconstruction of society, and plans for effecting this, common hopes and expectations as to the future of humanity, binding all very closely together. How strong these bonds of unity will prove, how far able to overcome the ties of race, and of inherited prejudices, and of political associations, time must show. But there are signs which indicate that, through the diffusion of socialistic ideas, there is now a basis being laid underneath the present institutions of Christendom, which will be deep and broad enough to serve as a foundation for a federation of States embracing all the civilized peoples. There is the feeling that such a unity of nations is a noble ideal which we may make real, and which appeals to what is best and highest in human nature, and especially to the generous aspirations of youth.*

national feeling shall be swallowed up. Nor can there be a thorough union between artisans and agriculturists in regard to the abolition of private capital. The fusion of different races and classes can be made only by their gathering around some great leader in whom they trust, and who will adapt his policy to the necessities of the case.

*How high are the expectations of some, may be seen by some extracts from a recent popular writer (Atlantic Mag., April, 1896): "There are unmistakable tendencies to international union. . . . Few thinkers will now smile at the prediction that international war will be made impossible, or doubt the coming realization of Victor Hugo's dreams of the United States of Europe. And this would signify nothing less than the final obliteration of national frontiers, the removal of all barriers between European peoples, the ultimate fusion of Western races

The belief in the possibility of a great political union embracing all States has been expressed by many writers, but it will be sufficient to refer to the German philosopher Kant, in his essay, 1774, "The National Principle of the Political Order," and his essay, 1795, "Eternal Peace." * He lays down in them certain fundamental propositions; first, "that all the capacities implanted in a creature by nature are destined to unfold completely and conformably to their end in the course of time." We may, therefore, expect to see realized "a political constitution internally and externally perfect, as the only State in which all these capacities can be fully developed, and the destiny of man on the earth be fulfilled." As this cannot be done while States remain in conflict, they must come at last under "a universal cosmo-political constitution." This will be effected by a federation of States. But before this they must become republican,—Kant distinguishes between republicanism and democracy,—and thus there may be established a system of international right founded upon public law, conjoined with powers to which every State must submit. Thus will come "the universal, international State,"—"a great political body such as the world has never yet seen." This will be the perfect order under which all the capacities of the human race will be developed. As individual men live in unity within the State, so all the separate States may live in unity within a great universal

into one vast social organism." And more than this: "The evolutional trend would seem to be toward universal brotherhood, without distinction of country, creed, or blood."

* Werke, Leipzig, 1868, Vol. VI, p. 408. See E. D. Mead, New England Magazine, June, 1896.

State. Then war will cease, and the nations dwell together in "eternal peace".

This conception of a federative Union, which agrees so closely with that foretold in The Revelation, was not based by Kant upon any belief in a revealed purpose of God, but on the principle that what ought to be will be. Believers in evolution see this Union in the future, as is said by Mr. Mead: "The evolution through which we are passing is an evolution to a great State of nations, a complete federation of the world." All holding this position will be ready to welcome the kingdom of the Antichrist as the culmination of human history.

In speaking of this federation of peoples no mention has been made of the religious bond, which in some sense is the most powerful of all. In virtue of it the Roman Church now rules over multitudes in every part of the world. Will religion become a bond of unity in the kingdom of Antichrist? Is there any form of religion which can take the place of Christianity, and become a world-religion? This question will be considered when we come to speak of the Church of the Antichrist.

But the question will arise, whether it is possible with the present advanced intellectual development of Christendom, and its great number of able statesmen and political philosophers, that any one man can attain to such supremacy of power?

In answer to this question it is to be noted that in the lower stages of civilization, and in the highest, individual men exert the greatest influence over their fellows, and become leaders. In a well-organized society, where all is fitly framed together by joints and bands, every man is kept in his place and limited in his action; and his personality, however marked, is comparatively of little importance. The strong and the ambitious thus restrained can render to the State better service through their greater energy. But in uncivilized communities where no such restraints exist, personal qualities find their full scope, and mark out the chiefs; and if there be one superior to the rest, he becomes the all but absolute leader. The same is true also of the civilized community when it reaches its last stage — the social-democratic. When laws and institutions are no longer reverenced as having religious sanction, when through continual changes they have no root in the traditions or love of the people, when rulers by popular election prove themselves incapable, when no surety or stability of legislation exists, and all are uncertain and anxious as to the future,— then there arises a general cry for a man. In the general disintegration it is only about a man that men can rally, not about abstract principles or written constitutions. All cry for one who, with a clear brain, inflexible will, and a strong arm, can serve as a centre of unity, and bring order out of confusion.

It is at the time of the end, when all elements, good and bad, are struggling together to the death, that this cry for the man becomes loudest; for all feel what is expressed by Carlyle, that "there is no other remedy for whatsoever goes wrong. There is but one man fraught with blessings to the world, and fated to diminish and successively abolish the curses of the world. For him make search, him reverence and follow; know that to find or miss him means victory or defeat for you." And as he is to be sought for, so he is, when found, to be obeyed and worshipped.

"He is above thee, like a god. . . . He is thy born king, thy conqueror, and thy supreme lawgiver." "To the primitive man the noble human soul was Divine, demanding worship." "Human worship everywhere, so far as there lay any worth in it, was of the nature of hero-worship." "Hero-worship, heartfelt, prostrate admiration; submission, burning, boundless, for a noblest godlike form of man; is not this the germ of Christianity itself?" "Hero-worship is the summary ultimate essence and supreme perfection of all matter of worship."

This sense of the importance of the man, as emphasized by Carlyle, is wholly in accord with his pantheistic philosophy. As humanity is Divine, he in whom is its fullest measure is the Divine man, the guide, leader, and ruler of all. And as there must be somewhere in the world such a man, one above all others, unless we suppose two or more exactly equal, he is to be sought out, and exalted to his true place, and obeyed and worshipped. Before him, when he shall appear, Carlyle, and all Pantheists, must bow down, and yield him "submission, burning, boundless." He will be to them "like a god, a born king, a conqueror, and supreme lawgiver." Who does not see in the Divine man of the Pantheists all the features of the Antichrist?

But the political supremacy of the Antichrist is not to be explained by his extraordinary personality, and the tendencies of the times, alone. There is, also, an invisible Power, of whom we know only through revelation, he whom the Lord called "the prince of this world." It is as invested with his authority, and endowed by him with superhuman powers, that the Antichrist rules. We read in The

Revelation (xiii, 2) that "the dragon gave the beast his power, and his throne, and his great authority." And the apostle Paul says that the coming of the Lawless One "is according to the working of Satan with all power, and signs, and lying wonders." It was, as we have seen, in the post-apostolic age, and with the false conception of the kingdom as already set up, that the Church, although she did not deny the existence of Satan, and a measure of activity on his part, yet affirmed that he was so far bound that he could offer no effectual resistance to her work in the conversion and rule of the nations.

It need not be said that, as the prince of this world, and as playing a most important part in human history, Satan lives no longer in the faith of many. How far the belief in his existence continues in Christendom, it is not easy to say; multitudes, doubtless, reject it as an idle superstition; and all the tendencies of modern thought run in this direction.

But if the existence of Satan and his power in the earth are a reality, it is more than folly to ignore them. To those who receive the Scriptures in their obvious meaning, and the teachings of the Church, "a kingdom of darkness," of which he is the head, is a reality. There are invisible powers who set themselves against God in all He would do for men; and who have control over men in proportion as they voluntarily yield themselves to their temptations. Against them mere unbelief is no safeguard; an incredulous and scoffing age is most easily befooled.

The Lord was tempted by the proffer of "all the kingdoms of the world" if He would pay homage to the tempter, and He refused with abhorrence. But Satan finds at last one who will willingly accept what he would give, and to whom he can transfer his throne and great authority. Many of the Christian fathers depicted this man as a monster, repellant in person, and stained with every vice. But we have seen ground to believe that the world will see in him one who represents in fullest measure its conception of human perfectibility; one worthy to be the leader of men, and their ruler.

By what successive steps Antichrist will attain to supreme power, it is not for us to say. But it is obvious that, as the son of his time, he must represent its beliefs, its needs, its aspirations. There must be a community of feeling between him and those who first gather around him. If the antichristian spirit is already widely prevalent, he will at once find many who will be his helpers and instruments in his further plans. Later, he may use force, as did Mohammed, and destroy all who will not submit to him. But it is contrary to the light which Revelation gives us, to suppose that his career is one of uninterrupted success. On the contrary, we seem to be taught that he early receives a check through the testimony of men inspired of God, symbolized by the "Two Witnesses" (xi, 8), who make known to the Church his true character and aims, and thus recall to their Christian faith many who had been deceived by him. At this time he is said in symbolic language to go down into the abyss, his power for a time obscured, and the nations bewildered in dark forebodings. But from this he soon emerges, full of satanic energy; and now crushes all opposition, and puts himself at the head of the nations.

In this rise of the Antichrist into power the world at large will, we may believe, see nothing supernatural, nothing wholly new to human experience. History records many instances of men, who, appearing as the representatives of new beliefs, new principles, new institutions, have overthrown the old, and attained dominion. What is necessary is that the old should have lost its hold upon many minds as outworn, and that the new seems better fitted to their needs. To this must be added the gift of leadership, the faculty of command. We might take from history many illustrations. The diffusion of Christianity through the Roman Empire, and the decadence of Paganism, gave to Constantine the opportunity of appearing as the champion of the new faith, and thus to attain to supreme power. Substantially the same conditions reappear to-day. The old Christian faith is struggling with infidelity in its many forms. Not a few are asking for a new religion. There is everywhere political discontent, social agitation; the peoples are saying: "We are weary of the old, it has disappointed us, it cannot save us, let us try the new." It needs only another Constantine; and a new order, political, social, religious, now rises upon the ruins of the old.

It is thus very possible that Christendom may see in the growing political ascendency of the Antichrist nothing that shows the hand of God in judgment, or any power of Satan; only the supremacy of the boldest, and strongest, and wisest. Those alone who believe the revealed word, and seek in the light of the Spirit to discern the signs of the times, will see that he is the predicted one to whom Satan gives his throne, and whom God uses as His rod to punish His disobedient people; others will see in his rule over the nations no more than their voluntary acceptance of him on the ground of his greater ability to further the general well-being. Not till the last stage of his career will his satanic character be fully revealed, and the Christians who have followed him turn back to their true Lord.

The duration of the rule of the Antichrist is brief. If the numbers, "forty and two months," "twelve hundred and sixty days," and "time, times, and half a time," or "three years and a half," are to be taken literally, we may conclude that his ascendency will be for a period of seven years — the first half spent in attaining power, the last in its despotic and bloody exercise. This is the judgment of many commentators, but no undue stress is to be laid upon such chronological conclusions.

As regards the extent of this kingdom, recent events which have brought China and Japan and other countries of the East into close relations with the Christian Powers, may have important bearings. The same may be said of the late division of much of Africa among the same Powers. Should there be a federation of the States of Christendom, its authority would extend over most of Asia and Africa; and through the present means of intercommunication this might be easily exercised and enforced.

Another marked feature of the present time is the revival of the Turkish Empire from its state of weakness and decay; and the growing zeal of Mohammedanism to extend itself among the Oriental peoples and African tribes. What the future relations of Mohammedanism to Christianity may be, it is not for us to foretell, but the present indications are that they will be those of bitter hostility.

Considering the movements and tendencies of the

time, democratic, socialistic, anarchistic, cosmopolitical, we find no difficulty in understanding how there may be a federation of States under one head, realizing the prediction in The Revelation of the union of the Ten Kings and the Beast. That these Kings act together in their persecution of the apostate Church, and " give their Kingdom unto the Beast, till the words of God shall be fulfilled," is expressly ascribed to His own action upon them: " For God hath put in their hearts to fulfil His will." (Rev. xvii, 16, 17.)

We may see in this union of the rulers of Christendom against Christ, the final fulfilment of the predictions of the second Psalm. " Why do the nations rage (tumultuously assemble), and the peoples imagine a vain thing; the kings of the earth set themselves, and the rulers take counsel together against the Lord and against His Anointed, saying, Let us break their bands asunder, and cast away their cords from us." R. V.

It is not a rebellion of the kings and rulers only against God and His Anointed King, but of the nations and peoples of Christendom. No longer will they be in subjection to any Divine rule. All laws and ordinances having Christ's name will they cast away. And the ground of this general rebellion is the deep hatred of the doctrine of human sinfulness, of which the cross is the symbol. This hatred becomes more and more intense as humanity seems to be ascending higher and higher in knowledge and power and goodness, and indefinite progress is open before it. The boasting of its great representative meets on all sides a welcome response: " I will ascend into heaven; I will exalt my throne above the stars of God. . . . I will ascend above the heights of the clouds; I will be like the Most High." (Isa. xiv,

13, 14.) But "He that sitteth in the heavens shall laugh; the Lord shall have them in derision." His King is the lowly One who humbled Himself, becoming obedient even unto the death of the cross; and now exalted to the Father's right hand, is the King of kings and Lord of lords; before whom every knee shall bow, in heaven and on earth and under the earth.

Of the political relations of the Antichrist to the Jewish people, little can be definitely said. In considering our Lord's teachings (page 18), we saw that He spoke of one who should come in his own name, whom the Jews would receive. This one is generally understood by commentators to be the Antichrist. But to what extent he will be received and worshipped by the Jews, and whether he will gather them again to their own land, are questions we cannot answer.

NOTE.— Some very recent remarks of Lord Salisbury (Mansion House Speech, Nov. 9, 1897) shew, in a striking way, how the nations are unconsciously co-operating with God in the fulfilment of His purpose. "The consent of Europe, or, as I prefer to call it, the inchoate federation of Europe, is a body which acts only when it is unanimous. But the difficulty of preserving unanimity is often great. . . . Remember that the federation of Europe is the embryo of the only possible structure of Europe which can save civilization from the desolating effects of a disastrous war. . . . The one hope we have to prevent this competition of the nations from ending in a terrible effort of mutual destruction, which will be fatal to Christian civilization — the one hope we have is, that the Powers may gradually be brought together in a friendly spirit on all questions of difference which may arise, until at last, they may be welded in some international constitution or federation which will give to the world, as a result of their great strength, a long spell of unfettered and prosperous trade and continued peace."

THE MORALITY OF THE FUTURE.

Morality has in the past been chiefly based upon the positive precepts of religion. This was the case with the earlier moral systems of antiquity. But, as the old religions lost their hold on men, a new foundation was sought for morality. This is seen in the case of the later Stoics, who presented a moral code quite independent of religion. The morality of Christendom is essentially Christian, based upon the positive commands of God, and of Christ and His Apostles. It is remarked by Prof. Jowett, that "of morality, as distinguished from religion, there is scarcely a trace in St. Paul's Epistles."

But, if our age is showing a disposition to put away Christianity as an authoritative revelation of the Divine will, and even to deny a personal God, can it retain Christian morality? Some seem to believe this, but the logical conclusion is that we must find some other basis for it, and this many are attempting to do. A supreme moral Lawgiver, they say, is not needed. If, as affirmed by J. S. Mill and M. Arnold, we can have religion without a personal God, why not also morality? Without believing in His existence, we may find right rules for human conduct. There is a natural as distinguished from a revealed morality, and this is all-sufficient for our guidance. We may give up Christianity and its code of morals, and yet find in Nature and experience definite rules for our moral action.

We meet here a matter of confessedly highest importance. Even those who say that society can exist and flourish without religion, admit that morality is indispensable. Upon what basis, then, shall it rest? A recent writer says (*Andover Review*, March, 1893) that "the theory of morals is undergoing a process of radical reconstruction. . . . We have come to a momentous crisis in the conception and treatment of morals. The old foundations of morality are gravely suspected, and the living generations are much at sea as to what are the proper principles." "If the great laws of morality are to retain their hold upon modern men, they must be put, like all other laws, upon a scientific basis." If this crisis is come,— and it finds confirmation on every hand,— we may well ask of those who deny a personal God and moral Lawgiver, What are the moral rules which they will substitute for the Christian code? Upon what basis will they rest, and what force will impel men to keep them?

Christian morality rests upon the facts of God's personality, and of the personality of man, and of rules of moral conduct made known by God for man's guidance. We are not concerned to ask how far under non-Christian religions a wholesome morality may exist; but what shall take the place of Christian morality in Christendom, if the fundamental facts on which it rests are rejected?

The first question which meets us is the relation of man to the two great realities of Nature and God, as now presented to us by modern science and philosophy. The position given him by Christianity in regard to both is one which permits freedom of moral action, though not one of absolute independence. As the creature of God, who has made him what he is, he must be dependent upon his Creator; but the relation is that of a person to a person. Christianity affirms the personality both of God and of man; and, therefore, man's life is a moral life which demands as its condition selfhood and self-activity.

In regard to Nature, also, his position is not one of absolute independence. He exists as a part of a great universe; but not in such dependence upon it, or so controlled by it, that he cannot act freely as a moral being.

If we now put aside Christianity with its teachings of God as personal and as the Creator, and of man's relations to Him and to Nature, can we give to man a place compatible with his moral freedom? Let us consider him, first, as a part of Nature, and ask in what sense he is a part, and whether Nature can teach him any code of morals.

I. Man as a part of Nature. That he is in some sense a part of it, no one can deny. He is a small item in the great totality of things. Is he so far under natural law that he is physically, intellectually, and morally, what the cosmic forces make him to be? And can we, from the study of these forces, find in Nature a Moral Order?

1. Atheistic Materialism. It scarcely need be said that this brings man wholly under material law, and denies a moral order. It can make no distinction between matter and spirit, for man in his whole being is the product of material forces, and his life can have in it no moral element.

2. The Evolutionary Theory of Morals. As evolution is now claimed to be "a great scientific

method, transforming every department of thought," its bearing upon man's relations to Nature must be noticed. It asserts that it can explain how man, from his state of animality, has become a rational and moral being; and that it can give, as the evolutionary process goes on, a higher and higher moral code. Let us then ask, What does evolution teach us as to the relations of man to Nature, and the existence of a moral order? Can we learn from it rules by which to regulate our lives?

It is here that the natural moralists disagree. As evolution can only justify its claims to explain the way in which the universe, including all moral relations, has become what it is, by shewing how morality has originated, many have undertaken the task. Let us, then, briefly consider the evolutionary theory of morals.

This theory is stated by Mr. Darwin in the plainest and briefest way.* According to him, morality has its root in the social instincts; and "any animal having these instincts, and with sufficiently developed intellectual power, will inevitably acquire a moral sense or conscience." The social instincts become stronger with time, and seek to be gratified because of their utility in the struggle for existence. As social, the animal soon learns to regard the plainer distinctions of property and right; and, as he rises in the scale of being and is humanized, he begins to regard the interests of others as well as his own. As his intellectual powers develope, so also his moral

* With the modifications of this theory by H. Spencer, "Data of Ethics," and L. Stephen, "Science of Ethics," we are not here concerned. For a statement of them, see the Essay by Prof. J. Seth, "The Evolution of Morality."

sense. The feeling of duty is begotten in him, and its voice becomes imperative. Thus, there is evolved a moral being. And, as he developes a higher and higher type of morality, all egoism or selfishness will at last die out. The interests of the individual and of the community will perfectly harmonize, for he will be perfectly adjusted to his environment. Then will there be no sense of duty, for the man will not be inclined to do anything which does not tend to the common welfare. Self-sacrifice, if this term may be here used, will be as easy as any natural action; all duty will be spontaneous and pleasurable. Thus evolution will, in the end, enable men to fulfil the apostle's injunction, "Let no man seek his own, but every man another's wealth."

Such is the theory which evolution presents to us of the genesis, the development, and the consummation of morality. We deal with morals as a branch of natural history. The ethical is the necessary outgrowth of the cosmical. Man, as he progresses up from his animal beginnings, will inevitably become a moral being. Under the action of the cosmic forces the moral nature is evolved and reaches its perfection.

But there are other evolutionists who do not recognize any moral purpose in Nature, and deny that the cosmic forces and the ethic are to be identified. We are told by Prof. Huxley ("Evolution and Ethics") that we "do not find in Nature any moral purpose. To morality Nature is indifferent; it is neither moral nor immoral, but non-moral. We see the absence of any relation between suffering and moral desert." Prof. Huxley sees two processes going on, the cosmic and the ethic. The first is not governed by moral ends, it evolves both good and evil; the second is in contradiction to the first, and looks to moral ends, and cannot be evolved from it. In the cosmic process, it is the best man, physically and intellectually, who survives; in the ethic, it is the best, morally. Thus, there is a continual struggle between the two, and one which must ever continue. "Ethical nature may count upon having to reckon with a tenacious and powerful enemy so long as the world lasts."

Thus here, according to Prof. Huxley, we have a dualism. Humanity is presented as a little independent cosmos within the greater cosmos, and ruled only by its own inner forces. Evolution is no longer a continuous process, supreme in all the realms of Nature; for man, who is its product, can, as ethical, assert his independence of its forces. He can defy, and in some degree set aside its laws. Non-moral and unconscious Nature has, in some incomprehensible way, produced the moral and conscious man. But he has no permanent place in the universe. His civilization and his morality are "artificial products," and must speedily pass away. God being put aside as non-existent, there are no duties to Him, only duties to man.

In the evolutionary theory of Ethics what is the ethical end? I must do right; but what is right? This, we are told, is the social good, or the general welfare; or in a larger sense, the improvement of the race. Here, then, we find our moral criterion. That is right which tends to benefit society; that is wrong which tends to its injury. But as we do not know intuitively what is for its benefit or injury, how shall we attain to this knowledge? It can be attained to only through experience. "The Moral Code," says Mr. Leslie Stephen, "is the result of practical experience." It is in this way that we must find out the laws which should rule our moral life. We are to note whatever experience has shown to be useful to society or the race, and to regard this as morally right, and all that is injurious as morally wrong. This is to base our morality upon the principle of utility — the public good.

But how are we to determine what is for the public good? The individual citizen cannot determine it for himself; it must, therefore, be determined by the State, or by society in its collective capacity. Whatever the State affirms to be for the general good, becomes obligatory upon its individual members. The moral code will, therefore, be whatever the State determines it to be. But how shall the State know what will be useful? Only by experience, and this must be the rule of its action. But experience is of the past. If that which has been tried and proved has not been satisfactory, and there is general discontent with the present, on what ground can the adoption of the new and untried rest? It is upon the belief that it will promote the social welfare. Thus the door is opened to legislative experiments of all kinds. The laws undergo continual changes, and thus lose their authority; and as they are the measure of morality, society plunges into a moral chaos. All is confusion; no one knows what is right or what is wrong. As of old in Israel when there was no king, there is no moral code recognized as authoritative by all, and "every man does what is right in his own eyes."

II. Man as a part of God. In what sense is he a part, and what shall we say of his moral code?

We have already seen the Pantheist's view of man's

relation to God. Denying the personality of God, he denies the personality of man, and with this all true moral action. He is so a part of God that he has no independent self-hood, and cannot oppose his will to that of God.

What is the ethical end? Not the development of society, but of the individual, his capabilities. Look within, not without. And this self-development must be the criterion of moral action. The Pantheist does not wholly deny that he is affected morally by the social influences around him, but he carries the standard of right and wrong in his own bosom. As expressed by one: "The only right is what is after my constitution; the only wrong, what is against it." The interests of society hold a subordinate place. What is useful to myself is good and right; what is injurious is evil and wrong. Having the voice of God within, — his "categorical imperative," — no authority can impose upon him a code of morals. Yet, as there cannot be a multitude of sovereign wills, there must be some moral arbiter. This the Pantheist finds in the State. The State, according to Hegel, is to be regarded as the highest manifestation of moral reason, and therefore the individual must conform to its decision his personal and private ends. "The State is Divine will." And others of the school speak in the same way. It is said by them, a man's first duty is the State; genuine morality is life in the State. A man cannot serve both the State and Heaven. It is the moral will as presented in the laws, customs, and institutions of a country, which is to be regarded as the supreme law of human conduct.

The morality of the future, so far as it ceases to rest on the religious elements now underlying it, must be built on Naturalism or on Pantheism. Each will have something peculiar to itself, but both have this formula in common: "Live according to nature," — meaning in the one case, learn the laws of the material world and live according to them; and in the other, know yourself as Divine, and live accordingly. Let us note in what these two moral systems, Naturalistic and Pantheistic, agree.

First, in denying to man free-will. In respect to moral freedom, it makes little difference whether man be regarded as a part of Nature or of God. If there is an impersonal Power, or Force, or Energy, which fashions and rules the universe, and which covers and controls all man's life, conscious and unconscious, it is of no importance what name we use, whether we say God, or It. If man is a part of Nature in the evolutionary sense, he is under the law of its movements, and is at any given time what it makes him to be. Unless he has a life of his own, and a self-determined activity, he can act only as he is acted upon by external forces. This is affirmed by Mr. H. Spencer. "Psychical changes either conform to law, [as he affirms,] or they do not; if they do, there cannot be any such thing as free-will." It is said by Mr. Balfour ("The Foundations of Belief"): "On the Naturalistic view, free-will is an absurdity." It is true that all men think themselves to act freely, but this is a mere delusion according to the natural moralists, of whose origin they can give no satisfactory account.*

* We are aware that not a few moralists deny that the freedom of the will really concerns ethics. It is no place here to enter into any discussion of the principles of the Determinists. The force of their reasoning seems to depend upon their definition of terms — such as Freedom, Necessity, Compulsion, Uniformity

As Naturalism, so Pantheism in all its forms, must deny man's moral freedom. God immanent in man is the real agent, the efficient cause of human action. It is said by Jouffroy ("Introduction to Ethics"): "Deprived of all proper causality, man is deprived at the same time of all liberty; and consequently can have neither a law of obligation, nor a controlling power over his own conduct." Whether we speak of "The Substance" of Spinoza, or "The Absolute" of the Hegelian school, or "The Cosmic Consciousness," we reach the same result; we have no real freedom, and a moral life is impossible. As said by Prof. James Seth: "If I am but a vehicle of the Divine self-manifestation, if in myself, in my own proper self-hood or personality, I am nothing, it is all illusory to talk of my freedom."

Secondly. The code of morals must be determined by the State. If the ethical end is the welfare of a community, this can be determined only by the State, and this on the ground of experience. If the ethical end is self-development, this is dependent upon a man's social relations,—to the family, to society, and to the State,—all of which are expressions of the Divine will, but the last in highest measure. Thus both moral systems agree in making the State the supreme moral arbiter.

Thirdly. Neither Naturalism nor Pantheism can give a permanent standard of morality. There are no fixed and unchangeable formulas in Ethics. We cannot, consistently with Evolution, speak of absolute right or wrong, good or evil. All is relative. The moral rules governing life must be correspondent to that stage of adjustment with his environment which a man has reached. Egoism, selfishness, is a virtue in a savage. It is only as the cosmic process advances that the ethic process can advance. A code of morals, therefore, must always be judged of by its suitableness to external conditions. Conduct which is right and good in one stage of adjustment, may be wrong and evil in another. Perfect morality is only reached when there is a perfect adjustment, and then, as we are told, the practice of morality will be as natural and spontaneous as to breathe. All sense of duty, or of obligation, will disappear at the completion of the evolutionary process.

This examination of the code of morals given us by Naturalism and Pantheism shows us: *a*, that it leaves no place for man's free-will; *b*, that it is ever changing; *c*, that it must be determined at any given time by the State upon the basis of experience; *d*, that in the last result it will be determined by every man for himself.

III. Let us now briefly contrast this morality of the future, Naturalistic and Pantheistic, with Christian morality. In this last we find three elements: *a*, a personal God, whose will is known, and is a law of human conduct; *b*, a sinful humanity, which, left to itself, rejects the moral restraints of the Divine law; *c*, a future life with its reward or punishment. None of these elements can find place in the scientific moral code of the future.

a. If there be no personal God, and no revelation of His will as a rule of human action, there is nothing to control this action but the physical forces around him. These do not act under the control of a personal Will, and to moral ends; it is mere assumption to speak of " a Moral Order " in the universe, or of " a Power that makes for righteousness." Man obeys these forces because he must, but in this obedience there is no moral element. Nature makes no distinction between good and evil, right and wrong, and we cannot say of any act that it is in itself immoral. The man, therefore, who follows Nature, may claim its authority for all kinds of conduct.

Putting aside all positive precepts of God as to human conduct, and having only the light of Nature as our guide, many practical questions of highest importance meet us. Let us take as an example the relations of the sexes. Why monogamy? Why not polygamy? There is no moral distinction to be taken. Either is good if demanded by the social welfare. What of the indissolubility of the marriage relation? Why shall not the marriage contract be dissoluble at the pleasure of the contracting parties? It is a question of social expediency only. Why should marriage be allowed to the diseased and deformed,—thus perpetuating sickly and abnormal types? Why should children, feeble and unhealthy, be so tenderly cared for and reared to be a burden and expense to society? If, as Darwin and Spencer tell us, the ethical end is "the rearing of the greatest number of individuals in full vigour and health," or "the improvement of the race," why make provision for and preserve in life the most imperfect types? And why build hospitals and homes for the old, the helpless, the incurable? To sacrifice the ethical end, the improvement of the race, to the feeling of personal affection, is not morality, it is sentiment.*

---

* It is suggested by Morison ("Science of Man") that "all habitual criminals be imprisoned for life, not as a punishment, but to prevent them from multiplying their kind." Other

As in the family relations, so is it in the relations of men to the State and its laws. Why is it immoral to disobey a law whose general utility is not self-evident? Why is it immoral to take from one who has a super-abundance, even if it be done by stealth or violence, and give to another who has nothing? Why in the State has not the woman the same right of suffrage as the man, and equal participation in all political offices? And if in the State, why not in the Church? It is a question of expediency alone, and this only trial and experience can decide.

b. A sinful humanity. Christian morality, recognizing man as having a fallen and sinful nature, easily tempted and led astray to evil, commands a strict control over it, and the subjection of its passions and appetites to the Divine law. But this sinfulness Naturalism denies. The natural moralist asks: "Where do I learn from Nature to repress any natural appetite or desire as in itself immoral? Nature says, gratify rather than repress. As the end of society is the good of the individual members, each, following nature, is to seek his own. Christianity, with its dualism of flesh and spirit, and its demand for the crucifixion of the flesh, is mere asceticism — a remnant of the primitive belief that God demanded human sacrifices. The cross as a symbol of human life must be put away." As said by one of this school,

writers of this school make it an objection to the Christian God that He is a God who forgives sins and is merciful, and prefer a natural law which is inexorable and makes no discriminations. This indifference to moral character marks in their eyes the perfection of righteousness, something better and nobler than Christianity can give.

"We are to put the ethics of self-development in place of the ethics of self-mortification."*

The Pantheist, who affirms that his humanity is a Divine humanity, can find no sinfulness in it, only ignorance and imperfection. Here, too, should be development, not repression. We are to act out what is within us, and accept no laws as binding on us that are not agreeable to our moral nature. We are told that we shall thus come to a morality far higher than any which Christianity can give us. It is said by Symonds ("Greek Poets"), who contrasts Greek morality with Christian, that the former rested on a belief in the moral order of the universe, and that this is better than that "which imposes upon us the will of a hypothetical ruler — our own creature — thus enslaving ourselves to our own delusions."

c. Immortality. Neither Naturalism nor Pantheism can make any positive affirmation of a life after death; and the logical tendency of both is to deny it. Some evolutionists put it wholly aside, as lying out of the range of scientific discussion; others affirm it on the ground that man is the end and crown of the evolutionary process. We are told by Mr. John Fiske, that "the psychical development of man is destined to go on in the future as in the past"; and

---

* A writer of great popularity, Prof. Renan, speaking of chastity says: "Later I saw well the vanity of this virtue, as of all the rest; I recognized that Nature cares not at all whether man is chaste or not. . . . I cannot rid myself of the idea that after all it is perhaps the libertine who is right, and who practices the true philosophy of life." A living novelist of wide reputation in a very recent book affirms that his heroine, in breaking the law of chastity broke an accepted social law, but not a law of Nature, and need not sorrow over her offense. (See Prof. A. Seth in Blackwood's Mag., May, 1893.)

by the Rev. N. Smythe, that "death is a necessary step in evolution"; and by Prof. Le Conte, that "without immortality the whole cosmic process is futile." But other evolutionists, like Darwin, see no proof that evolution gives any promise of a future life for the individual man; the race may make progress for an indefinite period, but the individual ceases to be. As a part of nature, the personal life is merely a passing incident in the endless evolution.

The position of the Pantheist Spinoza in regard to immortality was negative, and that of Hegel and of the modern Pantheists is in substance the same. Of the more recent writers, it is said by Mr. Bradley ("Appearance and Reality"), that "a personal continuance is possible, but it is little more." By many of the socialists immortality is most energetically denied.

What are the moral bearings of this disbelief in a future life? It is obvious that it must be to make the present life of supreme interest. This, with the better-constituted mind, may lead one to labour with greater diligence for the good of others. But upon minds narrow and selfish and sensual the effect must be to intensify the natural impulse to make the most of the present by full indulgence in all such pleasures as attract them. They will say: "Let us eat and drink, for to-morrow we die." As there is no life of blessedness hereafter, all must find their enjoyment in the present. Why then endure patiently the evils which bad government and an unrighteous social order bring, — the poverty and misery consequent upon them? Let the oppressed rise up against the oppressors; let the poor make the rich to divide their wealth; in fine, let all who feel that they are not having their part of the good things of life, take them, — by legislation if possible, or if necessary by violence. As there is no punishment hereafter, the fear of present punishment is the only restraint upon the fierce passions and raging lusts; and this fear diminishes as the number of the lawless increases, and the execution of the law becomes feeble and partial.

As the great part of our present social order rests upon the precepts and principles given in the Scriptures, their rejection would throw society into endless confusion. We may take as an illustration the subordination of woman to man. This is put by the Apostle (1 Cor. xi, 3) on the ground that there is a law of headship embracing Christ Himself. "The head of the woman is the man; the head of the man is Christ; and the head of Christ is God." As her head, the wife is to be subject to her husband. But we hear many voices, and among the loudest the voices of women, crying out against this subjection as arbitrary and oppressive. The two sexes should be put, so far as laws and institutions go, upon a footing of absolute equality.*

---

*It was said by Theodore Parker: "In all forms of religion the degradation of woman is obvious; it is terribly apparent in the Christian Church. . . . The Absolute Religion will give woman her true place." But experience has shown that the personal characteristics which fit woman for the place assigned her by God, and which make her a blessing to all when abiding in it, become potent elements of evil when perverted from their true ends. We have only to recall the women of the French Revolution, and of the late Commune, to see that none are so easily inflamed, so intemperate in their anger, so cruel in their enmity.

It will be noted that in the general religious ferment of the day, we find women most eager to pry into the mysteries of the unseen world. They, much more than men, have been ready to

So marked and general is the movement against the Christian doctrine of marriage, that it has been called by some, "the great revolt of women"; by others, "emancipation of women"; but all, whether supporting or opposing it, agree that it is most significant. Its friends affirm it to be the beginning of a new era in the world's history, when all the capabilities of woman will have full scope, and she will play a far more important part in the development of humanity than she has done in the past. But marriage must renounce any religious sanction, and be secularized. Perhaps we may yet see such an aversion to marriage as was seen among both the Greeks and Romans at the last stages of their civilizations. Even now, what has been called "experimental marriage" seems to be coming into favour.

If there be no immutable principles of morality, nothing is criminal but what the State declares to be criminal; or, in other words, only acts which are punishable by law.

It becomes, then, simply a question for the citizen whether he will obey the law, or disobey it and take the risk of punishment. It is evident that when this is the case, all proper moral restraints cease to have

---

accept spiritism, and to become mediums; to dabble in Theosophy; to fall into the delusions of Christian Science and Mental Healing, and become practitioners. All the realm of the occult has for them a special fascination.

It may be mentioned as one of the signs of the times, that a revision of the Bible by some women is now in progress in New York, in order to show that the present translation "destroys woman's self-respect, and makes her the slave of man." "The first step in the elevation of woman to her true position in the scale of being, is the recognition by the rising generation of a heavenly Mother, to whom their prayers should be addressed as well as to the heavenly Father."

power in a community; and all security of property and life is at an end. A condition of society will arise in which the Scripture predictions may be literally fulfilled: "The hand of every man shall be against his neighbour. The people shall be oppressed, every one by another." Respect for age and class and office vanish. "The child shall behave himself proudly against the ancient, and the base against the honourable."

It is readily seen that if it is given to the State to define in laws what is moral and immoral, right and wrong, just and unjust, its power over its citizens is supreme. If the foundations of Christian morality are undermined, and no other code of morals can be presented before man than those which Naturalism or Pantheism presents, the civil ruler has society absolutely under his control. It is his will which determines what the moral character of all human relations shall be, and can make virtue vice, or vice virtue. This is the condition of morals under the Antichrist. But the process of decay begins earlier, with casting off the laws of God and denying their authority. Domestic morality — including the relations of husband and wife, parents and children, brothers and sisters, masters and servants,*— is the first to be attacked. We see Christendom filled with unions and associations of all kinds, with their self-constituted and often tyrannous leaders, bound together to further their own special interests rather than the public good. The chasm between the several classes, and especially between the rich and the poor, widens; and a bitterness of feeling is engendered, which leads more and more to acts of violence and blood. Society

* See F. D. Maurice, "Social Morality."

perishes by the murderous hands of its own members, arrayed one against another.

As regards the moral relations of nations to one another, while much is said of peaceful arbitration, the real reliance is upon the strength of armies and navies. Considerations of right and wrong seem to be less and less powerful. Each at last consults only its own interests. Acknowledging in general terms the principles of international right, the Christian nations fight for territorial enlargement and commercial supremacy, and pay little regard to the rights of the less civilized peoples. Force is the supreme arbiter, and it is forgotten that there is a God of nations, who is a God of justice. In this condition of selfish isolation, each seeking its own, they easily are made subject to the Lawless One, who is able to bind them into unity and make his will the supreme rule of action.

Thus we may understand how the kingdom of the Antichrist may be full of moral disorder, and yet a strict political order be maintained. Like the leprous house which God would not endure in His land, and must be pulled down, and the stones and the timbers and the mortar be carried away (Lev. xiv, 45); so is it with his kingdom penetrated with the leprosy of immorality,— it must be broken in pieces, and be found no more, that the kingdom of righteousness may be established upon its ruins.

THE CHURCH OF THE FUTURE.

This phrase, the Church of the Future, has become quite common, and indicates that many, dissatisfied with the present condition of the Church, are looking forward to some reconstruction of it better adapting it to our own times. Probably no one of the existing Protestant bodies thinks that with its present organization and beliefs, it will become this Church; though some of the Methodists have occasionally intimated it of Methodism. That some common basis of doctrine and of action may ultimately be found on which all Protestants can stand, is, doubtless, the hope of many in the Anglican Communion; and there are those of High Church proclivities who are confident that, at some time, the Bishop of Rome will consent to give up his imperial claim, and to be recognized as only the first among the bishops. But the Roman Church is not likely to give up its pretensions; and as it has been the dominant religious body of the past, will assuredly strive to be such in the future; and, perhaps, believes that it will at last absorb into itself both the Greek and Protestant Communions, and become the one universal Church. What light the Scriptures cast upon these various expectations, will be later considered; at present let us note the several tendencies now active which point to a Church radically unlike the Christian Church, both as to doctrine and worship. The mediating Church of the Christian Socialists will also be considered later.

But before we proceed to enumerate these tendencies, we may ask whether we can speak of a Church founded on Agnosticism, or on the doctrine of the unknowability of God as it is affirmed in the evolutionary philosophy. Mr. H. Spencer, its chief representative, speaks of a religion and worship, and seems to look upon a Church of the Unknowable as one that lies in the future.

"The true religion," according to this philosophy, " is the consciousness that it is alike our highest wisdom, and our highest duty, to regard that through which all things exist, as the Unknowable." How, then, we ask, can it be the object of our worship? We cannot have any communion with it, we cannot pray to it, or have any feeling of affection or gratitude toward it; it teaches no duties, it gives us no help in the conduct of our lives. We have only "the one absolute certainty that we are ever in the presence of an infinite and eternal Energy from which all things proceed." But it is an Energy without feeling, working unconsciously and unintelligently in the universe. All is negative. To affirm any positive predicate is to know the Unknowable. As no creed can be made up of negations, nor men be united in worshipping congregations unless they have in common some positive religious belief, we ask, What is the element here that can serve as the foundation of any worship?

We are told by Mr. Spencer that this element is "the consciousness of a Mystery that cannot be fathomed, and of a Power that is omnipresent." But this consciousness can inspire no feeling of worship. The living God is in His essence a mystery, but we can know Him in His attributes. A fathomless mystery is a black abyss. As we look into it, we have not so much sentiments of wonder and awe, as an ever deepening feeling of terror and despair. We may, then, dismiss the Church of the Unknowable from our consideration, as one not likely to have any existence, at least as an organized body, in the future. Of those that aspire to be the Church of the Future, we may mention:

1. A Church based upon Natural Religion. It is said by its advocates that "whoever feels himself in the presence of a power immeasurably above himself, does truly believe in a God, and can truly worship Him. In Nature such a power is manifested, and it is unimportant whether men say God or Nature. We cannot love such a power in the highest sense of the term, as when we love a person, but we can find pleasure in the regularity and unity of its manifestations."

We may here, it is said, find a common ground where the worshippers of a God above Nature, and the worshippers of a God in Nature, may unite. Both believe that God is revealed in Nature, and therefore, if all worship of Him outside of Nature should cease, still all who see Him revealed in Nature can continue to worship Him. "The knowledge of Nature's laws and principles," we are told by the author of Ecce Homo, "is in the strictest sense theology." The relation in which the Church of Natural Religion stands to Christianity and its Church, is thus expressed: "We discard all distinctions between natural and revealed religion. Christianity is only one of the religions of the world; what is peculiar to it is not universal, what is universal is not peculiar. All the Messianic expectations,— expectations of Christ's return and judgment,— are not elements of a universal religion."

The Church of Natural Religion will have rites of worship, worship being defined as "habitual and permanent admiration;" and this worship will have elements not included in Christianity, and will assert the religious dignity of Art and Science, of Beauty and Truth. Its sphere will be larger than that of Christian worship, since Christianity exalts only goodness, and will embrace all that comes under the word Culture. Natural worship is the worship of whatever in the universe is worthy. Here, then, as we are told, is a broad basis on which all can stand who see in Nature a Divine power, and on this we may rear a universal Church.

It will at once be seen that as Nature does not teach us of any Incarnation and Atonement, the Incarnate Son and His work in man's salvation disappear. Those who believe in Him and approach God in His name as the One Mediator, and those who know Him not, can worship God with equal acceptance.

2. A Church of Humanity. This, accepting the agnostic principle of the unknowability of God, who cannot, therefore, be the object of our worship, finds such an object in Humanity; not human nature as seen in any particular individual, but in its totality, the sum of all the forces of individual men and women. To the objection, that this is by no means a perfect and a worthy object of worship, one of its chief advocates, F. Harrison, replies: "I am no optimist, I certainly see no godhead in the human race. . . . But this planet, and, so far as we know, this Universe, has nothing which is more worthy and

more inspiring of hope. . Divinities and absolute goodnesses, absolute powers, have ended for us." This writer accepts man as coming from the apes, and thinks him the more worthy of worship that he has climbed up so high.

Here, in a still higher degree than in the Church of Natural Religion, we may have worship without a God; His existence is not necessary to religion. If He exists, we know Him not. The highest of beings known to us is man; to Humanity, therefore, let our homage be paid, our prayers be addressed.*

Thus far, the Church of Humanity has found few votaries, and there is little probability of any considerable increase. Neither in its doctrine or polity or worship, does it meet the needs of the human intellect or heart.

3. A Church of pure Theism. This form of Unitarianism affirms its faith in one God, the Father, but wholly rejects Jesus Christ as an authoritative moral Teacher, and our Lord and future Judge. Of this Church, Theodore Parker and Miss Frances Cobbe may be taken as representatives. "The degree," says Miss Cobbe, "to which Christ has been allowed to supersede the Father in the heart of Christendom, is a very sad chapter in the history of religion." Jesus has, indeed, played a most important part in religious

* A few words from a prayer actually offered in one of the religious assemblies of this cult, will best illustrate the character of the worship: "We praise thee, Humanity, as for all thy servants, so especially for August Comte. Thou Queen of our devotion, lady of our loving service, the one shelter for all the families of mankind, the one foundation of a truly Catholic Church, to thee be all honour and glory." The benediction is given in the name of Humanity. This is the worship which Positivism would substitute for the worship of the living God.

history, and may be called "the Regenerator of humanity," but still we have very little knowledge of Him. The question, Who was He? still remains unanswered, and any definite answer is far in the future. "Who shall say how real is the ideal Christ?" The Father must now be restored to His true place. All distinctively Christian doctrine must be put away — the Incarnation, the Atonement, the Priesthood and Kingdom of Christ. The old Trinitarian Creeds must sink into oblivion; belief in prophecy, sacraments, and miracles must be given up. Traditionalism has lost its authority, and religion must rest upon the Divine authority of the conscience. "The faith of the future" must be founded on the consciousness of humanity, not upon a historical revelation. The fundamental canons of this faith of the future, as given by Miss Cobbe, are: "the absolute goodness of God, the final salvation of every created soul, the Divine authority of the conscience." Upon these can "the foundation be laid for a religion which may be truly the religion of Humanity. . . We shall have higher, truer, more loving ideas of God, and the current teaching will become unendurable. By degrees the old faith will fall into forgetfulness and disuse. The new shoot of vigorous faith will cause the old leaves to drop away almost imperceptibly. Men will only awaken to the fact that they have ceased to hold the old creed, when they have become firmly rooted in the new."

Thus, this theistic Church of the Future puts away with Jesus Christ all that is distinctive in Christianity, but will hold to the existence of a personal God. "Christianity," says Miss Cobbe, "may fail us, and we may watch it with streaming eyes going slowly down from the zenith where it once shone; but we must neither regret that it should pass away, nor dread lest we be left in the gloom. Let it pass away...... Already in the east there climbs the Sun." From Theodore Parker some quotations have already been made. The Christ of the Gospels and the Church, he affirms, must hold a subordinate place in the future. What is wanted is to teach and apply the Absolute Religion, and bring in a new religious life which "will not be controlled by the theology of the Christian Church."

4. A Church controlled by the State, or a State Church. Thus far, we have spoken of the tendencies looking forward to the formation of a Church radically unlike the Christian; but now we note another tendency. Probably, most men of to-day regard a State Church in the future, as at least very improbable. For many years the tendency everywhere in Christendom has been to separate the State and the Church, and thus give the largest legal liberty to all forms of religious belief. Is it likely that this tendency will be checked, and that the regulation of religion will become a matter of State policy? Before answering this question, we must briefly note the principles now presented in many quarters as to the province of the State in religious matters.*

In our examination of Socialism in its more advanced form, we saw that it demands, as its first step, the enlargement of the powers of civil government; and this enlargement embraces religion. Man, it is

---

* It is said by De Tocqueville: "I do not hesitate to affirm that among almost all the Christian nations of our day, Catholic as well as Protestant, religion is in danger of falling into the hands of the government."

said, must have a religion of some kind, and corresponding worship; and it is a matter so vitally affecting the moral order of a State, and the happiness of its citizens, that it cannot be left to individual control. The government has duties in this regard which it can best fulfil by treating religion in the same way that it treats education. It should establish places of worship in which some general principles of religion may be inculcated, and prescribe rites of worship in which the religious feeling may find an appropriate expression.

A Church so controlled by the State must, of course, be very broad, and its teachings will be mainly ethical rather than theological, but may or may not be positively antichristian; this will depend on the religious opinions of the government, and the development among the people of the antichristian feeling. But, with the present tendency to repudiate Christian doctrine, we cannot doubt that the higher dogmas of Christianity will at last have in it no place; perhaps not even the belief in any personal God. The future State will not formulate creeds, or attempt to prepare its citizens for a life after death; its aim is to make men better fitted for the duties of the present, and for this end it supports the Church. It is from this point of view that Prof. Huxley says: "I can conceive the existence of an established Church, which should be a blessing to the community; a Church in which, week by week, services should be devoted, not to the iteration of abstract propositions in theology, but to the setting before men's minds an ideal of pure, just, and true living; a place in which those who are weary of the burden of daily cares should find a moment's rest in the contemplation of the higher life which is possible to all, though attained by so few; a place in which the man of strife and business should have time to think how small, after all, are the rewards he covets compared with peace and charity. Depend upon it, if such a Church existed, no one would seek to disestablish it."

Not a few Socialists begin to speak in the same way. They affirm that, as religion has its root in humanity, and must be always a power in human life, its regulation properly comes under State control. If freed from superstition, made rational, and developed on its ethical side, it will be a help to the social order, and a bond of union to the citizens. Religious beliefs which are judged to be unfriendly to the highest development of man, or that hinder him from giving himself up with zeal to the improvement of the present life, will be frowned upon, if not absolutely forbidden. It is to make the earth a heaven, not to find a heaven elsewhere; it is this world, not any "world to come," that the hearts of all should be set upon; and whatever discourages men from labouring zealously for this end—the improvement of society —must be put away. Therefore, any disheartening doctrine of human sinfulness, any preaching of contentment with present evils, any labour in preparation for a future life, or any looking forward to a new and better order by the coming of Jesus Christ, must be regarded as inconsistent with the public good. All religions must be in harmony with the purpose of the State, and a help to it. No sects can be tolerated whose dogmas tend to unfit the citizen for his duties.*

* It is said by Tolstoi ("My Religion"): "To believe in a life to come unfits men to labour in the present, to renounce themselves, and to serve humanity. There is no real labour for the race so long as we believe in a future life."

The control of religion by the antichristian State, will be later spoken of when considering the Church of the Antichrist.

5. We have still to note the tendency looking to a Church which we may call a mediating Church, or that of the Christian Socialists who still wish to keep the higher truths of Christianity. It aims to establish better relations to the world by giving up much, both as to organization and doctrine, that has hitherto been held important; and by breaking down in great measure the walls separating the sacred and the secular, the Church and the world. The nature and bearing of this tendency will best be seen by some extracts from its prominent representatives, who, however, widely differ among themselves.

It is said by Canon Freemantle: "The notion of the Church will be profoundly modified when once men realize that the Church is not necessarily held apart from mankind by having different pursuits as its object, and a peculiar form of government enjoined upon it. The Church will be simply that section of mankind in which the Christian spirit reigns." "The Church of the future will make its worship bear upon the higher ends of life; or rather, it will teach that a true ritual is a holy life in all its departments, and thus it will merge itself more and more in general society; being ready, in the true spirit of its Lord, to lose itself that it may save mankind." "The main object of Christian effort is not the saving of individuals out of a ruined world, but the saving of the world itself." "If the Church is to realize God's kingdom in the world, it must occupy itself with all human relations; it embraces the whole social and political life, it must use the State for this purpose."

It is said by another: "The existing churches have been only shops in which the age has been working some piece that is to be fitted into its future. When that future shall be complete, these old shops will all be closed." "If Christ were now here, He would gather all upright religious lives into one multitude, and erase the lines that divide Jew from Christian, heretic from Protestant; He would teach a creed as wide as that of the poets and philosophers." Says another: "Organic connection with any historic Church, Roman or Protestant, has nothing to do with the question whether people are Christians. Civilization is the material incarnation of the faith of a people. True civilization is the growing universal kingdom of God." "The distinction of the sacred and secular must perish."

This mediating Church is likely to become largely popular, and to draw to itself those who, accepting more or less of socialistic doctrine, yet wish to combine it with the creeds and beliefs of the Church. It is an attempt which must ultimately fail, for the Church and the world cannot be reconciled; but it presents a show of peace and unity which is attractive to many.*

From this survey of the tendencies of the time, let us turn to ask what light prophecy gives as to the Church of the Future.

In examining the teachings of The Revelation, we

---

* It is not necessary to speak here of the religious organizations now springing up on all sides, such as "The Salvation Army," "The Labour Church," "The Civic Church," "The Christian Science Church," and many more. In some of them there are disconnected elements of Christian truth, but they are mainly ruled by the humanitarian or the pantheistic spirit.

saw that the Church was portrayed under the symbol of a woman; and this in two conditions, as abiding faithful to her Lord (xii, 1), and as unfaithful, a harlot (xvii, 1–). As a harlot, she is seen "sitting upon a beast, arrayed in purple and scarlet colour, and decked with gold and precious stones and pearls, having a golden cup in her hand full of abominations, and filthiness of her fornication." We have symbolized in this harlot the Church in the last stage of her apostasy, when she enters into an alliance with the Beast. That the woman is seen sitting upon him, foretells that at some period yet future there will be an alliance between him and the unfaithful Church, and that supported by him she will attain for a short time to power and honour.

We must clearly distinguish between the Church in this last stage and the Church of the Antichrist which is later in time, and not established till after her overthrow. It is in the Church as borne by the Beast that we may find the Church of the Future. Of the Church of the Antichrist we shall speak in the following chapter.

It is to be remembered, that although the apostasy may seem to be very general, yet that even in this darkest hour there are many who preserve their faith in God and His Son, and who constitute the true Church. We may believe also that many who, being for a time borne away by the infidel spirit of the age, and deceived by the wiles of the Beast and false prophet, had joined themselves in alliance with them, will be undeceived and return to their allegiance. We are told that at a certain juncture of affairs the cry is made: "Come out of her, my people, that ye be not partakers of her sin, and that ye receive not of her plagues." (The Rev. xviii, 4.) Those who heed this warning cry are God's true witnesses during the antichristian tribulation, — His Church, — even if all outward rites of worship may be forbidden.

It is not difficult for us, in view of the past and of the present tendencies to take from the Church all her prerogatives and authority, to understand how this final alliance may be brought about. The Church — and under this term we embrace all Communions, though the Roman through its stronger organization and numerical superiority may be the leading actor — has now presented to her the opportunity of regaining her former prestige, and a wider influence, by an alliance with the rising power of the Lawless One, whose character and purposes are not yet fully disclosed. The union of interests, ecclesiastical and secular, by the rulers in Church and State for their common advantage, has had many examples in the past, — notably in the case of Constantine and the early Christians, and recently in that of the first Napoleon and the Papacy. The present aspect of things shows us how this alliance may be effected. The day of popular rule in Christendom having come, ecclesiastics hitherto sedulous of royal favour, and all who seek the honour that cometh from men, begin to turn to the people. But Democracy is in its nature averse to any union of Church and State, and inclined rather to take from the Church her present possessions and endowments. Therefore concessions must be made by the religious rulers to the democratic spirit, its leaders must be propitiated. The Church will help them to power, if they will help her to maintain her traditional prerogatives against the growing antichristian forces.

We can now readily understand how, when the Beast shall begin to rise into eminence and strength as a popular leader, he may find in the Church for a time a most useful ally, and she find in him a serviceable friend. It is not likely that he appears at first in the character of a defender of ecclesiastical rights and authority; but rather as the saviour of society, threatened with destruction through social anarchy; and many of all Communions, terrified at the growing hostility to Christianity, will be ready to welcome help from any quarter. We see to-day, many who have no 'real regard for any form of Christianity, but only for their own interests as citizens, well disposed to lend an ear to the loud cries of the Roman Church that it alone can save society from its danger, and to grant it for this end some part at least of its old civil prerogatives.

Thus we see that condition of things already preparing in which may be fulfilled the prophecy of the woman sitting upon the Beast, but which waits for a fuller development of the antichristian spirit. Such an alliance with the secular power, as has been already said, is that sin of fornication in His espoused wife which the Lord will not forgive; and which is here seen in its most offensive form, since he to whom she gives her Lord's prerogative, is "full of names of blasphemy." To enter into an alliance with him is the culmination of her sin, the final development of the apostasy. That the apostate Church still preserves the outward forms and shews of her former Christian standing, is seen in the symbols used — her vesture of purple and scarlet, her ornaments of gold and precious stones and pearls, and the golden cup in her hand. But in this cup is not the consecrated wine; it is "full of abominations and filthiness of her fornication," the "wine of her fornication with which the inhabitants of the world have been made drunk."

This reign of the apostate Church, upheld by the Beast, is probably of short duration. His alliance with her ends so soon as his power is sufficiently consolidated to enable him to cast her off, and to show forth his hostility in her destruction (xvii, 16). But it is probable that the Church will regain, as a barrier against the destructive anarchical tendencies of the times, in part at least, her old place in Christendom. Upon this ground Rome is already regaining some of her old influence, and Protestantism feels the need of consolidating its many sects. It is remarked by M. De Tocqueville, that our posterity will tend more and more to a single division into two parts—some relinquishing Christianity entirely, and others returning to the bosom of the Church of Rome. But whatever ecclesiastical authority may thus be regained, it will be moral and spiritual only, till the Church makes alliance with the Antichrist, and the power of the State is at her command. The question whether the words (xvii, 6), "I saw the woman drunken with the blood of the saints, and with the blood of the martyrs of Jesus," refer to the past, or to persecutions to follow upon the alliance, and still future, and which are to be carried on in the name of Christ against all those who do not recognize the supremacy of the harlot, is one which time must answer. To most, imbued with the tolerant spirit of our day, all future religious persecution will seem incredible; but wherever the claim of absolute spiritual supremacy is still affirmed, any attempt to exercise it must necessarily lead to bloody persecution.

We thus find in the Church of the Future not any one of the present existing churches becoming dominant, nor any of those, which, rejecting more or less of Christianity, aspire to this place; but that one yet future, symbolized by the woman sitting upon the Beast. Under what special conditions this alliance may be brought about, we cannot foresee. There may be rapid changes in the ecclesiastical relations of the churches to their respective States, and to one another, which, when they take place, will make the fulfilment of the symbolic prophecy seem wholly in the natural course of events.

The purpose of the Beast in this alliance being to gain personal power, when his end is attained, his hostility to the Church as Christian breaks forth. Aided by the ten kings, who are now his allies, he acts as the instrument of God's judgment. "These shall hate the whore, and shall make her desolate and naked, and shall eat her flesh, and burn her with fire." Now the way is prepared for the Antichrist to establish his own Church, a church founded on the Divinity of man, and which shall be co-extensive with his kingdom.

THE CHURCH OF THE BEAST AND THE FALSE PROPHET.

The Apostle John, who saw "a beast rise up out of the sea," saw also "another beast coming up out of the earth, and he had two horns like a lamb, and he spake as a dragon." (The Revelation, xiii, 11.) There is no reason to question that this beast, like the first, is an individual man, though both have others of like spirit acting with them. He is called (Rev. xix, 20) "The false prophet," and with the beast is "cast alive into a lake of fire." As we have seen, the sea is the symbol of the peoples where the popular will is supreme, and all is unstable; the earth is the symbol of an established and more stable order. The coming up of the second beast out of the earth seems to show that he represents a traditional past, which still has a measure of solidity and authority. His two horns like a lamb may indicate an outward semblance to Christianity; but his speech as of a dragon shows whose servant he is, and by whom inspired.

We now ask, what are the relations of the second to the first beast to whom power has been given over all nations? We may say in general, that he is the ecclesiastical head of the antichristian kingdom. To this end all the necessary authority is given him. "He exerciseth all the authority of the first beast in his sight." (Rev. xiii, 12, R. V.) The object of this ecclesiastical administration is, to make "the earth, and them that dwell therein, to worship the first beast." In addition to the power of punishing with death all who refuse this worship, he is able to deceive men by the proofs he gives of the actual possession of superhuman power, in the doing of great signs or wonders. Of these is mentioned, "the making of fire to come down from heaven on the earth in the sight of men." This was the sign which the Lord refused to give to the Pharisees. (Matt. xvi, 1.) Having thus created faith in himself as endowed with superhuman power, he induces those dwelling on the earth, whom he has deceived, to "make an image to the beast." This term "image," though usually applied to a single person or thing, is applied in the Epistle to the Hebrews (x, 1) to an institution, and is so used here. This image, set up by the false prophet, is not, as many have said, a material image like that of Nebuchadnezzar, of the precious metals or of stone, which he is able to endow with life, or a marble bust of the beast, which speaks; but a form of ecclesiastical polity or church organization. The life — $\pi\nu\epsilon\hat{v}\mu a$ — given it so that it can both speak and act, is the influx of that evil spiritual power which makes it the counterfeit of the Church, both as to word and work. As the Holy Ghost came down at Pentecost from Heaven, and dwells a living power in the Church, so into the image of the beast enters the spirit from the pit.

Now appears the Church of the Antichrist, not as a mere external ecclesiastical organization, or a society of men bound together by a common hatred of Christianity, but an organism filled with demoniacal power. Invested with all secular authority, the false prophet and his hierarchy can present their religious system and worship for universal acceptance. All men must receive some mark as a sign of submission; and if this be refused, they must be slain.* (It may be that those spoken of, xiv, 12, 13, may be those slain at this period. See also vi, 11.) None will be permitted to buy or sell, or, in other words, to receive or dispense any grace of God through His appointed ordinances, now superseded by the ordinances of Satan. (xiii, 17. See Matt. xxv, 9.) The first beast is to be the object of worship, and all other worship is forbidden. Antichrist is now "seated in the temple of God, exalting himself above all that is called God, or that is worshipped," thus fulfilling the words of the Apostle Paul. (2 Thess. ii, 4.)

Having this prophetic outline of the Church of the

* The early Fathers said much of the persecutions under the Antichrist, of their fierce and bloody character. Referring to these, it is said ("Discussions and Arguments") by J. H. Newman: "In persecution the Church begins, and in persecution she ends. . . . Let us then apprehend and realize the idea that a persecution awaits the Church before the end, fiercer and more perilous than any which occurred at its first rise. Further, it is to be attended with the cessation of all religious worship. So the Fathers understood the taking away of the Daily Sacrifice."

Of the persecution (Rev. xvii, 6), something has already been said. It would seem that this is instigated by the woman, although it is carried into effect by the Beast. Whether this persecution is past or future, is for time to decide; but apparently it does not take place till the alliance of the Church with the Antichrist has been consummated. But whether past or future, it must be distinguished from the last persecution under the Antichrist in that it is confined to the saints and martyrs who reject her authority; the last extending to all dwelling on the earth who refuse to worship the Beast.

Antichrist, let us ask on what basis it can be built, and how far it will be fitted to be a universal Church.

1. Let us first ask, putting aside all revealed religion, what principle lies at the basis of a universal or catholic religion? It is that the religious element is an essential element in human nature; and that there must be, therefore, among all people some forms of belief and of worship, and these are capable of continual development. The great problem is how to give this religious element as now developed its simplest and most easily received form; and thus obtain a creed and worship which may be truly universal. To obtain these, we must put off from the many existing religions all that is local and national and temporary, and keep only what is common to the race, and therefore permanent. The universal creed can express only the beliefs common to all,— the first or elemental principles of religion. Many may believe far more, but their beliefs cannot be imposed upon others, or form part of the one creed.

2. The first and chief element in a religious belief is its conception of God. A God to be worshipped by all, must be known of all. We are now come to a time when the conception of Him is through science and philosophy so enlarged that all anthropomorphic limitations, as of personality, will, intelligence, are to be done away, and we come to an indeterminate and universal Being.

"The race," as we are told, "has been long reaching forward to such a conception of Deity." Primitive Polytheism has given place to Henotheism, Henotheism to Monotheism. But Monotheism retains the dualism of God and nature, of nature and man; and therefore must give place to Monism, and thus come to an absolute unity. In this way we reach a conception of God which may be universally received, being stripped of all that is particular and distinctive and transient. The world can now conceive of a God who is an Infinite and Eternal Energy or Principle working in nature and man. But the eye sees him not, the understanding does not comprehend him, theology cannot define him, the imagination can form no image of him. He is the Inscrutable, the Unknowable, the Inconceivable, yet the Omnipresent and Omnipotent. Now have we come to the idea of a God, — a Power, or a Principle, which, we are told, may be the chief element in a universal religion. No earlier age could have come to such a conception; it is the product of the latest and highest development of science and philosophy.

3. But what religious emotions can such a conception of God awaken in men? And under what forms of worship can they be expressed? It may be admitted that a feeling of wonder and awe may fill the heart in the presence of "this Infinite and Eternal Energy." But such a feeling could not express itself in prayer or in any positive acts of worship; nor would it have any real influence on the conduct of life. There is nothing spiritual or even moral in it. None of those feelings which the Christian conception of God as our Father awakens, — filial love, holy fear, dependence, trust, gratitude, a sense of sin, hope of future blessedness in higher communion with Him,— can be awakened by a belief in an impersonal and unknowable First Cause. Worship of such a deity would be empty and unmeaning. The human soul, conscious of its weakness, craves communion with Persons, and cannot be put off with

laws or powers. Neither the "Energy" of the Evolutionists, nor the "Substance" of Spinoza, can take the place in the heart of a personal God.

How then in an age which denies a personal God can we find an object of worship? Such an object modern Pantheism gives us. As God is in all men, and becomes self-conscious only in man, he in whom the Divine is most manifested may be an object of worship. The pantheistic church may conceive of God as an impersonal spiritual Principle, and yet find in a man such a manifestation of the common Divinity that all the world may be called to worship him. The Church of the Antichrist may therefore be in its essential principles pantheistic, and yet find in a man a Divine head to whom all are to pay their homage and to be obedient. Of the nature of this worship something will be said later.

Thus our age has reached a conception of God on which may rest a universal religion, embodied in a universal Church. And this Church can have its rites of worship, full of life and power. We have already in germ all the conditions necessary for the building of the Church of the Antichrist; but this cannot be accomplished till he appears as its head, and the work of organization has been effected by the false prophet.

We are now prepared to consider the tendencies and movements of our times which point forward to this Antichristian Church.

1. Of the pantheistic conception of God, and of His relation to men, sufficient has been already said. This unity of the Divine and human in man lies at the foundation of the many antichristian movements

for unity which we see in all regions of human thought and life, political, social, religious.

2. But we are now concerned only with religion, and the tendencies to universalism as opposed to particularism. In the Christian Church many are weary of its divisions and crying aloud for unity; and in the non-Christian bodies many are manifesting the desire to have only one religion, one church, one worship. Accepting as an incontestable fact that the human race is making continual progress, and that though religions may die, religion will live and develope forever, they affirm that the future must bring with it in time a universal Church. It is said by one of this school: "Instead of religion passing away, we are in the time of its re-birth. There is to be a more magnificent religion, a grander church, than the past has ever dreamed of. . . . We are getting ready to build the new temple in which God shall manifest Himself as He has not in the past, and that shall be full of light and love and peace for all mankind."

That expectations of this kind are becoming very general, ample proof is found in the sermons and lectures, and in the popular theological literature of our day. But a more significant sign is seen in the recent assembling at Chicago of "The World's Parliament of Religions,"* the first of its kind ever held.

---

* "The World's Parliament of Religions," held at Chicago, 1893. Of this it is said by its historian, Dr. Barrows, that it continued seventeen days, and 150,000 people during this time attended its sessions. "It was full of the highest religious enthusiasm from first to last . . . And at times the scenes were Pentecostal." It has been proposed that these parliaments be held regularly, and much is now said of one to be held at Paris in 1900 at the same time with the proposed great International Exhibition. It

It contained many men of great learning and ability, and of high ecclesiastical positions. A Roman Cardinal commended it as "worthy of all encouragement and praise." And an Archbishop said: "The conception of such a religious assembly seems almost like an inspiration." A Protestant Bishop spoke of the movement as "a grand one, and unexampled in the history of the world." Other Bishops and Protestant clergymen spoke in the same way. It was said by one: "It has been left to the mightier spirit of this day to throw the gates of the Divine Kingdom wide open, and bid every sincere worshipper in all the world, of whatever name or form, 'welcome.'" And by another: "A Pentecostal day is come again, for here are gathered devout men from every country under heaven, and we do hear them speak the wonderful works of God. And so is fulfilled in a sense more august than on Pentecost itself, the memorable prophecy in Joel (ii, 28) of the one coming, universal religion." And by another: "This Parliament marks the first step in the sacred path that shall one day bring the truly humanitarian and universal religion."

These extracts, which might be many times multiplied, show how, under the attractive guise of a religion which shall embrace all men, and bind them into one great religious brotherhood, the way is preparing for the Antichristian Church. Starting with the principle that all men are alike the sons of God, and are

is said by one of its chief promotors that "the Parliament of Religions has just begun to live," and by another, that "it has come to stay." Such assemblies of religious leaders, Christian and non-Christian, may, therefore, have an important part to play in the religious history of the future.

sincerely striving to find Him, all religions have a claim to recognition as having in them more or less of truth. And as the knowledge of God is continually enlarging with the progress of the race, no one religion can say that it has the absolute truth. There should be, therefore, from time to time, assemblies of the chief representatives of all faiths, that through comparison and discussion they may gradually attain to the pure truth, and agree upon a universal religion.*

Thus we have set before us a universal religion and a world-wide Church; how are they to be attained? In the Parliament there was not an agreement of opinions, but the general expression of the non-Christian members was, that they were to be attained by the elimination of all that is particular and temporary in the several religions; retaining only what is common to all, and so permanent. To this the orthodox Christian members could not assent, for this would be renouncing essential Christianity as founded in Christ. It was for them a difficult position. Either they must say, Christianity has the absolute truth, and is, there-

* Of the four great religions which are now confronting Christianity, the Hindu, the Mohammedan, the Confucian, the Buddhist, all striving to be world-religions, one has recently written: "Victory cannot be expected to incline to either side, until there has been an intelligent study by each of the sources of the other's strength, an appreciation of the spiritual and social needs which it has met, and an absorption by the one that has most inherent excellence and power of assimilation." How long a time may be needed for this study and final absorption, the writer does not say. It is the law of evolution applied to religion; the best will survive, and the process may demand a few centuries, more or less, or even hundreds of them. But what of the purpose of God in His Son, whose words to His Church are: "Watch, for I come quickly."

fore, to be accepted of all; or it has not, and is itself
seeking after more truth. But if it has the absolute
truth, why convene the representatives of other religions to compare and discuss their partial truths?
They must in the end receive its teachings.*

But if Christianity has not the absolute truth and
is seeking after it, and convenes the Parliament
to this end, then its representatives must meet the
representatives of other religions on the same plane,
and recognize them as teachers having the same
right to teach as themselves.†

Thus Christianity appears before the world as one of
many religions,— having, it may be, more truth, but
still without the element of universality. For this
end it must be modified, and these modifications must

---

* It may be said that something was gained if the non-Christian religions were put in close and direct contrast to the Christian, and their relations to it thus shown. But this involved the clear and direct presentation of Christianity as the absolute religion to which all must come. Such a presentation was not made.

It need not be affirmed that the Church in her present condition of division and doubt can teach all truth, but that her Head *is* the Truth, and the Spirit of Truth, however hindered, still dwells in her; and that, therefore, through her alone the perfect revelation must be made, and she become in full reality the light of the world. To her light all must come.

† It is said by a recent writer : "The appearing of Christianity in the Parliament can mean nothing less than a voluntary abdication of all exclusive claims to be the only true and revealed religion." The same inference seems to have been drawn by many of the non-Christian members, and they returned to their homes feeling that the true way to attain to a knowledge of God is by a scientific comparison of religions, and the selection of the best in each, not by the acceptance of Christ and His work and teachings. Some are reported to have said that Christianity had so lost its hold upon the people of the United States that a good opportunity was offered for the diffusion of the Eastern religions.

be in the direction of universalism. It must give up what is peculiar, that it may be in harmony with the common religion. As the Incarnation, based on the Trinity and realized in the Person of Jesus Christ, is the great distinctive feature of Christianity, this is especially an obstacle to be put away. It is, therefore, of great interest as a sign of the times to note how the orthodox members of the Parliament acted in regard to it. We may, without injustice, say that it was in large measure kept out of sight, at least as regards the Person of the Incarnate Son, and His place as the Living Head, and the present Ruler and Teacher of the Church, and through her of the world. To His place as a religious teacher long since dead, no objection could be made by the non-Christians; some would have admitted Him to be the greatest of all past teachers. But the presentation of His claims in His own words, and affirmed as present realities by the Christian members, would have brought to a speedy end its discussions as to the way by which to attain religious truth. How could they come to a knowledge of God while disowning or ignoring Him who said: "He that hath seen me hath seen the Father." "No man knoweth who the Father is but the Son, and he to whom the Son will reveal Him." "I am the Way, the Truth, and the Life; no man cometh unto the Father but by me." "I am the Door; by me if any man enter in he shall be saved." Can He who spake these words be put out of sight when men assemble to consult how they may know God? Is it "sectarian" to repeat them? If true, must not those assembled have, as the first step, bowed down before the Son and besought Him to teach them of the Father? How could they expect to know Him when they denied or ignored the Son whom the Father had sent to make Him known, and who alone can reveal Him?

We have dwelt longer upon this Parliament of religions because it gives us an illustration how the way may be prepared for the Church of the Antichrist. The first and great step is the deposition of Christ from His supreme place as the Incarnate Son, now living and having all authority in heaven and earth, the one Image and Revealer of God, and His degradation to the place of an ethical and religious teacher; and then, the rejection of His teachings as now outgrown. This change is gradually effected by the silence of the Church as to His Person and present offices as Priest and Lord, and by dwelling on His teachings, comparing them with those of other teachers, so that the world learns to think of Him only as a religious instructor. This forgetfulness of His absolute supremacy was illustrated in the Parliament. It was assumed by its conveners, that, although it had not met in His name, and although some appearing as His representatives denied His Divinity, His Atonement, His Resurrection, yet that He was well pleased, and would fulfil His promise to be "in the midst of them." It was assumed that although He is the Head of the Church, and had prayed that all its members might be one in Him, yet that He is not displeased to see them arrayed under sectarian banners, teaching contradictory doctrines, having little or no communion or fellowship with one another, and rejecting His appointed bonds of unity. It was assumed that all He had spoken of the future of the Church, its temptations, its trials, its perils, its falling away, and His warnings of the sore judgments He would send upon it, might be safely ignored, and only visions of prosperity and peace be set before it. There are no calls to repentance which they should heed.

Thus we see how, through the silence of the Church as to her Living Head and His prerogatives, He passes gradually from the thoughts of men. As to all present offices of teaching and rule, He becomes practically non-existent. He is far off, and is silent because He cannot speak by the Holy Ghost. We must go back, it is said, to His work in the past. We have His earthly teachings in a book ; let them be our guide. But there is no agreement as to their meaning. Shall we take the interpretation of the early disciples ? But why ? Age gives wisdom, and the nineteenth century is better able to interpret them than the first. We are not to be bound by the letter. In spirit Christianity is a world-religion ; let us make it so by striking out all that is particular and exclusive. To this end let us study all religions and widen our Christianity; let us enlarge the Church to take in, not only the baptized, but all seekers after truth of every creed ; so shall we attain a universal religion and a universal Church.

Thus forgetting that the Person of Christ, the Incarnate Son, — very God and very Man, — is far more than His past works and teachings, important as these may have been, and forgetting that He has much more to do and to teach in completing redemption, the Church grieves and dishonours Him when she substitutes those for His present headship and guidance.

Not any personal Christ under the limitations of space and time, but His all-embracing spirit of philanthropy, is what many now seek. The next step is to affirm that no one, Jesus Christ or another, can stand for ever as mediator between humanity and God; for this is a denial of God's fatherhood, and of man's Divine sonship. The limitations of Christianity as represented in Christ must be put aside. Thus the absent and silent Christ has already become to many the dead Christ; and the way is thus prepared for him who shall present himself as the great and living Power upon the stage of religious action.

All studies in comparative religions, which are necessarily limited to a few scholars, can end only in forming schools of philosophy, not in a universal church. For this there must be a personal centre of unity, a head, and an inspiring energy which only some superhuman indwelling power can give. Thus the Antichristian Church becomes the analogue of the Christian with its Divine Head, and the indwelling Holy Spirit; and can exercise a spiritual sway over the minds and hearts of men. The mark which its head puts upon the foreheads and right hands of his followers, is the symbol of their unity with him, and of the submission of both thought and action to his will.

It is only as an organism — the image to which breath is given — that the worship of the Antichristian Church can retain its hold upon its worshippers. Without this inbreathed life from the pit, all its services would be artificial and hollow, and all men would soon weary of them. The worshippers must be made conscious of a Power not of themselves, and yet working in and upon them, and overmastering them. The vague feelings of wonder and awe awakened by the presence in the universe of a mysterious and inscrutable Energy of which the evolutionists speak, now, through satanic operations, take definite forms and become real; and can express themselves in rites and acts of worship which hold the worshippers by a mighty spell. This spiritual energy, manifested in highest degree in the Antichrist himself and in the false prophet, is seen also in all the ecclesiastical orders, in his evangelists, his prophets, his priests. They are made to speak and do things of which they are at other times incapable. There are inspirations, ecstasies, tongues, miracles. There is spiritual power in every ordinance, his falsehoods are not empty deceptions, his blasphemous words burn like fire. There may thus be kindled a fervour of faith, an evangelistic zeal, a high religious exaltation, which will rival those of the early days of the Church. To his worshippers Christian worship in the power of the Holy Spirit may seem in comparison tame and lifeless. (See 2 Thess. ii, 9–12.)

To this worship, full of living power, let there be added all that science and art can do to make its outward forms and rites impressive. Let there be temples, stately and majestic, on which all that architectural taste and skill can do has been expended; the master-pieces of painting and of sculpture, priests in their splendid vestments, music that calls into play the capacities of all musical instruments and of all human voices,— in a word, all that our advanced civilization can add of magnificence and beauty to religious services,— and we may understand what power of attraction will be in this worship for those who will not bow their knees in humble adoration before the Father and the Son, confessing their sins and pleading the merits of the sacrifice offered upon the cross. The cross as a symbol of salvation from sin will disappear, and some symbol expressive of the Divinity

of man and of the greatness of his aspirations will
take its place and be the symbol of the new age. Men
will say: This is the religion for which the world has
waited so long; not a Christianity narrow and exclusive, but all-embracing, universal as humanity. This
is a worship worthy of the dignity of man.

We have yet to ask as to the time of the setting
up of the Antichristian Church. It is not till the
ten kings have consummated their alliance with the
Beast, and become the obedient executors of his will.
(Rev. xvii, 16, 17.)* They give their kingdom to
him, and the last act of judgment is then accomplished.
"These shall hate the whore, and shall make her
desolate and naked, and shall eat her flesh, and burn
her with fire." The way is now prepared for Antichrist to manifest himself in the fullness of his pride,
and to show himself to the nations not only as the
International king and supreme ruler, but also as God.
Now is brought into his service and made his chief
instrument, the false prophet who, as the ecclesiastical head, may stand to him in a relation not unlike
that which Napoleon wished to establish between
himself and the Pope.

* Whether the number "ten," as the number of the kings in
union with the Beast, is to be taken literally or symbolically,
cannot be positively said. Ten, like seven, is a symbol of completeness, but in a different way; seven implying that that to
which it is applied is complete of its kind, or fulfilling its idea;
ten, that a certain definite order is completed, the number perfect. As applied to the kingdoms of the world regarded in
hostility to the Kingdom of Christ, we have the ten toes of the
image and the ten horns of the fourth beast in Daniel (ii. 41;
vii, 7); the ten horns of the dragon and of the Beast. (Rev.
xii, 3; xiii, 1.)

The ten kings may be the heads of ten kingdoms into which
Christendom will be ultimately divided; but this only the event
can show.

We call to mind, says Renan ("Religious Hist. and Crit."), those proud words ascribed to Napoleon: "I meant to exalt the Pope immeasurably, to surround him with pomp and homage. . . . I would have idolized him; he should have lived near me. Paris should have become the capital of Christendom, and I would have directed the religious as well as the political world. It was a device for binding together all the federative parts of the empire, and for holding in the bonds of peace all that remained outside. I would have held my religious as well as my legislative sessions. My councils would have represented Christendom; the Popes would merely have presided at them. I would have opened and closed these assemblies, and approved their decisions, as Constantine and Charlemagne had done."

With Napoleon the establishment of a church was a purely political matter — as he said: "The people must have a religion; and this religion must be in the hands of the government." But the Church of the Antichrist stands in a much closer relation to him. There is a spiritual unity, the operation of Satan, whereby it becomes in a sense his body.

Of the downfall of Babylon notice has already been taken in considering the teachings of The Revelation. In point of time it probably precedes the work of the false prophet. The universal Church is based upon the universal kingdom. "Power was given him over all kindreds, and tongues, and nations; and all that dwell upon the earth shall worship him, whose names are not written in the book of life of the Lamb." Now in anticipation of Him who is to come, he seats himself a priest upon his throne. (Zech. vi, 13.)

But the time of his triumph is short. He comes who will cast out the prince and god of this world, and redeem His inheritance from its pollutions, and establish righteousness and peace in all the earth. "And I saw heaven opened, and behold a white horse; and He that sat upon him was called Faithful and True. . . . And out of His mouth goeth a sharp sword, that with it He should smite the nations. . . . And I saw the Beast and the kings of the earth and their armies gathered together to make war against Him that sat on the horse, and against His army. And the Beast was taken, and with him the false prophet. . . . These both were cast alive into a lake of fire." (Rev. xix, 11–20.)

And now begins the last stage of the Lord's redemptive work,— to "put all enemies under His feet," during which He acts as Judge and King. "And He that sat upon the throne said: Behold, I make all things new." When redemption is completed and the heavenly order fully established, He gives up the Kingdom to the Father, "that God may be all in all." Beyond this, prophecy is silent. In the present state of our religious knowledge no revelation of that future condition could be intelligible to us. We must ourselves be lifted up into that higher knowledge of God and of His purpose which the resurrection life will bring.

SUMMARY AND CONCLUSION.

In the preceding chapters (passing over the Preface and Introduction) we have seen what the Scriptures, and especially the Lord and the Apostles, have declared respecting the religious condition of the Church and of the world at the time when the Son returns from Heaven. It is a time when faith in Christ has failed in many, and their love grown cold, and iniquity abounds. The Apostles, who saw very early in the Church the beginnings of an apostasy, foretold that it would continue and increase, and finally bring forth as its product the Man of Sin, the lawless one. As the purpose of God in the Kingdom of His Son approached its realization, the hostility of the world would become more determined, and would find its last embodiment in the man who would stand as the great representative of fallen humanity, against Christ the representative of the redeemed humanity.

In considering the apostasy, we have seen its root in the loss of the first love, whereby a separation was made between the Lord and the Church,— the Head and the body, — and He was hindered in the exercise of His headship. Through the same loss of love, the Holy Ghost, sent by the Son, was unable to fulfil His mission. After a time the expectation of the Lord's speedy return passed away, and also the hope of it; and the Church made it her work to bring all the world under subjection to Christ before His return.

Thus the history of the Church has not been that of a community of one heart and mind, carrying out the will of its Head under the guidance of the Holy Ghost, and steadily growing in love, holiness, wisdom, and power; but of a community divided against itself, forgetful of God's purpose, filled with ambition to rule in this world, and covetous of its pleasures and honours. The Holy Ghost has not been able to do His full work in the Church, and therefore her witness to the world has been partial and feeble. The Head, though nominally honoured, has passed more and more from the thought of the Church as her living and ruling Lord, and from the knowledge of men as the King of kings.

We have seen in the movements and tendencies of the present time the preparation for the final fulfilment of the Scripture predictions. Modern pantheistic philosophy is leavening the public mind with its denials of a personal God, of man's moral freedom, and of immortality. Modern science, particularly in its evolutionary phase, is denying a Creator and a creation, and can find in the Universe no Divine purpose, only an endless evolution, in which man appears for a moment as a shining bubble, then disappears for ever. The Bible is put aside by many as a book outgrown, with its doctrine of sin and its legendary miracles and history. Much of modern literature is imbued with the pantheistic spirit, or is critical and skeptical, and, when not positively irreligious is indifferent to religion.

We have seen how the Man of Sin can demand for himself as God the homage of the world, because of the belief that humanity is itself Divine, and he is the highest expression of that Divinity. The line of distinction between God and man being effaced, no mediator between God and man is needed. Christianity must cease to be regarded as a redemptive system, having the cross as its symbol, and calling to repentance. The Church is not the community of those partaking of Christ's resurrection life, but embraces all men as by nature the sons of God.

We have seen the last form which the Church assumes in alliance with the powers of this world, as symbolized by the woman on the beast; and the judgments which come upon her through their final hostility. After her overthrow arises the Church of the Antichrist, which he will make the universal Church, co-extensive with his kingdom; and which will be full of spiritual power through the energy of Satan.

We have seen the growing tendency among the nations of Christendom to recognize their common interests, and make these the basis of a political unity,— the brotherhood of nations built upon the brotherhood of man. The outlines of a great confederacy are coming more and more distinctly into view, which, when it is perfected, will have Antichrist as its head, and thus make him the great ruler of the world. But his reign is of short duration. He, with the false prophet, perishes, and the returning Lord establishes His Kingdom of righteousness, which will fill the earth and never end.

If what has been said of the teaching of prophecy in regard to the Apostasy, and of its consummation in the Antichrist, and of the present antichristian movements and tendencies of the times, be true, we must ask, What truth needs to be most strongly and distinctly proclaimed by the Church for the defence of her children? Beyond question, it is the doctrine of the Incarnation. This is the great peculiar doctrine of Christianity, and distinguishes it from all other religions. It is one which tests the faith of men in the highest degree, for it affirms the union of Deity and humanity; and this not as an abstract doctrine, but as realized in the Person of Jesus Christ, and in Him alone. No words can express the transcendent nature of this union; no finite mind can comprehend its bearings, not only on the history and destiny of man, but on the history and destiny of the Universe, and of all created beings forever.*

To the devout and thoughtful mind, seeking to know the relations of God to men, and discerning spiritual things, what inexhaustible depth of meaning lies in the words: "The Word was made flesh, and dwelt among us." What awe-inspiring mystery, and yet what clouds of glory, surround His Person who is Very God and very man, for whom all things were made, the one central figure of the Universe, who binds all worlds and all creatures into unity,— the visible Image of the invisible God.

Let us, then, put ourselves face to face with the

---

* It is here assumed as the teaching of the Scriptures and belief of the Church, that this union of natures is without end. The Apostle Paul speaks of "the day when God will judge the world in righteousness by that Man whom He hath ordained," and of the "one Mediator between God and man, the Man Christ Jesus" (Acts xvii, 31; 1 Tim. ii, 5). His humanity, though glorified, is not changed as to its essential elements. His body is the body which was transfigured on the mount, which came out of the sepulchre, and in which He will return to judge the world, and is the norm of the new material creation.

fact of the Incarnation, and consider our relations to it as a present reality. Our belief as to the future of Christianity will depend upon the answer that we make to the question: Is the Son of the Virgin, who died upon the cross, now the risen and glorified Man seated at the right hand of the Father, and the possessor of all power in heaven and in earth? It is a question of fact, which must be answered with a yes or no. Let us first suppose it to be answered in the negative, and note the consequences that must follow.

If the death of Jesus was the close of His ministry, then Christianity as a system of doctrine, religious and ethical, must rest upon His earthly teachings as recorded in the Gospels. His mission ended upon the cross. He did not rise from the dead; He did not ascend into Heaven; He was not made the Head of the Church; He did not send down the Holy Ghost; He is not our great High Priest. Since His death He has been with the other disembodied saints in Paradise, waiting for the resurrection; and has stood in no other personal relations with men than they. He has had no part in the history or government of the world. And if it has been so in the past, we must believe that it will be so in the future. He will not come again to judge the world, to raise the dead, to change the living, and to reign in righteousness.

Christianity, then, resting wholly as to its doctrines upon Christ's earthly teachings, can have only that measure of truth which He Himself possessed and taught. Did He teach His disciples the perfect, the absolute truth, to which no addition can ever be made? No one will say this. If He had all truth, the revelation which He could give of God and of man's relations to Him was limited by the spiritual capacity of the disciples, and by the stage then reached of the Divine purpose. "I have yet many things to say unto you, but ye cannot bear them now." If His voice was silenced in death, Divine revelation could not cease. Others must follow Him in all generations who could lead men into new and higher realms of spiritual knowledge, and make known more of God, His perfections, and His purpose.

The denial of the present existence of the risen Lord, fulfilling His offices as the Head and Teacher of the Church, thus takes from Christianity its claim to be the one, true, permanent, and universal religion. As He takes His place among other religious teachers of the past, distinguished only by the greater measure of religious knowledge which He was able to teach, His teachings must necessarily be supplemented and modified by the teachings of others in subsequent times. It is only when we see in Christ "The Truth," and the one Teacher of all truth, that Christianity can affirm that it has all truth, and therefore is the one universal and unchangeable religion. Himself in Heaven, "the same yesterday, to-day, and forever," He has continued to teach His Church through the Holy Ghost dwelling in her, so far as she had an ear to hear; and all further knowledge of God in all the ages must come through Him.

The Church, then, must plant herself firmly upon the fact of the present existence and offices of the Incarnate Son in Heaven, if she will defend her children from the deceits of the Antichrist. It becomes, therefore, a matter of greatest interest to ask how far those who bear the name of Christ believe in their hearts that Jesus, risen from the dead and made immortal, is now the actual possessor of all power in Heaven and in earth. This is the professed faith of the Church, and affirmed in her creeds, and daily reaffirmed in their worship by millions. It would be presumptuous for any one to say how far this profession of faith is not sincere; but there are many indications that there are multitudes in Christendom who refuse to accept the statements of the creeds in regard to the Incarnation. They accept the Lord as a religious teacher sent of God, but reject Him as the One Incarnate Son, risen from the dead, and the present living Lord. Let us note some of the grounds on which this rejection rests.

We may note first the intellectual difficulties which the fact of the Incarnation presents. The Lord's words to St. Peter: "Flesh and blood hath not revealed it unto thee, but my Father which is in Heaven," teach us that the intellect cannot comprehend it. Considering the transcendent nature and the inexpressible greatness of the Incarnation, it is not strange that the scientific mind, seeking to bring all things under law, doubts or openly denies it. Philosophy, also, is baffled in its attempts to bring it within its own domain. The evolutionist can make the Incarnate Son no product of evolution. Both the stupendous character of the fact itself — the union of Deity and humanity in Jesus Christ — and the manner of its realization, present difficulties even to faith which become greater as men, under the influence of the spirit of the time, learn to judge all things in the light of the intellect and not of the Spirit.

We cannot, therefore, be surprised that on the ground of its intrinsic intellectual difficulties, the doctrine of the Incarnation, as it has been held by the Church, and with it the fact of Christ's present existence and prerogatives, is very widely rejected in Christendom. If not wholly rejected, modifications of it are proposed, as we have seen, which essentially change it, and leave us only a shadowy image in place of the risen and glorified Lord.

If it be objected, that as the great Creeds of the Church remain unchanged, their statements as to the headship and rule of the Incarnate Son must be taken as sufficient proof that they are really believed in; it may be replied, that evident proof to the contrary is found in the very imperfect appreciation, if we should not rather say the cold indifference, with which His relations to the Church are regarded by her. When we consider the Divine Majesty of His Person, how great is the honour He gives the Church in that He condescends to stand in closest relationship with her as her Head and High Priest! Without Him, the source of her life, the moving spring of all her activity, her Teacher and Defender and Ruler, she is nothing. We may therefore expect to see her exalt Him and pay Him the profoundest homage, and take herself the place of lowest humility, and strive to obey in everything the intimations of His will. What faith should she have in His words, what fear of His displeasure, what sacrifices should she make for Him, and what joy should she feel in the hope of seeing Him, and of being made like Him!

How unlike this is the reality. As regards the history of the Church, can we see in it the proof that she has had any just appreciation of His headship, and of the high exaltation thus given her, and of the duties it imposed upon her? How little has her conduct before the world been in sympathy with His heavenly dignity, His all-embracing love, His Divine peace. How could the conception of His Kingdom as an earthly kingdom, whether under the rule of a single priest or of a multitude of priests and laymen,— Satan still reigning in the earth, and the Church continuing under the law of sin and death,— have been thought worthy of Him, the immortal and glorified Lord? Such low conceptions of the Kingdom must be based on low conceptions of the King. The Apostles who were with Him in the holy mount, and were eye-witnesses of His majesty, could never have believed that the honour and glory which He received from the Father could be set forth by a bishop of Rome or of Constantinople, or be parted among a multitude of Councils and Convocations and Conferences. He cannot establish His Kingdom upon the earth under the curse; He must first make it new. Those who shall reign with Him must first be made like Him in resurrection life and power.

Whatever we of to-day may say in our creeds of Christ's Divine Person and present offices and authority, our disregard of His commands and promises testifies against us. This is strikingly shown in the neglect of His utterances respecting His return. To watch continually for the returning Lord, that they may have their high calling ever before them, and so be kept from the love of this present world, is His command; but what has been the attitude of the Church toward His return? For many weary centuries the successive generations have been groaning and weeping under the law of sin and death; famine and pestilence and war have made the earth a great graveyard; crime and oppression have filled it with prisons and dungeons; yet only from a feeble few in all the centuries has the cry been heard: "Come, Lord Jesus, come quickly." And to-day, when crowded cities are full of vice and misery, when nations are beating plowshares into swords and pruning-hooks into spears, when famine and pestilence mock at the skill of statesmen and physicians, when the roaring of the discontented and restless peoples is like the roaring of the sea, and men's hearts are failing them for fear; do we hear prayers and supplications addressed to Him that He would come and save us? Papal encyclicals, pastoral epistles of bishops, missives of the clergy to their flocks, missionary reports and addresses, are either wholly silent, or speak with bated breath of His return as an article of faith indeed, but as something that does not practically concern us, and not to be prayed for or desired. We hear not the voice of the poor widow crying: "Avenge me of my adversary," — but the voice of one proud and lifted up, saying in her heart, "I sit a queen, and am no widow, and shall see no sorrow."

The words of the Lord respecting His return are more than a command to watch; they are a promise of the new and Heavenly Order which He will then establish. It seems scarcely credible that with any true belief of the Lord's present existence in glorified humanity,— the Man in whom manhood is raised to the head of all creature being,— and that He waits with earnest longing to give to His children this perfected and immortal life, and to make all things new; He yet has been unable to awaken in their hearts any real and earnest response. How are the thoughts of all to-day set upon the improvement of the old, the progress of the race, the development of humanity.* With what interest is every scientific discovery heralded, every invention that makes human life more endurable; but with what chilling indifference are all words received that tell of the Heavenly Order which He is to establish. To be made like Him at His coming, and so to share in His glory and blessedness, seems to have no attraction for most who bear His name. Deliverance from the law of sin and death through resurrection or translation, seems too much for faith to grasp; the disembodied state, or the natural and gradual evolution of humanity in the course of the ages, is all that can be believed.

If the children of God truly believe that the Incarnate Son,— Himself the Heavenly Man, made immortal through resurrection,— has promised to return speedily and take them up into the fellowship of His glory, how can we explain it that they do not everywhere desire and pray for the fulfilment of His promise? We can account for it only on the ground that His present existence as the risen and glorified Lord is not to them a reality ; and therefore there is no living hope of their own resurrection, and no longing for the new heaven and earth. Christ being no more

---

* In the true sense of the term "humanitarian," the Christian Church is the highest of all humanitarian institutions, for in it should be shown the love to men of the Father and of the Son. But as the term is now currently used, it means the good of humanity without reference to God and to His purpose in man. Humanitarianism has become a synonym for the philanthropy which looks only to the present life and the welfare of men on the earth, and therefore occupies itself with the improvement of present moral and social conditions. A life after death, and preparation for it, is not within its province.

seen as "the First-born from the dead," "the Beginning of the new creation," they soon learn to say that the only new order we may expect is a moral one, wrought in the spirits of men, but having nothing to do with material things. He has taught the world the noblest principles of religion, and illustrated them in His own life, and these are ultimately to revolutionize society and new-create the world; but beyond this we may not go.

With this wide spread of unbelief in the Deity of Christ, and in His place as the one Mediator between God and man, we see the strong and increasing tendency to make humanity Divine, and thus to make any mediatorship unnecessary. Christianity presents God in the Person of the Son descending into humanity, first to redeem it from sin and death, and then to lift it up into heavenly light and glory. Antichristianity presents humanity as in its nature Divine, beginning indeed in animality, but continually ascending, and revealing more and more through the ages its Divinity. We stand at the parting of the ways. The time has come for a final decision to be made. Will the Church have the Lord return, and bring with Him the Heavenly Order, beginning with the resurrection of her members and completed in the new heaven and earth; or will she have a development of the present earthly order, a gradual improvement of the race? Before her stand Christ and Antichrist: One, the representative of a humanity first redeemed and then glorified; the other, the representative of a humanity which needs no redemption, but is itself Divine. Between them the choice must be made.

All the tendencies and movements of the time are

toward the denial of the need of any Saviour from sin, of any living Lord, and of any coming Judge. Can the Church offer any effectual resistance to these tendencies and movements? She cannot, unless she first make the existence of her Head a great reality to herself, and be so filled with the Spirit of truth and of unity that she can bear witness of Him unto the world in the fulness of faith. No one will say that she can now bear such a witness.

Could we suppose that at this stage in the history of the Church a council could be held of her chief leaders of all the divisions to formulate a creed, how much of the statements of the present creeds would be retained? Would there be agreement even upon the Apostles' Creed? We cannot doubt that there would be many dissentients, and many more in respect to the Nicene Creed. Still worse would it fare with the Athanasian. It may be questioned whether any statement of the doctrine of the Incarnation could be made, except one so vague and general as to allow the largest liberty of interpretation. That the Incarnate Son, raised from the dead, Lord of all, is now the Head of the Church, would beyond doubt, in many quarters, call forth the strongest opposition.

It is in this loss of faith in the great central fact of Christianity, its corner-stone, that we find the special preparation for the Antichrist. Doubtless, in times past many have professed to believe it who did not truly believe it; and in these we see the hypocrisy re-appearing which was so marked and general in the Lord's day,— not conscious, but unconscious. The Scribes and Pharisees thought that they believed the Scriptures and kept the Law, till the Lord condemned them by showing them in His own Person the true nature of faith and obedience. Thus in the past many have thought that they had faith in Christ as the living Lord, and in all His prerogatives, and rendered Him all obedience and honour. But in our day large numbers, under its stimulating antichristian influences, have awakened to the consciousness that they do not truly believe in Him as the present Incarnate Son, and can no longer affirm it in their creeds and worship. An avowed denial takes the place of a quasi-belief. And many more seem to be moving rapidly to the same result.

It was said many years ago by C. Maitland, ("Apostolic School of Prophetic Interpretation"), that "in the day of Antichrist, besides the unequalled trouble, death, and perhaps bodily torment, there would be also the torture of sickening doubt, of writhing and racking despair. The grounds of faith will be so obscured as to render argument hopeless. . . It will be a man's first difficulty to realize the faith for which he is called to suffer. . . For in that day Christianity will seem to the world to have been a dream." A recent writer already quoted speaks of Christianity now seeming to many as "a parenthesis in the world's story, a dream that is passing away." It is the Spirit of truth alone who can make the promises of God a reality to us; and if He be grieved and depart from us, our faith cannot comprehend them,—they become to us empty words. And as it is with His promises, so with His threatenings of judgment. We hear them unmoved. Even the words of awful meaning spoken by the Lord: "There shall be great tribulation, such as was not from the beginning of the world to this time, no, nor ever shall be," awaken in many no fear, no dark forebodings, no repentance for the sins which bring upon us such overwhelming judgments.

The duty of the Church to the world is plain. She must affirm with far greater distinctness and vigour than she has done since apostolic days, the prerogatives of her Head; and warn the world that He lives to whom the Father has given all authority and dominion in Heaven and earth; and that He will not always suffer His authority to be derided, and His Father's name to be blasphemed. As the sense of sin diminishes, so also the fear of Divine anger. Therefore will the judgments upon the scoffers and blasphemers be the more terrible, "when He shall be revealed from Heaven with His mighty angels in flaming fire."

Upon His unfaithful children He will also bring sore judgments, but in love; not for destruction, but to purify them. The "wood, hay, and stubble" will be burned, but the "gold and silver and precious stones" will survive the fiery trial. The foolish virgins will pass through the Great Tribulation, but be delivered, and stand at last joyful in the presence of their King. Antichrist and his armies being cast out of the earth into the lake of fire, all nations will worship the Father through the Son; and the Church will sit with Him on His throne, and throughout all the earth be holiness, righteousness, and peace.

NOTES.

I.

The following quotations from Dr. Howison's Introduction to "The Conception of God," by Prof. J. Royce, 1897, — seen too late to be referred to in the proper place, — will serve to confirm the statements already made as to the wide influence of the Theism of the Hegelian school:

"That this conception of an immanent God is a fact affecting not only the world of technical philosophy, but also the world of applied theology and practical religion, it is enough to cite in evidence the writings and influence of the late Prof. Green in England, of the brothers Caird in Scotland, of Prof. Watson in Canada; and in the United States, besides its presence in various modified forms in the philosophical chairs at the leading universities, the preaching of Phillips Brooks, the philosophical inducting of the National Commissioner of Education, the noticeable book of Prof. Allen, 'The Continuity of Christian Thought,' the public declarations of Dr. Strong, the writings of Dr. Gordon, 'The Christ of To-day' and 'Immortality and the New Theodicy,' and the Lectures by Prof. Upton, 'Bases of Religious Belief,' 1893. Idealistic Monism pervades the religious influence of all these minds, gives them its tone, and tinges deeply the New Theology, as it is termed, wherever this appears, be it among Anglicans, Presbyterians, Baptists, Methodists, or Unitarians, or even among the progressive Romanists. One finds clear traces of it in the 'liberal' theological seminaries in almost every denomination. A significant fact of the same kind is in the irenical essay by Mr. John Fiske, 'The Idea of God,' and its extraordinary popular success."

Dr. Howison adds: "The pervasion of pure literature by this fascinating theme is not to be overlooked in recounting the causes of its present prevalence. It has filled, especially, almost the whole realm of poetry, from the days of Goethe. The English poetry of the century is alive with it. Wordsworth, Shelley, Keats, Tennyson, Browning, Arnold, — it seems to be the ceaseless refrain of all their song. Nor, to turn to the essayists, may we forget Carlyle; nor in his theistic moods, Emerson."

NOTES.

II.

From a book which has very recently appeared,* some brief extracts may be made confirming what has been said in the remarks upon Socialism:

"The specific system of production and distribution is the point of issue for every social movement . . . The present movement is directed to the establishment of communal ownership, that is, to a socialistic, communal order of society in place of the existing method of private ownership." The present system, the capitalistic, is now face to face with its antagonist, the communistic. "This condition of things, not slowly grown, but developed as if by magic." The reason of this rapidity of development is that "there has never been another time like ours of such entire change in all the conditions of life. All is in a flux, economics, science, art, morals, religion." But, notwithstanding this and the differences amongst the social agitators as to their action, the socialistic movement is steadily gaining in unity and strength. "The movement of different lands approaches more and more to an unanimity."

But it is the attitude of Socialism toward Christianity that here chiefly concerns us. Of this Prof. Sombart says: "Leaving out of consideration the English working-man, the proletarian movement is doubtless strongly anti-religious." And this opposition is both theoretical and practical. "Not only has an enthusiasm for scientific materialism taken hold of the proletariat with special force, but also the enthusiasm for unbelief has been greatly helped in its development by the instinctive feeling, or the clear consciousness, that in the materialistic conception of the world lies the germ of a mighty revolutionary force well suited to drive authority from all spheres of life. . . . One of the conditions of the very existence of the proletariat lies in a tearing asunder of all the old points of faith. . . . So long as men try to support monarchy and capitalism, using the Christian Church for this purpose, the social movement must become anti-ecclesiastical, and thus anti-religious." "But if Christianity be presented as non-partisan in its social influence, or as directly social-democratic, then there is no reason why this movement should retain its anti-religious character. Whether Christianity is adapted to the needs of the proletariat, I do not dare to say." But Prof. Sombart

* "Socialism and the Social Movement." By Werner Sombart, Prof. in University of Breslau. Trans. G. P. Putnam's Sons, New York, 1898.

thinks that it can only be adapted to this end by removing from it all its ascetic elements (or, in other words, the doctrines of sin, of the cross, and of punishment), "for the proletarians shew no inclination to allow the good things of life to be taken from them."

The sum is that, as the present economic system rests on Christian ideas, Christianity must be put away when the new system of communism shall come in.

III.

While history never repeats itself, we often find relations in the past which cast light upon similar relations in the future. The dealings of Napoleon with Pope Pius VII, in the establishment of the Concordat, 1801-2, may serve to give us clearer conceptions of a new Concordat, perhaps not very remote. We quote a few sentences to shew how the Papacy may be a most useful instrument in the hands of one who should succeed in making the Pope his friend. In his book, "The Church and the French Revolution," (Trans., 1869,) Mr. E. De Pressensé says: "Religion is always considered by Napoleon from the political point of view as an instrument of government. The priests appeared to him eminently useful to tighten the cord of obedience in his States. He said: 'The people must have a religion; and this religion must be in the hands of the government.' But Napoleon would not deal with a multitude of priests, they must have a head, one with authority over all; and with this head he would deal. Controlling him, he controlled all. He said: 'I have need of the Pope, he will do what I wish . . . A Pope is necessary to me . . .' The first Consul—that is, himself—nominates a hundred bishops, the Pope institutes them, they nominate the parish priests, the State pays them."

It need not be said that since the Vatican decree of the Pope's supremacy and infallibility, the Roman Church is wholly under the control of its head, and must follow whithersoever he leads. If he be deceived by the wiles of him who will come with all cunning craft, and become his friend and ally, a wide door is opened in Christendom to the arch-enemy, whose destructive progress can be resisted only by such individual witnesses as God may raise up. Of course, the Papal advocates will say that the Pope cannot be deceived, and will never form any alliance with the Antichrist, but be his greatest enemy. This, however, we must leave to time to shew.

ALPHABETICAL INDEX.

Abbott, L., 187.
Agnosticism, the term,—relation to Hume and to Kant, 123 ; negative only, 126 note.
Allen, Prof., "Continuity of Christian Thought," 139.
Anarchy, 270.
Andover Review, 285.
Antichrist, or Antimessiah, — meaning of the term, xx.; beliefs concerning him in the early church, xxi. *et seq.* ; an individual, xxii. ; term applied to the Papacy, xxiv.; Reformed Confessions, xxv.; present Protestant beliefs indefinite, xxvii. ; in Roman Church, xxviii.; Antimessiah in Old Test. 3 ; teaching of the Lord, 18 ; teaching of St. Paul, 28 ; terms applied to him, 35; His claims to Divinity, 37 ; relation to Satan, 38; as head of the nations, 264 ; His church, 319; His destruction, 336.
Antiochus Epiphanes, as type of Antichrist, 6.
Apostasy,—its meaning, 30; St. Paul's teaching of, 30; beginning seen in his day, 29 ; its origin in loss of love, 31, 79 ; a hindrance to its full manifestation, 39 ; Antichrist its final product, 29, 35.
Apostles, their relation to the Head, 93 ; rejection of their authority, 94 ; consequences of this rejection, 95.
Arius, 242, 249.
Armilus, 6.
Arnold, M., 172, 207.

Atheism, the term, 121 ; sets aside all religion, 122.
Atlantic Mag., 273 note.
Augustine, St., 108.

Babylon, a symbol, 55 ; union of church and state, 57 ; a mystery, 59; separation of the faithful from, 60; destruction by the beast, 60.
Balfour, J. H., 292.
Barrows, Rev. Dr., 325 note.
Bax, E. B., 232.
Beast, a symbol, 5; in Daniel, 5; in the Revelation, 61; distinction of the heads and horns, 62 note; his blasphemy, 63; his worship, 64 ; his deadly wound, 65; his kingdom, 66; destruction of, 66.
Bellarmine, Card., xxviii.
Bengel, J. A., 21 note.
Bernard, T. D., 80 note.
Bertholdt, D. L., 5 note.
Bible, modern criticism of, 169, 182 ; denial of its great facts, 171, 208; said to be superannuated, 176; as a book for literary study, 177 note ; the Old Test., a millstone, 177, criticism of the New Test.; 178 ; its facts unimportant, 179 ; loss of faith in, as preparing the way of the Antichrist, 183 ; revision of, by women, 300 note.
Bishops, popular election of, 91 ; the Roman bishop's claim to have universal jurisdiction, 95
Bowen, Prof., 133.
Bradley, F. H., 298.

Briggs, C. A., 8.
Brooks, Bishop, 151, 153.
Browning, R., 209.
Buchanan, Jas., 137.
Burton, E., 37.

Caird, E., 134, 137.
Caird, J., 134.
Carlyle, T., 184, 205, 236, 276.
Chadwick, 246.
Christ, Messiah, importance of His person and work, 20 ; as man raised from the dead and made immortal, 73 ; His resurrection life given to the church, 74 ; His headship, 75 ; His work in heaven as the High Priest, 76 ; His future work, 149; His pre-existence, 191; place as now living in the thought of the church and the world, 240 ; denial of His Divinity, 242, 243 ; denial of His teachings as true, 245 ; and of the perfection of His moral character, 245, 246 ; growing disparagement of His person, 247.
Christlieb, Prof., 137.
Church, the Body of Christ, an election, 71 ; not a continuation of the Jewish church, 72; close union with its Head, 73, 76; its organic unity, 75 ; the means of His manifesting Himself to the world, 77 ; the dwelling place of the Holy Ghost, 98 ; His work in it, prophetic utterance, 99 ; His voice silenced, 100 ; the evils which have followed, 100; the church of the future, 303; various forms, 305 ; the church and socialism, 221 ; alliance with the beast, 314 ; the church of the beast and false prophet, 320 ; pantheistic, 324 ; the universal church, 325 ; its rites and worship, 332 ; and see 354.
City, a symbol, 55; the heavenly Jerusalem, 56.
Clifford, Prof., 165.
Clough, A. H., 210.

Cobbe, Miss Frances P., 245, 307.
Coleridge, S. T., 255 note.
Comte, A., 307 note.
Contemporary, The, 209.
Cook, G. W., 212.
Creation, 185 ; this denied, 186; with origin of the world evolution nothing to do, 187 ; creation and evolution antagonistic, 188.

Daniel, the prophet, 5, 6.
Darwin, Chas., 187, 287.
Deification of Man, 198.
Delitzsch, F., 6, 9.
Democracy, 264 ; how preparatory to the Antichrist, 265 ; affinity with pantheism, 254.
Descartes, 127.
De Tocqueville, A., 203, 204, 254, 267, 309, 317.
Dorner, Prof., 124, 146, 147.
Draper, J. W., 189.
Dualism, see Monism.

Eadie, Prof., xxii., 28.
Earth, 192, 195.
Elijah, the prophet, 96 note.
Eliot, George—Miss Evans, 212.
Ely, Prof., 222, 227.
Emerson, R. W., 165, 206, 257 and note, 262.
Estius, xxv.
Ethics, see Morality.
Evolution, substitutes an infinite and eternal energy for a personal God, 185 ; its goal the perfecting of man, 166 ; place of death, 175 note.

Fairbairn, A. M., 137.
Feuerbach, 132, 164.
Fichte, 129.
Fiske, John, 166, 190.
Fornication, spiritual, 54 ; the harlot in alliance with the beast, 55.
Fremantle, Canon, 227, 312.

Godet, F., 48, 180 note.
Goethe, 187 note.
Gog, 7.
Green, T. H., 184.
Greswell, E., xxi.

ALPHABETICAL INDEX. 357

Haeckel, E., 189.
Hamilton, W., 124.
Harrison, F., 306.
Hartmann, 188.
Hase, K., xxv.
Hedge, F. H., 248 note.
Hegel, 130, 145.
Hegelian Philosophy, 186.
Heine, H., 205, 262.
Hewitt, A., xxviii. note.
Humanity Divine, 150; the archetypal man, 151.
Humanitarianism, 347 note.
Hume, D., 123.
Hutton, R. H., 205, 207, 257.
Huxley, 123, 188, 197, 288.

Image, of Nebuchadnezzar, 5; of the Beast, 320.
Immanence, Divine, 141; as distinguished from transcendence, 142; God immanent in all, 143; all men His sons in same sense as Jesus Christ, 144; basis of a new Christianity, 146, 352.
Incarnation, its purpose, 194; God incarnate in His only-begotten Son, not all men, 143.

Jerome, 9 note.
Jouffroy, Prof., 298.
Jowett, B., 5 note, 28 note.

Kant, I., 123, 274.
Kingdom of God, 103; Hebrew conception of, 104; Apostolic conception of, 105; post-apostolic conception, 107; identified with the church, 108; the Roman bishop, as Christ's vicar, supreme ruler, 108; the world subdued to Christ before His return, 111; its relations to evolution, 166; to socialism, 222; how preparatory to the kingdom of Antichrist, 225.
Kingdom of the Beast, 264; political supremacy, 277; endowed by Satan, 278; duration of his rule, 281; extent of his kingdom, 282.
Kings, the ten, 282, 318.

Kropotkin, 270.
Külpé, 254 note.

Labour Associations, 273
Lawless One, 85.
Le Conte, Prof., 298.
Literature, its religious character, 202; as democratic, 203; as agnostic and pantheistic, 204; essayists, 205; poets, 208; novelists, 210.
Longfellow, S., 246.
Luther, xxv.

Maitland, C., xx., 350.
Maitland, S. R., xxii.
Malvenda, F. T., xix., xxviii.
Manning, Rev. Dr., 206.
Mansel, H. L., 125.
Marriage, 295, 299.
Martineau, Jas., 151 note, 187, 197.
Materialism, 122, 286.
Maurice, F. D., 151, 227 note.
Mead, E. D., 275.
Mill, J. S., 187.
Monism, tendency to, 120; denial of dualism, 126; spiritual 132; material, 189.
Morality, Christian, its basis, 285; natural morality, 286; evolutionary theory of, 287 — the ethical end, 289; pantheistic morality, 290 — the ethical end, 291; man' sfree-will denied, 292; morals determined by the state, 293; denial of human sinfulness, 297; morality as moulded by the antichristian spirit, 301.
Morell, 129, 130.
Morison, J. C., 198 note, 295 note.
Morris, William, 210.

Napoleon, 272, 335, 354.
Nations, the unity of, desirable, 271, 273; anticipations of Kant, 274; how to be realized, 276; the ten kings united under Antichrist, 282, 334 note.
Nature, terms natural and supernatural, 74 note.

358   ALPHABETICAL INDEX.

Neo-Kantianism, or Hegelianism, 184.
Newman, J. H., xxii., xxviii.

Orr, Mrs., in *Contemporary Review*, 209.

Pantheism, defined, 126; no dualism, 126; "the substance" of Spinoza, 127; the supreme ego or self of Fichte, 129; Schelling, 130; Hegel, undetermined Being, the absolute, 131; development of the Idea as God, 132; power of pantheistic philosophy, 137; effect upon Christianity, 139, 146; immanence of God, how far pantheistic, 141; a general incarnation, 142, 143; God and man essentially one, 147; the Son eternally man, 151; a Divine humanity in God essentially pantheistic, 152; humanity consubstantial with God, 157; both forms of neo-christianity preparing the way of the Antichrist, 158; pantheism and democracy, 254; inflates the mind, 257.
Parker, T., 176, 245, 299 note.
Parkman, Francis, 58 note.
Parks, Rev. Dr., 157.
Parliament of Religions, 325 note; utterances at, 326; points to a universal religion, 327; place of Christ in, 329.
Pessimism, 133.
Pfleiderer, 125 note, 169.
Philosophy, modern pantheistic, 119; its progress, 138.
Polychrome Bible, 183.
Press, periodical, 213; religious, 217 note, 218.

Renan, 165, 297 note, 335.
Revelation—Apocalypse, its author and purpose, 52; its symbols, 53; the bride, 53; Babylon, 55; the beast, 61.
Revolution, atheistic, 253; pantheistic, 255, 256; pantheism breaks with the past, 257;

prepares the way for a new social order, 259; presents a new religion, 259; its revolutionary forces, 262.
Robertson, F. W., 157.
Rossetti, D. G., 210.

Saisset, M. E., 137.
Salisbury, Lord, 288 note.
Satan, 38, 64, 113.
Schaff, P., xxv.
Schäffle, A., 221.
Schelling, 129.
Schopenhauer, A., 133.
Science, modern, its tendencies, 186; H. Spencer on creation, 188 note; place of the earth in astronomy, 193; effect of, on spiritual receptivity, 197.
Scudder, Vida, 210.
Sea, as a symbol, 68.
Seth, A., 134, 147.
Seth, James, 145 note, 287 note.
Simon Magus, 37 note.
Smith, Goldwin, 177.
Smythe, N., 175 note.
Spencer, H., 185, 188 note, 292.
Spinoza, 127, 141.
Stephen, Leslie, 126 note, 165, 289.
Stern, C., xx. note.
Stevens, G. B., 47 note.
Swinburne, A., 208 note.

Ten, symbolic meaning, 334 note.
Tennyson, A., 166, 208.
Tertullian, 39.
Tiele, Prof., 37.
Todd, J. H., xxii.; 5 note.
Tolstoi, 311, note.
Tucker, Rev. Dr., 226.
Tyndall, Prof., 122, 187.

Upton, Prof., 134, 145.

Van Dyke, H., 208.

Wenley, Prof., 137.
Whitman, Walt, 204 note.
Wordsworth, Bishop, xxii., 29, 48.
Wordsworth, William, 205.

www.ingramcontent.com/pod-product-compliance
Lightning Source LLC
Chambersburg PA
CBHW070958160426
43193CB00012B/1825